# THE NEGRO AND THE COMMUNIST PARTY

# THE NEGRO
## AND THE
# COMMUNIST
# PARTY

*by*
**WILSON RECORD**

STUDIES IN AMERICAN NEGRO LIFE
*August Meier, General Editor*

**ATHENEUM**

NEW YORK

1971

*Published by Atheneum*
*Reprinted by arrangement with The University of North Carolina Press*
*Copyright, 1951, by The University of North Carolina Press*
*All rights reserved*
*Library of Congress catalog card number 76-162279*
*Manufactured in the United States of America by*
*Halliday Lithograph Corporation, West Hanover and Plympton, Massachusetts*
*Published in Canada by McClelland and Stewart Ltd.*
*First Atheneum Edition*

# ACKNOWLEDGMENTS

I am indebted to a number of people for generous assistance in the preparation of this study, chief among whom are Mr. Horace R. Cayton, Dr. Charles A. Gulick, Dr. Guy B. Johnson, Dr. Carl Landauer, Mr. Seaton Manning, Dr. C. Wright Mills, Mr. Henry Lee Moon, Dr. Robert C. Weaver, and Mr. John Schulter, and Dr. Donald Coney and the staff of the University of California library.

To Dr. Gulick I am especially grateful for sound suggestions and patient counseling in the organization of the manuscript. Dr. Johnson carefully reviewed the study in its initial stages, offering encouragement and advice and supplying much hard-to-get data on the Communist Party in the South. Mr. Moon and Dr. Weaver made valuable comments concerning general content and factual detail and called attention to a number of earlier omissions. Mr. Schulter with a background of long experience in the labor movement, supplied many fruitful observations on the Communist Party and the trade unions.

Most of all I am indebted to my wife, Jane Cassels Record, to whom this book is dedicated. Her ideas concerning emphasis, content, and style are embodied in every page of this book. Its dedication to her is small compensation for the time and energy she devoted to its completion.

WILSON RECORD

Berkeley, California
September, 1950

# CONTENTS

# ABBREVIATIONS

| | |
|---|---|
| AFL | American Federation of Labor |
| ANLC | American Negro Labor Congress |
| AYC | American Youth Congress |
| CAWIU | Cannery and Agricultural Workers Industrial Union |
| CIC | Commission on Interracial Cooperation |
| CIO | Committee for Industrial Organization |
| CPA | Communist Political Association |
| CRC | Civil Rights Congress |
| FEPC | Fair Employment Practice Committee |
| ILD | International Labor Defense |
| ITUCNW | International Trade Union Committee of Negro Workers |
| IWW | Industrial Workers of the World |
| LSNR | League of Struggle for Negro Rights |
| MOWM | March on Washington Movement |
| NAACP | National Association for the Advancement of Colored People |
| NNC | National Negro Congress |
| NPCASD | Negro People's Committee to Aid Spanish Democracy |
| NRA | National Recovery Act |
| NUL | National Urban League |
| RILU | Red International of Labor Unions |
| SCHW | Southern Conference for Human Welfare |

| | |
|---|---|
| SNYC | Southern Negro Youth Congress |
| STFU | Southern Tenant Farmers Union |
| SU | Sharecroppers Union |
| TUEL | Trade Union Educational League |
| TUUL | Trade Union Unity League |
| UAW | United Automobile Workers |
| UNAVA | United Negro and Allied Veterans of America |
| UNIA | Universal Negro Improvement Association |
| YCL | Young Communist League |

# THE NEGRO AND THE COMMUNIST PARTY

# I

# NEGRO PROTEST AND RADICAL IDEOLOGY: A PERSPECTIVE

---

NOT since the Civil War has the Negro question in the United States figured so prominently in national and international affairs. No longer is it a question peculiar to one distinct economic and cultural region of the country; it is nation-wide, extending from Boston to Birmingham, from Seattle to Savannah, from Detroit to the Delta. And no longer is it an exclusive concern of the United States; it occupies the close attention of countries all over the globe—China, India, Russia, and the various colonial states of Africa and South America. It is not likely to decline in importance. On the contrary, it will perplex us until such time as we achieve some fundamental resolution of the conflict between our democratic values and our undemocratic treatment of more than 15,000,000 American Negroes.

Evidence of the growing importance of this question is everywhere at hand. Newspapers devote considerable space to reporting and editorializing on its various aspects. Political parties develop serious schisms because neither spokesmen nor followers can agree upon a program to deal with it. Government agencies continually intervene in an effort to achieve workable answers to certain of its specific manifestations; as, for example, in employment and housing. Scholars devote their full energies in efforts to learn more about its different aspects. More recently it has received wide attention among educators who are convinced that their special instruments can make some contribution in providing the answer. The courts are continually forced to render new interpretations of the law, indicating that traditional answers, however sanctified by custom and precedent, are not final.

The churches are no longer able to ignore their dilemma when the idea of Christian brotherhood is posed against the doctrine— and their own practices—of racial superiority. Many American universities are now weighing their ideals of scholarship and equality of intellectual opportunity against their practices of exclusion, quota systems, and more subtle forms of discrimination against Negroes. Throughout many phases of American life, and the main body of institutions through which it is carried on, we are having to confront the Negro question. The answers being offered are varied and frequently contradictory, but they *are* answers of a sort, indicating quite clearly that the fundamental question will not solve itself and cannot be ignored.

Not only is a large body of Americans, including practically all Negroes and many whites of various religious, social, and political convictions, demanding a more equitable solution, but throughout the world the United States is being judged on the basis of the answers it provides. A lynching in Georgia is not ignored by textile workers in Bombay. A race riot in Detroit does not escape the notice of the dock worker in Shanghai. The existence of our Negro ghettos is known to the Chinese peasant and the South African mine worker even though many Americans continue to ignore it.

During World War II we appealed to such people for support in a struggle against a régime that posed a theory of racial superiority as part and parcel of a program of world domination. We are appealing to them now in our world-wide opposition to what many regard as an equally repugnant ideology; we seek their support against a dire threat to our national interest and to the democratic potentials of other countries. We are making promises. We are offering some guns, some butter, and a little hope. The colored races over the world are likely, however, to judge us by what we do and not by what we say. Their loyalties and decisions will be shaped in part by what is done about the Negro question here at home. As the world becomes smaller, our neighbors not only can look over our back fence; but they also can examine the contents of our closet. Many of them—black or yellow or of some other hue—will not like what they see.

For more than three hundred years there has been a "Negro problem" in America. It had its origins in the slavery system; but the decay of southern feudalism, its political and military defeat in the Civil War, and the "liberation" of the Negro did not provide a final answer. While our national growth during the past century has resulted in a continued extension of rights and privileges to the common man, the Negro has tended to remain isolated from the main stream of American life, holding a second-class citizenship that displays many aspects of the old slave order from which he presumably was freed.

Almost from the beginning of the enslavement of the Negro in the United States, individuals and groups raised their voices in protest against it. Their motives were economic, religious, ethical, and political. Their proposed solutions were frequently conflicting. Some wanted to expropriate the owners and return the slaves to Africa. Others wanted to liberate the blacks but establish them in a separate area and culture of their own. Still others, few in number, demanded that the Negro slaves be freed and accorded the same rights and responsibilities as other citizens. Thomas Jefferson was convinced of the innate inferiority of the Negro race, strongly suspecting that it was a part of the "natural order of things." Abraham Lincoln looked with favor on colonization schemes proposed during the immediate pre-Civil War period as a solution of the Negro question and of the impending conflict between the rising industrial North and the feudal South. Even the most ardent abolitionists were none too clear about the social role of the Negro as a free man. Few of them visualized his liberation in the context of equality. I do not wish here to explore the slavery controversy or weigh the positions of the contending forces; I merely want to note that from the beginning there was opposition to the slavery system, and groups of varying disposition organized to eliminate it.

But the most ardent opponents of the slavery system were the Negroes themselves. Contrary to the conceptions of many earlier (and even some recent) historians, the Negro did not passively accept his bondsman role.[1] From the earliest times revolts and uprisings occurred in the southern slave areas. For example, in September of 1663 Negro slaves on the plantation of John Smith of Gloucester County, Virginia, organized an extensive conspiracy among both slaves and white indentured servants. The plan was betrayed by one of the planter's favorite servants, and a number of the conspirators were executed. Succeeding efforts to throw off the slavery yoke were met with similar reprisals.[2] But violent repression did not end Negro unrest, and more and more of the military and police power of the South had to be given to keeping the Negro in his slave status. Free Negroes in the North were prominent in the abolition movement, frequently manning the underground railways which moved a constant stream of runaway slaves to the havens of the North. Thousands of Negro troops served with the Union forces during the Civil War.

More recent literature on ante-bellum protest movements indicates that, though slaves generally lacked organization, leadership, and weapons, they were often willing to risk their lives in revolt against the institutions of slavery. Again I do not wish to explore the details of such movements or attempt to measure their significance; I merely want to note that throughout the slavery period Negroes actively struggled for their freedom and that their efforts were viewed sympathetically by some white groups, particularly in the North. These developments were of significance, as I shall attempt to show later.

When the Emancipation Proclamation was issued, it was a limited and piecemeal document. But the response of the Negro slaves justified the hopes of northern political leaders and Union army commanders, some of whom appreciated the military potentials of Negroes and the political implications of their being freed. Negroes responded in many instances by turning on their white owners, running away to enlist in the Union forces, or serving the various Union armies in the field in non-military capacities. Had a more intensive effort been made to arm them and enlist their services in combat, thousands more probably would have joined the Union forces.

With Reconstruction came the temporary political enfranchisement of the freed Negroes. The charge that this new power was not understood and frequently abused has, of course, some basis in fact. However, more recent studies balance these charges with new data and insights. While political corruption was not uncommon in the Reconstruction program, the fact remains that under Reconstruction leadership a number of southern states adopted more modern constitutions and enacted progressive social legislation. Realizing that democratic growth depended on a better informed citizenry, the Reconstruction governments hastened the setting up of free public schools for both Negroes and poor whites.[3]

Local governments in some instances were democratized and no longer represented the will and interests of the plantation owners. There was a redistribution of legislative representation, and the poorer and more backward sections were given a stronger voice. Efforts were made to establish an independent system of courts, with a clearer distinction between the judiciary and the executive. The ante-bellum tax structure, which bore most heavily on free Negroes and poor whites, was reorganized; plans were drawn, and in some cases carried out, for the establishment of a new set of public service institutions.[4]

But political emancipation was not paralleled by economic freedom. The large plantations were not broken up. The freedmen and the poor whites did not obtain land in sufficient quantity to break effectively the hold of the traditional plantation system. The program of the Radical Republicans, temporarily successful immediately after the war, was not carried through to its logical economic conclusion. The Federal authority failed to crush the basic economic institution of the South; on the contrary, after a decade or so, under the strong influence of the victorious capitalist-industrialist élite, the Federal government accepted the plantation system as a subordinate part of the national economy.

Thus the abolition of slavery and the feeble efforts to implement the economic program which this implied did not bring full freedom to the Negro in the United States. His northern liberators soon abandoned him to his former masters, refusing to face the social and political implications of the sudden manumission of millions of blacks or to assume the responsibility of providing the conditions for their full citizenship.[5] The Negro quickly lost whatever independent economic foothold he had gained during the Recontruction period. Legal and other institutionalized barriers were erected to "keep him in his place." Where such instruments proved ineffective, illegal violence was widely and systematically employed. His newly won political enfranchisement was at first curtailed and later, for all practical purposes, abolished. At the close of the Reconstruction period he was neither slave nor free, neither alien nor citizen. He was the Negro in the United States, with the great task of becoming a free and equal human being still to be accomplished. He was a question, which has since rested heavily on the American conscience and left a heavy imprint on all the major areas of American life.

After the Reconstruction period the Negro question declined in importance as the major resources of the nation were directed toward the conquest of a continent and the building of a gigantic industrial apparatus and business system. The great bulk of Negroes remained in the South as tenants and sharecroppers, attempting to survive under a new form of servitude built on the ruins of the old. Survival under such circumstances required the development of attitudes of compromise and accommodation, the outward acceptance of an inferior status in a white-dominated culture, and strict conformity to the detailed rules of the southern racial pattern. Protest impulses were held in check; organization and political action were possible only with the approval of the dominant whites.

There developed among the mass of Negroes a psychology and a point of view that were perhaps best articulated by Booker T. Washington. The Negro was to accept the biracial system and his subordinate status. He was to seek advancement within the confines of his segregated black world. He was to develop the friendship of influential whites and use their assistance. By cultivating habits of hard work, thrift, and honesty he was to demonstrate his claim to wider acceptance and better treatment. Above all, he was never to present any organized challenge to the existing order of things or engage in movements which might be regarded by whites as detrimental to their economic and political interests.[6]

During this time the only organization that really reached down among the grass roots of the race was the church. Like other Negro institutions its survival was ultimately contingent on its acceptance by the whites. It was conservative in the extreme; its appeals were emotional; its eyes were fixed on another world —after death. It held fast the valves of Negro protest and piped the stream of revolt harmlessly into the clouds. It recognized the oppression of the Negro people, and spoke eloquently of their trials and tribulations. But it preached salvation after death and sang of the glories on the other side of Jordan.[7]

The labor movement which emerged during and after the Civil War left untouched the mass of Negroes. One of the earliest labor challenges to the growing power of corporate wealth was the National Labor Union. A resolution adopted at its 1869 convention declared: "American citizenship for the black man is a complete failure if he is proscribed from the workshops of the country," and further that, "the National Labor Union knows no North, no South, no East, no West, neither color nor sex on the question of the rights of labor." But this pronouncement and organizing efforts were largely in vain. Negro laborers, and particularly those in the South, could not be expected to rally behind issues of currency reform and political action when they had no currency and no vote. The aims of the National Labor Union were too vague and far removed, not only for the Negro worker but, as it shortly proved, for the white as well.[8] By 1871 the National Labor Union, for all practical purposes, had ceased to exist.

The Knights of Labor likewise emphasized the importance of organizing together Negro and white workers. The Knights made some headway in the South, particularly among craftsmen and dock workers in the major port cities. They did not succeed in eliminating racial prejudice in the labor movement, but they attacked the problem with more vigor than most of their predecessors. They confronted the task with a reservoir of idealism, firm belief in the solidarity of all labor, and confidence in the possibility of achieving industrial brotherhood. But as the organization succeeded in drawing more and more craftsmen into its ranks, it faced the problem of reconciling their aims with those of the movement as a whole, and this was where it failed. The attitude of the Knights of Labor on the Negro question stands out in sharp contrast to that of its immediate successor, the American Federation of Labor.[9]

It was unfortunate that the emancipation of the Negro and his emergence as a relatively free factor in the labor force coincided with the growth of job consciousness and the craft form of organization in the American labor movement. While the American Federation of Labor initially emphasized the unity of labor regardless of race and even refused to affiliate organizations adhering to discriminatory policies, within a short time it modified its position and permitted the various crafts to determine independently the courses they would pursue. The result is too well known to be detailed here. It is sufficient to say that as the craft organizations sought to limit the labor supply and establish job monopolies, they found a convenient instrument in race prejudice and employed it on a large scale; and ultimately, it was incorporated as a central point of numerous constitutions, by-laws, or rituals.[10]

At the time, the AFL was not set up to organize the mass of unskilled and semi-skilled workers. Negro industrial laborers fell into these categories. The AFL, of course, had no interest in, or instruments for, the organization of tenants and sharecroppers, groups in which the bulk of the Negro labor force was concentrated. In those cases where Negro industrial workers were organized by affiliates of the AFL, it was frequently on a separate local (or auxiliary) basis. Thus the labor movement developed its own biracial system and surrounded it with a set of institutions and rationalizations, many of which have persisted to the present time.

From the close of the Reconstruction period until after the turn of the century there were no significant race movements among Negroes. Individuals who found themselves revolting against the southern scheme of things had few alternatives. They could migrate to other sections in search of wider opportunities and a more congenial environment. But they could protest in the South only at the risk of being lynched by the whites and ostracized by the more "accepted" leaders of their race. They could find no meeting ground with the lower-class southern whites, with whom, under other circumstances, they might have made common cause against the southern political edifice and the plantation system on which it rested.

Some efforts were made to organize "Back to Africa" schemes, frequently with the assistance of conservative white elements, but all of these attempts were sporadic and small-scale. A few Negro intellectuals and artists spoke out eloquently against the oppression of their people, but they lacked organizational ties that would have connected protest with action. Most Negro political leaders were closely tied to the Republican Party; along with Douglass, they felt that the "party was the ship and all the rest the sea." Riding on the prestige of Lincoln, the Republican Party could usually take Negro support for granted, placating colored leaders with promises and a little patronage. The Negro population, concentrated in the South where it was disfranchised, had not yet gained the political voice that was to come with the great migration of World War I and afterward.

It was not until around the turn of the century that a few Negro intellectuals repudiated the philosophy of Booker T. Washington and embarked on what was then a radical program for Negro rights. The Niagara Movement organized by W. E. B. DuBois and a handful of Negro leaders in the North around 1905 represented the first clean break. Its purpose was to form a national protest organization, with branches in a number of states, to wage a fight against segregation and discrimination in all its forms.[11] It was extremely critical of Booker Washington, who, along with his many white friends, in turn vigorously opposed it. The Niagara Movement floundered for a few short years and then passed from the scene.* A few years later a number of

* Of the Niagara Movement leaders Henry Lee Moon observed: "Their cause was just, their motives pure, their goals noble and practical; but they were perhaps too far removed from the masses to inspire them to action—too conscious of their own privileged position as black élite. Among the limited intelligentsia they created a considerable stir, stimulating and inspiring the young men and women of their own class whom Dr. DuBois called the Talented Tenth. They failed, however, as completely as earlier efforts to build sustained support among any considerable number of Negroes, the vast majority of whom were ground down to the prosaic, day-to-day business of surviving in a hostile environment." Henry Lee Moon, *Balance of Power: The Negro Vote.* (Garden City: Doubleday and Company, Inc., 1948), p. 100.

its leaders were instrumental in organizing the National Association for the Advancement of Colored People, which took over a number of important points in its program.[12]

A few years after the establishment of the NAACP, it became apparent that a wider program unifying a larger number of Negroes in protest movements was highly desirable. The NAACP accordingly was instrumental in convening the first Amenia Conference, so named because it was held on the estate of Joel E. Spingarn at Troutbeck, near Amenia, New York. The Conference was attended by approximately one hundred white and Negro leaders. It was hoped that a great amount of unity of thinking would emerge as a result of the deliberations and that the NAACP would be assigned the task of putting any new program into operation. The Conference adopted a number of resolutions which declared: (a) all forms of education were desirable for Negroes and should be encouraged; (b) Negroes could not achieve their highest development without complete political freedom; (c) the advancement of Negro rights demanded a high degree of understanding and working unity among Negro leaders; (d) the South presented special problems and it was necessary for race leaders of the two sections to work closely together. These and other resolutions suggested the need for unity of Negro protest, but it was not achieved at the first Amenia Conference. The second such meeting was not held until 1932.[13]

It was also around the turn of the century that the Socialist movement in the United States entered its most significant period of growth, a development that was not halted until the outbreak

---

Of the same group Bunche has said: "The leaders of the Niagara Movement were the black "radicals" of their day. In a sense they were tougher than the young post-war radicals who later cropped out in the twenties. The "Messenger" of the later period, the Communists and others of radical or radical-racialist bent, were not subject to the same pressure and resistance exerted against the Niagara Movement. Time and the Negro had moved on, the country had become accustomed to hear the Negro make demands. But these early leaders were pioneers, and they boldly staked out civil rights claims for the Negro, the majority of which have not yet been realized." Ralph J. Bunche, *The Programs, Ideologies, Tactics and Achievements of Negro Betterment and Interracial Organizations*, p. 22. Unpublished manuscript prepared as a part of the preliminary researches for Myrdal's *An American Dilemma*. Available at the Schomburg Collection of the New York City Public Library.

of World War I. Predicating their program on a Marxist analysis, the Socialists saw their task as the organization of workers, not only for improvement of wages, hours, and working conditions, but also for taking over a collapsed capitalism and building upon it the new Socialist commonwealth.

They stressed the solidarity of labor. They were at first extremely critical of the American Federation of Labor for dividing the American workers along craft and race lines. But the Socialist Party, as Debs frequently pointed out, had "nothing special to offer Negroes." For the Socialists the real differences among men were class and economic. The oppression of the Negro was merely an extreme form of the oppression of all workers. The Negro suffered because he was a worker; not because he was black. The Socialist Party had no distinct theory of the Negro question. It lacked the special approach and techniques which were later to be employed by the Communists.[14]

While the Socialists welcomed Negroes to their ranks, they were never successful in enlisting any large number. Through the years Negroes had become justifiably skeptical of those who courted their support for various reform schemes, and the Socialist program did not appear exceptional. Negroes were too preoccupied with staying alive and praising God (in that order) to give time to the building of the new society. Coupled with this was their reluctance to invite the stigma of radicalism when the stigma of race was already overwhelming. The failure of Socialists to challenge the southern biracial system as such and directly, in its own terms, was further proof to radically inclined Negroes that the Socialist Party was just another of many white-sponsored "do good" organizations. The fact that it did proper deference to southern mores by organizing separate locals below the Mason-Dixon line did not enhance its appeal to Negroes.

Beginning in 1905 the Industrial Workers of the World embarked on a program of organizing the unskilled and semi-skilled workers in agriculture as well as manufacturing in the United States. Believing in the solidarity of all labor and in the class struggle, and visualizing also a Socialist commonwealth violently ushered in by the general strike, the "Wobblies" drew no racial lines.[15] Negroes were organized together with whites in the lumber camps of Louisiana, the docks of Philadelphia, the wheat fields of Kansas, the grape ranches of California. The IWW was extremely critical of the craft and race policies of the AFL and saw in them the betrayal of the unskilled and Negro workers. A number of Negroes served as IWW organizers, the most prominent being Ben Fletcher, who was jailed with Haywood, Chaplin, and others for his opposition to World War I.

While few Negro (or white) members of the IWW comprehended its philosophy of revolutionary syndicalism, they could understand its militant demands for pay increases, better working conditions, and other goals immediately connected with the job at hand. The IWW, in spite of the hysterical claims of those who saw in it a threat to home, fireside, God, and country, never achieved a large Negro membership. It had few locals in those areas where the bulk of the Negro labor force was concentrated, and Negro members probably never constituted more than five or ten per cent of the total. The failure of the IWW to secure Negro support was the result, not of its racial policies, but of fundamental weaknesses in the organization itself.

The period from the end of Reconstruction until World War I was characterized by determined efforts on the part of a number of labor, radical, and race movements to do something about the "Negro problem." But they accomplished relatively little, and the end of the period found the conditions of the Negro similar in most respects to those at the beginning. The Negro population was still concentrated in the Deep South, under the firm domination of the white ruling class of the area. A few migrations of Negroes to the North and East had taken place, but they made no real imprint on the distribution of the Negro population.

With the exception of the young and untried National Association for the Advancement of Colored People, there was no important Negro protest organization through which black citizens could struggle for their rights. The Supreme Court in a lengthy series of decisions had given judicial sanction to the biracial system and the resulting practices of segregation and discrimination. The Negro worker was still at the bottom of the economic ladder whether on the farm or in the factory. There was no significant political movement having a mass base among workers and farmers with whom he could cast his lot. The Washington philosophy, though it had been questioned by some and directly challenged by others, was still the dominant influence among Negro leaders and intellectuals.

World War I had a terrific impact on this state of affairs. For the first time there were significant migrations of Negroes from the South to the cities of the North, East and Middle West. There were employment opportunities for Negroes in industries from which they had previously been excluded. There was an awakening of race and national consciousness among large segments of the Negro people, the emergence of a new psychology. It found expression in the form of rejection of the traditional role assigned the Negro and evoked a demand for rights rather than a request for privileges. It was strongest, of course, among those Negroes who migrated to the North and East, but in various and sundry ways it seeped through the cotton and magnolia curtain.[16]

For the first time the Negro had some bargaining power. He was needed to help win the war: to serve as a soldier, to work in war production industries, to produce the food for victory. In World War I, as later in World War II, the moral dilemma of fighting for democracy abroad while oppressing the Negro at home rested heavily on the American conscience. Concessions were granted, promises were made, and in spite of the violent anti-Negro reaction following the end of hostilities, certain permanent gains accrued to the American Negro.

World War I brought about a fundamental change in the Negro question in the United States. With race riots occurring in Chicago, Detroit, and other cities, it was no longer possible to speak of the Negro as a southern problem, or entrust its solution to that region. The Negro problem became national in scope, assuming the basic forms that it displays at present. It now had many implications. Trade unions could no longer ignore the Negro worker, for he was a threat to their job control and security. Political parties had to reckon their election chances with an eye on the Negro vote. Radical movements became aware that though the Negro had been frequently thought of as an obstacle and a liability in the past, he was now a resource to be developed, a force to be turned to account, an important potential to be organized. Those Negroes who remained in the South, still a significant majority of the total, discovered that they were not completely without influence, and in important areas of the South, political re-enfranchisement of the Negro began to get underway. Their fellows outside the region gave them aid and comfort, attempting to use their political power at the national level to force changes in the southern racial pattern. National race organizations established branches in the South, challenging the inalienable right of southern whites to do as they saw fit with the Negro.

This was the highly dynamic race relations scene which confronted the Communists when they organized in the United States shortly after the end of World War I. In Russia the revolution of November, 1917, had resulted in the establishment of the dictatorship of the Communist Party. Similar revolutionary movements in adjacent countries were temporarily successful but later defeated. Out of the Russian revolution grew the Third International, with a program of immediate proletarian world revolution. On the assumption that world capitalism was on the verge of collapse, the Communists launched a series of movements in the industrial countries and among the colonial peoples urging them to join with the proletariat of the respective imperialist powers in ridding themselves of their common capitalist masters.

Most of these movements died a-borning; others were crushed after limited temporary success. The remainder, although unable to obtain power, nevertheless survived and were manipulated by the Comintern in furtherance of its revolutionary program. The Communist movement in the United States was extremely weak. It started as a small underground organization composed of dissident Socialists, syndicalists, anarchists, some radical foreign-language groups, and a hodge-podge of unattached intellectuals. Completely misreading the signs of labor and racial unrest in the United States, and under the charismatic spell of the Russian movement, the Communists prepared, at least on paper, an extremely ambitious program for immediate realization of the proletarian dictatorship.

Taking their lead from Lenin's analysis of imperialism and the national and colonial questions, they proposed to direct much of their energy toward development of the oppressed Negro into a revolutionary force. Because Negroes were the most exploited group in the United States, they were thought to be one of the greatest potential resources for the Communist program. The Negro, the Party maintained, not only would be in the vanguard of the proletarian forces at home; but he would also be instrumental in awakening and leading the colored races of the rest of the world in the struggle to overthrow capitalism. While preceding radical movements in the United States had placed no special emphasis on the Negro question, usually subordinating it to an economic class analysis, the Communists proposed to make it one of the focal points of their program tactically.

Since the inception of the Communist movement in the United States, the Negro question has been prominent in the Party program. Special organizations have been set up within the Party to deal with it; continual efforts have been made to develop a Negro leadership; a stream of special books, pamphlets, and papers on the Negro question has flowed from the Party press. An elaborate theory of the Negro question has been worked out. A substantial portion of Party resources has been given over to propaganda and organizational work among Negroes. All of this is striking evidence of the importance which the question holds in the local and world strategy of the revolutionary Communist movement. To trace the development of the Communist Party program on the Negro question, to examine certain of its historical and theoretical origins and the means whereby it has been implemented, and to evaluate it in terms of its contribution to the achievement of a more complete citizenship for the Negro in America is the purpose of this book.

# II

# THE EARLY PATTERN OF RED
# AND BLACK, 1919–1928

IN the United States radical movements with a general Socialist orientation have always had to consider the Negro question in formulating their analysis of capitalist society and in advancing programs for its fundamental change. This is true for three reasons. First, such movements usually seek to establish a working-class base, and the Negro is a significant portion of the labor force. Second, Negroes suffer more than any other racial group from social and economic exploitation, and their special plight is posited as a manifestation of the fundamental characteristics of capitalism. Third, because Negroes are numerically important and especially exploited, they are regarded as either an important resource or a distinct liability for those who would reconstitute American society along radical lines, depending on the particular program to be advanced.

During the period from 1901 to 1920 the Socialist Party of the United States was the foremost advocate of a radical reorganization of the American economic structure. It enrolled thousands of members. It established an elaborate organizational apparatus, with local and state branches scattered throughout the country. It supported an influential press that turned out newspapers, magazines, books, pamphlets and other propaganda on a large scale. It entered politics and was able frequently to elect its candidates to local and state offices. Its nominees for president and vice-president rolled up an impressive number of votes in several elections.

After World War I its influence lagged. It was torn by suicidal factionalism. Many of its dissident followers withdrew or were expelled, and some of these helped organize what eventually became the Communist Party of the United States. One of the principal causes of this fatal split was a difference of opinion on the Russian revolution of October, 1917, and the question of supporting or opposing the newly established dictatorship of the Communist Party.

In approaching an examination of the Communist position on the Negro question it is necessary to review briefly certain developments in the earlier Socialist program. The Socialist Party was never a unified organization. There was no rigid "line" to which all members were expected to adhere or any strict and sure "discipline" for the dissenters. When the Socialist Party was organized in 1901 by the amalgamation of the Social-Democratic Party and dissident elements of the Socialist-Labor Party, a minimum program was agreed upon. But this "unity" was brief, if it ever existed at all. It soon became obvious that there were fundamental differences between the moderates, with a non-revolutionary, non-violent program for realization of the Socialist commonwealth, and the left-wing elements, who favored more drastic measures in ridding America of capitalism.

The history of the Socialist Party during this period is from one point of view the history of the struggle for power between these two factions and their sympathizers. It is not necessary here to trace the details of this series of internecine conflicts. It is important to note, however, that during practically the entire period the moderate elements held the upper hand. Officially, at any rate, they were in control, although frequently unable to direct the actions of the opposing factions and individuals.

The fundamental differences within the Socialist Party never really centered around the Negro question. There was some criticism of the reluctance with which Party leaders approached the economic and political organization of Negroes, but this criticism was exceptional rather than focal. While there was serious disagreement on political action, the role of trade unions, the use of violence, opposition to war, and cooperation with other parties, the Negro question was not a source of serious factionalism. Most

Socialist Party members were agreed that the exploitation of Negroes was only an extreme form of the exploitation of all workers under capitalism. It was not basically a problem of "racial antipathy or social caste." It was a working-class problem, whose solution was possible only through Socialism.

The Socialist Party, however, did not completely ignore the question, as the following resolution adopted at the organizing convention in 1901 indicates:

*Whereas*, The Negroes of the United States because of their long training in slavery and but recent emancipation therefrom, occupy a peculiar position in the working class and in society at large;

*Whereas*, The capitalist class seeks to preserve this peculiar condition, and to foster and increase color prejudice and race hatred between the white worker and the black, so as to make their social and economic interests to appear to be separate and antagonistic, in order that the workers of both races may thereby be more easily and completely exploited;

*Whereas*, Both the old political parties and educational and religious institutions alike betray the Negro in his present helpless struggle against disfranchisement and violence, in order to receive the economic favors of the capitalist class; be it therefore,

*Resolved*, That we Socialists of America, in national convention assembled, do hereby assure our Negro fellow worker of our sympathy with him in his subjection to lawlessness, and oppression, and also assure him of the fellowship of the workers who suffer from the lawlessness and exploitation of capital in every nation or tribe of the world; be it further

*Resolved*, That we declare to the Negro worker the identity of his interests and struggles with the interests and struggles of workers of all lands, without regard to race or color, or sectional lines; that the causes which have made him the victim of social and economic inequality are the effects of the long exploitation of his labor power; that all social and race prejudices spring from the ancient economic causes which still endure, to the misery of the whole human family, that the only line of division which exists in fact is that between producers and the owners of the world—between capitalism and labor; and be it further

*Resolved*, That we, the American Socialist party invite the Negro to membership and fellowship with us in the world movement for economic emancipation by which equal liberty and opportunity shall be secured to every man and fraternity become the order of the world.[1]

The resolution summed up the Socialist analysis of the Negro question in the United States, an interpretation that was to change little during the subsequent two decades. While the Party "invited" the Negro to join in the movement, it never took the necessary steps to enroll him as an active participant. Debs, as the presidential nominee of the Social-Democratic Party in 1900, had called for the organization of all workers in the United States regardless of race, color, or sex, and had demanded the full enfranchisement of the Negro; but later, as one of the foremost spokesmen of the Socialist Party, he declared: "We have nothing special to offer the Negro, and we cannot make special appeals to all races. The Socialist Party is the party of the working class, regardless of color—the whole working class of the whole world." [2]

Had the Socialist Party set out to win the support of the Negro workers after 1901, it would have had to develop special techniques and methods for approaching them. It would have been necessary to analyze the specific problems confronting Negroes as a racial minority and not merely as workers. The Socialists would have had to work closely with the institutions through which Negroes could be reached; for example, the churches, the lodges, the Jim Crow unions, and the small protest groups. It would have had to concentrate its efforts in the South, for it was there that the vast majority of the Negro population was to be found. Actually, very little was done. There were a few Negroes in separate Party locals in the South. Negroes were admitted to Party units outside the area, usually on an equal basis, but the total number was never significant. The Negro question was not even discussed at the conventions of 1904 and 1908.

The strength of the Party was in the industrial centers of the North and among Populist elements of the Middle West and Far West. Up until World War I few Negro workers lived in the main areas of Socialist strength. But there were portents of the great migration from the South as early as 1910, and a few Socialists emphasized the implications of the new migrants for the labor and radical movements. The Party was criticized for its failure to deal more realistically with the Negro question. Some insisted that it was no longer possible or advisable to dismiss the matter by turning an idealistic phrase.[3]

It would have been necessary for the Socialist Party to have played a much more positive role in the American trade unions in order to bring about the organization of Negroes on an economic or political basis. The 1912 convention called upon the trade unions to organize the unorganized on an industrial basis without regard to race, color, or sex. However, it hedged its demand with reservations indicating that the Party was content to let the unions themselves determine the areas and strategies of organization. The Party was anxious for recognition as the political arm of the American labor movement and was willing to leave the latter's economic aspects to the craft organizations. As a result, it refused to act through the instrument which alone would have given it a chance to reach the Negro working class. As Spero and Harris pointed out:

Because it confined its effort to the political arena and refused to grapple with trade-union issues, the party made it impossible for its teachings to reach the rank and file of the most articulate sections of the workers. It thereby destroyed its effectiveness even in the chosen field of politics. In spite of its declarations of class solidarity, it could not hope to win the Negro worker politically without first capturing him economically and educating the unions to the necessity of organizing him as chief among the unorganized and excluded.[4]

The Party did make some headway among Negro intellectuals, particularly in New York City. Chandler Owen and A. Philip Randolph, as editors of the *Messenger*, were the principal spokesmen of this small group which pushed the Socialist program among Negro workers. But the mass of Negroes remained indifferent to, even unaware of, Socialism.[5] Their political orientation was pragmatic rather than doctrinaire. An organization that proposed to speak in behalf of Negro workers without being able to break with the racially prejudiced craft unions made no sense.

As already mentioned, the October Revolution in Russia made a tremendous impression on the Socialist movement in the United States. Many of the left-wing members of the Party openly supported the new Communist régime and believed that their own revolutionary doctrines were largely confirmed by events in Russia. They accordingly made plans to swing the Party behind such a program and affiliate it with the Communist International as a part of the world revolutionary Socialist program.[6]

The moderate group, however, was still in control of the National Executive Committee of the Party. It proceeded to expel those locals advocating an Americanized version of the Russian revolution. Although the moderates retained official control of the Party, they lost some two-thirds of the membership. The left-wing groups held a national conference in June, 1919, and divided almost immediately on the question of whether to organize a separate Communist Party or attempt to capture the Socialist Party from within.

The majority group set up a national council for realizing the latter aim, while the minority organized a committee for a Communist Party. In August of that year the dissident elements— those who had previously broken with the Socialist Party and those who remained behind to "bore from within"—agreed to form the Communist Labor Party. However, members of the earlier organizing committee, now led by the Russian Federation, a section of the old Socialist Party, considered themselves the "purer" Communists and formed a second revolutionary organization, the Communist Party. In 1920, on the orders of the Communist International, these parties were merged to form the United Communist Party. This was an underground organization; however, in late 1921, again at the direction of the Communist International and over the objections of some American Communists, it came into the open as the Workers Party, but still maintained an underground apparatus. Although from the outset there were bitter factionalism and personal-power struggles in the new organization, the firm control of the Communist International was never seriously threatened. As a matter of fact, the Comintern's hand was strengthened because it could play one faction against the other, as in the Foster-Ruthenberg controversy.[7] Later when the Workers Party became the Communist Party of the United States, control by the Comintern was even more complete.

As early as 1920 the Communist Party organized by the Russian Federation had addressed itself to the Negro question, declaring:

The racial expression of the Negro is simply the expression of his economic bondage and oppression, each intensifying the other. This complicates the problem, but does not alter its fundamental proletarian character. The Communist Party will carry on agitation among Negro workers to unite them with all class conscious workers.[8]

This view that racial oppression was an expression of "economic bondage" and that the solution of the problem was to be found in the unity of the Negro "with all class conscious workers" was similar to that of the Socialists. This theory, though subsequently elaborated by the Workers and Communist parties, was not seriously altered until the Sixth World Congress of the Communist International in 1928.

The significant difference in the Socialist and Communist programs on the Negro question centered around the role the latter was to play in over-all strategy. The Communists were convinced that in failing to emphasize the Negro problem the Socialists had committed a serious blunder; consequently, they were determined not to repeat it. Whereas the Socialists had regarded the Negro as a deterrent to effective organization of the American working class—or else, for all practical purposes, had ignored him—the Communists regarded him as an asset.

Several factors will explain this. First, the Communists were much impressed by racial unrest in the United States during the immediate post-World War I period. The great Negro migration during the war had brought hundreds of thousands of Negroes from the rural South to the industrial centers of the North and East.[9] This provided Negroes an economic and political base such as they had not had previously. The migrants, experiencing the freedom of a northern industrial environment, were losing their fear of the white man and were inclined to demand rights rather than request privileges.[10]

There was a growing race consciousness among Negroes in the South as well as in the North. It found expression in the Garvey and other protest or escapist movements. Because unrest had not only affected the Negro middle classes but had even boiled up from among the workers, the Communists believed that it could be turned to account for their program. Negroes were also developing a political consciousness, although in the metropolitan areas this had led to support of the old-line machines.[11] The Communists believed that in time this growing political awareness would lead the Negro worker to a realization of his fundamental interests in a revolutionary program.

The Communists in the United States were also impressed by the role that racial and national minorities had played in the Russian revolution and its aftermath. The fact that the Bolsheviks, with a "Leninist program of self-determination," had been able to win at least the neutrality, if not the enthusiastic support, of a number of cultural and ethnic minorities was considered to be one of the main chapters in the revolutionist success story. The Communists exhibited an almost childlike faith that the Negro in the United States would be won to their cause on the basis of the Leninist race and national policy in Russia. Here, they thought, was a program that could not be dismissed as a utopian scheme, even by the Negro with his deep skepticism. Consequently, in their appeals to the Negro, they placed heavy emphasis on the role of colored races under the Communist régime.

The Communists in the United States were in full agreement with Lenin's analysis of imperialism and the national and colonial questions. Even had they wanted to differ, it would have been on pain of being disinherited by their rich uncles in the Kremlin. Revolutionary movements in the colonies were lacking in organization and leadership. The Communists believed that Negroes in the United States could be trained to assume an important role, not only in the proletarian revolution of the United States, but in the national liberation struggles of the backward imperialist colonies as well. One spokesman of the Workers (Communist) Party put it this way:

Every attempt to make the struggles of the Negro masses in the United States a purely national question, to isolate it from the struggle of the Negro race in all of imperialism's colonies and spheres of influence, or even isolate it from the struggles of ALL the darker-skinned peoples is to play into the hands of the ruling class. Equally true it is to say that any misunderstanding of the common interest in, or attempt to draw a line of separation between, the world proletarian revolutionary struggle and the liberation movements of colonial peoples and racial minorities, leads straight to disaster.[12]

In particular the Communists were bent on the organization of workers in northern industry and the development of a revolutionary race leadership among them. It was emphasized that:

> From among the American Negroes in industry must come the leadership of their race in the struggle for freedom in the colonial countries. In spite of the denial of equal opportunity to the Negro under American capitalism, his advantages are so far superior to those of the subject colonial Negroes in the educational, political and industrial fields that he is alone able to furnish the agitational and organizational ability that the situation demands.[13]

The Communists were particularly anxious to enlist the support of the Negro organizers who had been active in the Industrial Workers of the World, since they were the only ones with any experience in a working-class revolutionary movement. If Negro workers were impressed by the Party's estimate of their leadership potentials, they did not display it by flocking behind the red banner, or by assuming important positions in the organizational apparatus.

The general contrasts, then, between the Socialist and Communist programs on the Negro question may be summarized as follows:

1. The Communists had a theory of revolutionary overthrow of capitalism, whereas most Socialists proposed to use legal nonviolent means.

2. The Communists saw Negroes as an exploited minority with distinctive characteristics, as a historical, cultural, and racial group whose support was to be secured on the basis of special appeals and propaganda. The Socialists likewise recognized these characteristics, but defaulted in drafting any specialized approach to colored workers.

3. The Communists blocked out for the Negro in the United States a special revolutionary task and, in addition, visualized for him a central role in colonial liberation movements. The Socialists,

being a non-revolutionary group, had no such ambitions for the Negro or any other racial minority.

4. The Communists, even at this early stage, were part of a highly centralized, tightly controlled, and well disciplined revolutionary apparatus. The Socialist movement in the United States was a loose amalgamation of various groups and factions. Prior to World War I it had been affiliated with the Second International, which in turn was a loose federation of diverse, and at times conflicting, Socialist movements in Europe and America.

5. The Communists could claim to their advantage the achievements of the Russian revolution and the "liberation" of the various race and national minorities by the Bolsheviks; and for a considerable time there was little contradiction of such assertions. The Socialists were in no position to "point with pride" to such an achievement. On the contrary, while they approved certain aspects of the program of the Communist dictatorship, they were critics of the means whereby it was carried on.[14]

It is not surprising that the Communists placed heavy emphasis on the Negro question. From the very beginning they attempted to develop a revolutionary Negro leadership; they undertook special studies of Negro problems; they supported a special Negro press, from which poured a constant stream of propaganda. A substantial portion of their time and resources was devoted to work among Negroes. What perhaps is surprising is that, in spite of all this, they made practically no headway among the race— with workers, farmers, or intellectuals. Just prior to the Sixth World Congress of the Communist International in 1928, the Central Executive Committee of the Communist Party of the United States declared:

...the party as a whole has not sufficiently realized the significance of work among the Negroes and that the work among the Negroes should be considered not as a special task of the Negro comrades but as one of the special revolutionary tasks of every Communist, of the whole Party.[15]

The failure of the Party to advance among Negroes during the period from 1921 to 1928 is further attested by a breakdown of the membership figures. Total membership in 1928, according to Party spokesmen, who would be inclined to exaggerate rather than minimize their figures, was 14,000. Of this number, 9,300 were regular dues-paying members. Party membership had grown at the rate of about 1,000 per year since 1925. Negro membership in the Party was estimated at only 150 to 200, although it was claimed that an additional 300 had recently made application. Jack Stachel, the organization director, complained that little recruiting had been done among Negroes in the urban-industrial centers of the North, the localities from which the Party proposed to draw its Negro "cadres." Party functionaries were admonished to concentrate their recruiting activities among Negroes and "by the next convention we should have at least 2,000 Negro workers in our Party." [16]

The Party's failure to make significant gains among Negroes during this period cannot be attributed to lack of effort. It failed because it slavishly followed the line laid down by the Comintern, even though this approach proved to be strikingly unrealistic for the U.S. The extent to which the American Party accepted external criticism as valid for the U.S. is indicated by a quotation from Lovestone:

The Communist International is the outward, the real form of the international unity of our Communist movement. Decisions of the Communist International are the expression of one international experience on the problems of the different national parties. The value of this experience lies not only in the fact, that in the form of Comintern decisions, it corrects wrong policies, but also, and most important of all, it conveys this international experience in the form of theoretical and practical lessons to the Party concerned. When a Comintern decision reverses a policy of a national party it is done on the basis of an experience that was not at the disposal of the body which decided the original policy. [17]

To understand why the Comintern approach met with indifferent success one must raise certain basic questions. How did the Communists view the Negro social structure in America? What did this point of view imply for their specific program? How did they attempt to organize Negro movements? What organizations did they establish among Negroes, and how did they operate? What attitudes did they take toward moderate Negro organizations and the non-revolutionary Socialists? What role was projected for the Negro Communist within the Party? These questions will be considered in the remainder of this chapter.

The Communists became aware, after quick disappointment in attempting to organize Negroes into a revolutionary party, that the black social structure was similar in many respects to that found in American culture as a whole. There was an extremely small Negro upper class, a somewhat larger middle class composed of small businessmen, professionals and intellectuals, and a large working class made up of laborers and sharecroppers. It became apparent that there was no approaching Negroes in the mass as a homogeneous racial group with a common social and economic outlook.

The Communists came to believe that their only chance of building a Negro following was through focusing on the lower class. During this period they were extremely hostile toward the Negro middle class and the moderate protest and betterment organizations the "black bourgeoisie" supported. (It was only later, when the Negro question was approached as a "national" problem, that they conceded that the Negro bourgeoisie could make some positive contribution to Negro "liberation.")[18] The Party accordingly concentrated on Negro industrial workers and made one or two feeble attempts to build organizations among farmers and sharecroppers in the South.

Prejudice against the Negro, the Party maintained, was a result of two factors—his background in slavery and the conscious efforts of the capitalist class to perpetuate racial antagonisms in order that the American working class could be permanently split on a racial basis. Racial prejudice was fomented not only by American capitalists; it was a common device of imperialism everywhere. Negro workers were to be united with the white workers in the United States and with the colored peoples in the colonies for a decisive struggle against capitalism. The Negro bourgeoisie, the Party insisted, was under the control of the dominant white economic interests and therefore was to be opposed.[19]

Negroes in American industry, the Communists believed, encountered opposition based on artificial grounds. There were no inherent differences, physical or mental, between Negroes and whites. One of the tasks of the Party was to work within the trade union movement to educate the white workers to an acceptance of Negroes as equals. The possibility of organizing Negro and white workers together, the Party held, had been demonstrated on numerous occasions by the Knights of Labor, the National Labor Union, and the Industrial Workers of the World. The role of Negroes was to be broadened now because:

> The American Communist Negroes are the historical leaders of their comrades in Africa and to fit them for dealing the most telling blows to world imperialism as allies of the world's working class is enough to justify all the time and energy that the Workers (Communist) Party must devote to the mobilization for the revolutionary struggle of the Negro workers in American industry.[20]

Emphasis was placed on full equality, social as well as economic. "Our Party," declared the platform of 1925,

> must work among the unorganized Negro workers, destroying whatever prejudice may exist against trade unions, which is being cultivated by white capitalist and the Negro Petit-Bourgeoisie. . .Our party must make itself the foremost spokesman for the real abolition of all discrimination of the as yet unorganized Negro workers in the same union with the white workers on the same basis of equality of membership, equality of right to employment in all branches of work and equality of pay.[21]

And Earl Browder, in a bid for Negro labor support, emphasized the uniqueness of the Communist program on the Negro question, saying:

> The Communist attitude toward the Negro and his problems differs from that of the bourgeois sentimentalist who proclaims himself "a friend of the Negro," as it does from the dastardly propaganda of race hatred. The Communists meet the Negroes as comrades, unite with them in close organizational co-operation to realize our common tasks, and wage war upon bourgeois-cultivated prejudice.[22]

The role of Negroes in the world proletarian struggle was continually linked to the immediate organizational tasks in the United States. Thus, the 1925 report of the Central Executive Committee of the Workers (Communist) Party declared:

The aim of our party in our work among the Negro masses is to create a powerful proletarian movement which will fight and lead the struggle of the Negro race against exploitation and oppression in every form and which will be a militant part of the revolutionary movement of the whole American working class, to strengthen the American revolutionary movement by bringing into it the 11,500,000 Negro workers and farmers, connect them with the struggles of the national minorities and colonial people of all the world and thereby further the cause of the world revolution and the dictatorship of the proletariat.[23]

It will be recalled that after 1923 the Communists followed a strategy of "boring from within" the American labor movement. In implementing this strategy for the Negro question the Party set the following goals:

1. To link specific racial demands of Negroes to economic and political struggles of the working class.

2. To organize Negro workers under Workers (Communist) Party leadership.

3. To penetrate all separate Negro trade unions or Negro locals of American Federation of Labor affiliates.

4. To develop among Negroes a favorable attitude toward the trade union movement and, where possible, bring them into existing organizations.

5. To fight for the admission of Negroes into current trade unions on an equal basis.

6. To advance the principle of industrial unionism as the surest technique of reaching and organizing Negro workers.

7. To strengthen the Trade Union Educational League and extend its influence among the Negro and other trade unions.

8. To build the American Negro Labor Congress and establish local branches throughout the country.

9. To strengthen the International Labor Defense and place it directly in the fight for the legal and civil rights of Negroes.

The Trade Union Educational League was the principal Party instrument for work among the trade unions, and upon it fell the responsibility of carrying out the Negro program in the industrial labor field. As conceived by the Party, the TUEL's principal aims were to:

1. Direct all eligible Party members to join whatever unions

were at all subject to penetration by the "boring from within" tactic.

2. Organize Party "fractions" within the unions and within the League itself.

3. Build the League into a broad left-wing working-class movement.

4. Stimulate the development of a broad "progressive" block within each of the unions where the Party had members.

5. Form alliances with dissident groups within the trade unions and direct their opposition toward the existing bureaucracy.

6. Use the regular electoral machinery of the unions to capture offices and place revolutionists in positions of control, especially in the executive and editorial branches.

7. Agitate for the formation of a labor party, and support both amalgamation moves and political action on the part of trade unions.[24]

Special emphasis was to be placed on work among Negro unionists, for it was from among this group that revolutionary race leadership was to be drawn, not only for the movement in the United States, but for the rest of the world. The draft program of the TUEL presented to the Third World Congress of the Red International of Labor Unions declared:

The problem of the political and industrially disfranchised negroes [sic] shall occupy the serious attention of the League. The League shall demand that the Negroes be given the same social, political and industrial rights as whites, including the right to work in all trades, equal wages, admission into all trade unions, abolition of jim-Crow [sic] cars, restaurants, etc. The League shall issue a special pamphlet dealing with negro workers.[25]

The League's most significant gains were made in the needle trades organizations, where racial discrimination was at a comparative minimum. In actual practice, the Negro program was frequently subordinated to the more immediate tasks of securing organizational control. Frequently the TUEL's efforts to change the racial policies of the crafts led only to a more determined effort on the part of these unions to continue their traditional practices.

In 1925 the Central Executive Committee of the Workers (Communist) Party proposed building a revolutionary Negro labor organization. Negroes from separate and mixed trade unions, from different factories and industries, a few known for their activity in behalf of the race, and a selected number from "progressive" and semi-intellectual Negro organizations, were to be invited to join. The purpose was to create a national, Party-controlled apparatus that could direct the work of a series of local committees in bringing Negro workers into the trade union movement and building a Party base among them.[26] As a result, the American Negro Labor Congress was convened in Chicago during the latter part of October, 1925.

Prior to the first meeting its Communist sponsorship was widely publicized, and the organization was bitterly attacked by the Negro press and moderate Negro leaders. It was publicly repudiated by a number of non-Communist trade union leaders who had earlier given it their indorsement. Only about thirty delegates were present at the first meeting; only a few trade unions, practically all of which were under Communist control, sent representatives. No Negro farmers or sharecroppers were present. Federal unions affiliated with the AFL sent no delegates, and William Green bitterly attacked the Congress as another disruptive Communist device. The Congress in turn assailed Green and the AFL for its anti-Negro stand in shelving a resolution on Negro equality at the previous convention.[27]

It is rewarding to examine the program mapped by the first American Negro Labor Congress, for it anticipated certain policies that were to be followed by the Communists during the United Front period beginning in 1934. The Congress proposed first to establish in cooperation with other Negro organizations a local branch in each of the major industrial centers. The locals were to be composed of representatives of Negro and mixed trade unions and certain other "progressive," non-worker organizations. Their purpose was to influence the policies of unions toward admission and equal treatment of Negro craftsmen and laborers. A second aim was to promote among Negroes an acceptance of trade unions, which the former viewed with justified skepticism or outright hostility. Branch organizations of the ANLC were never to function in the name of the Party. Tendencies among Party functionaries to use the Congress locals as mere instruments for building the basic Communist organization were to be discouraged; the initial efforts, at least, were to be directed toward building an agency representative of all "progressive" elements in the white as well as the Negro community. Dual, revolutionary labor unions for Negroes were to be established only as a last resort.*

The ANLC made little headway in establishing the proposed local branches. The Party frequently lacked any nucleus that could have constituted a base for organizing drives. Where such committees were formed they had difficulty in obtaining the support of other Negro organizations. Moderate groups such as the NAACP and National Urban League branches were reluctant to undertake any kind of joint program with an organization whose Communist origin and control was apparent from the beginning. Party members themselves, while offering the right hand of unity to non-Communist groups, were bitterly attacking them with the left. For example, Robert Minor declared:

[The NAACP is...] an organization resembling in its pattern the ancient abolition society and breathing the spirit of the white philanthropists in benign collaboration with colored bishops and lawyers, and, of course, the white Republican politician of the border states and other parts where Negroes can vote and where anti-lynching speeches can be made.[29]

Negro members of AFL affiliates would have no dealings with the Congress, perhaps because the AFL had declared its intention of taking drastic measures against members identified with the

* Charles H. Wesley writing a short time after the formation of the ANLC suggested that if Negroes continued to be rebuffed by the white-controlled craft unions in the American Federation of Labor, the black workers would attempt to build their own separate organizations. He thought that the ANLC portended such a move. [Charles H. Wesley, *Negro Labor in the United States* (New York: Vanguard Press, 1927), p. 279.] However, it was not the aim of the Communist Party at the time to undertake organization of separate unions for Negroes. It was not until after the Sixth World Congress of the Communist International in 1928, which forced the American section to abandon its "boring from within" tactics, that revolutionary dualism was again the order of the day for the Communists. This minor error on Wesley's part should detract in no way from his pioneering study of Negro labor in this country.

ANLC.[30] Perhaps a more important factor, however, was the basic conservativism of Negro unionists, which differed little from that of their white fellow members. The Communists were to learn, and learn the hard way, that the Negro working class, like Negro society generally, reflected the values and patterns of the dominant white institutions.

But the Communists, initially at any rate, hailed the ANLC as a great success, Robert Minor declaring again that:

> This was the first American Negro workers' convention. It had a reverberation of considerable magnitude among the Negro masses. It laid the basis for an unprecedented mass organization. It showed that there have developed among the Negro workers a number of strikingly able young leaders. For the first time it has thrown among the confused, misled, and swindled Negro toilers a program adapted to the class character of the Negro masses. There is every reason to believe that upon the basis already laid there can be a Congress of ten times the size and mass representation within another year.[31]

Subsequent events were to prove that such great expectations were completely groundless. The ANLC in fact never amounted to much more than a paper organization, though it continued a more or less formal existence until 1930, at which time it was "transformed" into the League of Struggle for Negro Rights.

The dismal failure of this organization was later admitted by the Party itself in James W. Ford's observations:

> Although there was a large migration of Negroes into industry, their organization into trade unions was weak, and their class consciousness was not widespread. There was a natural suspicion of trade unions among Negroes because in most cases these unions were led by white leaders who carried out the policies of the ruling class of Jim-Crowism and segregation in the labor movement. The American Negro Labor Congress was faced with a most difficult task which it undertook to the best of its ability.
>
> There were shortcomings in meeting this task. The A.N.L.C. was too narrow in its approach. For the period of its existence it was almost completely isolated from the basic mass of the Negro people; this short-coming was carried over into the League of Struggle for Negro Rights. The class content of the program of the A.N.L.C., which was essentially

correct, was, however, not carefully adapted to the feelings and moods of the Negro people. The local councils were too rigid. Instead of uniting broad masses of the Negroes through their organizations, the councils were built on the basis of individual memberships composed in almost all cases of those people and individuals who were dissatisfied with the existing organizations and were breaking away from them completely. In many cases members of the councils were class-conscious white workers, but together with their Negro brothers, were separated from the broad masses, and knew little or nothing about their broad problems and their life. In many cases sincere Negroes were driven away from the organization by bad methods of work.[32]

During the same year that the Communists formed the ANLC they also began building the International Labor Defense. It was only one of a number of similar organizations built by the various sections of the Communist International for legal defense; it was affiliated with the Red International of Class War Prisoners Aid. Its general purpose was to defend radicals, and particularly Communists, in the courts by use of the regular judicial procedures and by "mass pressure." At the very outset the ILD displayed a special interest in cases involving Negroes—whether the individuals were politically radical or not.* It was keenly aware of the propaganda value of identification with Negro victims of injustice; it had plenty of opportunities in the United States. It sought to enlist Negro support around a series of specific cases and gained wide prominence during the early 1930's as a result of its participation in the Herndon and Scottsboro cases.

The fact that the ILD was determined to concentrate on the field of Negro rights was further evidenced in the fact that William L. Patterson, a Negro lawyer and journalist, was eventually named to the position of Executive Secretary. Patterson, an able executive and writer, had visited Russia during the mid-

---

* The ILD itself gave as reasons for its formation: "The encroachment of local agencies upon the constitutional rights and civil liberties, the activities of extra-legal organizations such as the Ku Klux Klan, Silver Shirts, etc., in restricting the freedom of activity of people because of race, nationality, creed, color or class." Ralph Bunche, *Programs, Ideologies, Tactics and Achievements of Negro Betterment and Interracial Organizations*, p. 708. Unpublished manuscript prepared as a part of the preliminary research for Gunnar Myrdal's *An American Dilemma*. Available at the Schomburg Collection, New York City Public Library.

1920's, undergoing, along with a number of other American Negroes, special training in Communist schools in Moscow. The Party also viewed the ILD as an instrument for providing helpful experience for American Negro Communists in preparing them for revolutionary leadership in the colonial areas as well as in the United States.

From the time of its formation in 1925 the ILD adhered closely to the Communist position on the Negro question, incorporating the theory of self-determination in its program after the Sixth World Congress of the Communist International in 1928. Writing in 1941, prior to the dissolution of the ILD—and its later replacement by the Civil Rights Congress—Ralph Bunche observed:

> The program of the ILD, however, like that of the Communist Party must reflect the national interest of the Soviet Union, and it is thus subject to the many vagaries typical of the American Communist Party. Its interest in the Negro is purely a tactical one dictated by political expediency.[33]

The technique of mass pressure represented no new method of fighting for the rights of radicals and minority group members in the courts. The Industrial Workers of the World had employed it very effectively in their dramatic free-speech fights in the West and later in defense of the "Wobblies" jailed under the espionage and sabotage laws of World War I.* This was one reason why the Communists were anxious to have former IWW members serving on the initial executive committee of the ILD.[34] The experi-

---

* Ralph Chaplin describes the IWW technique in attempting to obtain amnesty for the "Wobblies" remaining behind bars in 1923: "In this biggest and most important of the I.W.W. defense drives we proposed to employ every device that the organization had worked out and perfected in its long experience. As everything depended on the raising of huge sums of money for propaganda, we insisted that the defense machinery of the I.W.W. be put into high gear at once. Our next step was to compile and publicize the long list of 'front men'—the statesmen, writers, artists, poets, educators, and churchmen who had espoused the cause of amnesty. Then, with the aid of our speaking staff, backed up by suitable slogans and tons of well-prepared literature, we proposed to concentrate the fire of nation-wide mass protest on Washington. To my knowledge it was the first time in American history that the techniques of mass pressure were used on a national scale, with all the stops pulled." Ralph Chaplin, *Wobbly: The Rough and Tumble Story of an American Radical* (Chicago: University of Chicago Press, 1948), pp. 329-330.

ences of such old-line "Wobblies" as Ralph Chaplin and Elizabeth Gurley Flynn would fit in well with the kind of program the ILD envisioned.

The Communists, in line with their class theory, viewed the American courts as instruments of the capitalists. The courts' principal function, they maintained, was to place at the disposal of the ruling class the physical force of the state, to be used in protecting bourgeois interests against the demands of the workers. Individual workers could expect no justice from such tribunals; the latter would respond only to a display of militant solidarity. The International Labor Defense attempted to use this technique in all cases and to make court trials the occasion for exposing the capitalist-controlled judges and juries while spreading its own doctrine of class struggle.

The Communists had still another reason for organizing the International Labor Defense. Since its formation in 1910, the National Association for the Advancement of Colored People had held an uncontested position as spokesman for Negroes in their fight for legal justice and civil rights. At the time, the NAACP was composed largely of individuals from the white and Negro middle classes. It was not hostile to labor but lacked any important ties with the trade union movement. Its aim was to secure by judicial and legislative action a more equitable role for the Negro in the major phases of American life. It was opposed to the Communist program, and had consistently refused to be drawn into any joint activity with the leftists. Consequently, a characteristic feature of the ILD program during the period from its formation until 1936 was its uncompromising opposition to the NAACP. The *New Masses* thus summarized:

... the I.L.D. composed chiefly of workers, understands that there are two classes, and that the courts belong to the ruling class. The N.A.A.C.P. under the dominance of white and Negro bourgeois reformers, attempts to deny the conflict of class interests. The I.L.D., based on class struggle, knows that mass pressure upon the courts fundamentally affects the court's decision—in the same sense that mass pressure by strikers fundamentally affects the employers' position on wages, hours, living conditions. The N.A.A.C.P. is an instrument to conceal these class truths.[35]

It is surprising that the Communists, with their emphasis on the Negro question, made no great effort to organize Negro tenants and sharecroppers in the South, who even after World War I still represented the bulk of the Negro population and labor force. But until 1928 Communist activity below the Mason-Dixon line was practically nil. Party spokesmen had emphasized the importance of obtaining a foothold among southern Negroes, and some plans had been drawn. Organizers were dispatched on exploratory expeditions, and Communist journalists frequently reported on the conditions of these Negroes for the *Daily Worker,* the *New Masses, The Workers Monthly* and *The Communist.* None of this led to any real organizational effort. It was not until around 1930, after the new revolutionary line had been laid down by the Third International, that the Communist Party of the United States set out to build an organization among southern Negroes.

Several factors account in large part for the earlier default. First, as already mentioned, the Communists concentrated their organizational efforts among the urban Negroes in the North, believing that they would have to have a foothold among this more advanced group before making efforts to reach their more exploited and backward brethren. Second, they were also concerned with the development of Negro leadership for the revolutionary struggle in the colonies and proposed to draw it from the Negroes in northern industry. Third, the tasks of organizing Negroes in the South were much more costly and dangerous than elsewhere, and the Party lacked the resources and the courage (and a lot of both would have been required) to attempt the organization of black tenants and sharecroppers into a revolutionary movement. Fourth, there were lacking among Negroes in the South established agencies that would lend themselves to the "boring from within" technique being followed by the Party at the time.[36] Communist hostility to religion generally and to the Negro church in particular closed the doors of one of the few institutions in the South through which they might have approached the colored sharecroppers and laborers.* The Com-

---

\* "Damn the church and damn religion," said a Communist spokesman at the Chicago meeting of the American Negro Labor Congress in 1925.

munists did not make any sustained effort in the South until the Sixth World Congress of the Communist International decreed that Negroes in the Black Belt were a "nation" and directed their organization in a "national liberation" movement.

One index to the "line" being followed by the Communist Party of the United States at any given time is the attitude it takes toward other organizations. This is particularly true in the case of the Negro question. During the period from 1919 to 1928 the Party took a definitely hostile position toward practically all moderate Negro organizations. The NAACP and the National Urban League in particular were vigorously condemned. There was some basis in fact for such criticism. The NAACP had been extremely cautious in its legal and legislative work for Negroes during the early 1920's, and the National Urban League had played a questionable role in a number of the large industrial strikes during the immediate post-war period.

James W. Ford was a delegate to the 1926 convention of the NAACP as an advocate for the American Negro Labor Congress. He submitted a resolution calling for the formation of inter-racial commissions in each locality, to be composed of representatives of the NAACP, Brotherhood of Sleeping Car Porters, and other labor organizations. These committees would attempt to break down local obstacles to the full admission of Negroes into trade unions and promote among black workers an acceptance of the union movement. The NAACP rejected the resolution but took no anti-labor position in doing so.

The Party assailed the NAACP for rejecting the Ford proposals, which were also the demands of the American Negro Labor Congress. The failure of the NAACP to take favorable action was explained by the Party in terms of the former's social composition: middle class intelligentsia "for the most part who are unable or unwilling to see that the strength and driving power of the Negro race in America is its working class—the only class among the Negroes which possesses great universal strength and economic power." [37]

The main objections of the Communists were that these moderate organizations of the middle class were essentially non-revolutionary institutions. By emphasizing devices such as the courts, legislative action, and interracial education, the Party maintained, the black "reformists" obscured the basic class and economic character of prejudice. Since there was little opportunity to apply the "boring from within" tactic in these groups, the Party answered with open opposition and dual organization. At a later period both the NAACP and the NUL were to be regarded quite differently.

Another organization which the Party sought to influence during this period was the Universal Negro Improvement Association. The Association and its ultimately nationalistic ideology came to be known as the Garvey Movement. Its founder and guiding spirit was a West Indian immigrant, Marcus Garvey, who during World War I began agitation among Negroes migrating into the urban-industrial centers of the North. During the post-war period he was successful in articulating and capitalizing upon the mass discontent among Negroes, particularly among the recent migrants to the North. However, the Garvey Movement reached out into all areas of the country, even the South.

In its earlier days the Garvey program embodied many elements of a radical working-class ideology. Within a short time these items were obscured by an increased emphasis on race consciousness. It was at this time that the "Back to Africa" idea became the principal plank in the UNIA program. Garvey then took the position that Negroes in the United States would never be able to obtain their rights as citizens. Racial antipathy, he held, was so wide-spread and intense in America that no possible remedial programs could overcome it. Negroes would be able to find equality only in a country of their own—a country with a Negro government, institutions and culture.

Garvey was a highly skilled demagogue and organizer, basing much of his appeal upon a glorification of dark skin as opposed to many light-skinned, established, middle-class Negroes. He appealed to the rank and file of the race over the heads of their conservative leaders, particularly the churchmen. Garvey injected religious appeals along with his more specifically political demands, and in this way he was able to lend an emotional dimension to the movement which many of his followers had formerly found only in the churches. As Drake and Cayton point out:

With his emphasis on the "proud tradition of the African past," upon "race pride," and particularly upon the virtue of "blackness," Garvey put steel into the spine of many Negroes who had previously been ashamed of their color and of their identification with the Negro group. Before his time, such things as colored dolls or calendars with colored families and heroes were a rarity; today they are common place. Garvey didn't get many Negroes back to Africa, but he helped to destroy their inferiority complex, and made them conscious of their power.[38]

Garvey's main strength lay among the lower and lower-middle class Negroes, who found in the promises of a new land an escape from the harsh realities of segregation.

Garvey built a number of subsidiary organizations through which he proposed to carry out his "Back to Africa" scheme. Among them were the Royal African Legions, the Black Star Line, and the Black Cross Nurses. The UNIA reached its peak strength around 1925; then, torn by internal strife and the jailing (and later the deportation) of Garvey himself, the movement began to disintegrate. Within a few years it was dead for all practical purposes.[39] * Just how dead is evidenced in the fact that during the depression period it was unable to turn to account the discontent of the Negro masses for any kind of "Back to Africa" program.

The Communists at first were not opposed to the Garvey organization. They were anxious to develop a race and national consciousness among Negroes as well as to ally the race with the working class. The Party was greatly impressed by the lower-

* There is considerable disagreement among students of Negro protest concerning the strength and influence of the UNIA. Cayton and Drake (*op. cit.*, p. 752) state that: "Several million American Negroes were once dues-paying members in the UNIA." William Pickens of the NAACP claimed that Garvey never enrolled more than a million members. Kelly Miller, a Howard University professor, placed the number at four million. (Myrdal, *op. cit.*, p. 748.) Even if we take the lowest estimate, the character of the Garvey Movement as a mass organization remains. It is important to remember that the UNIA emerged and prospered in the face of opposition by practically all the "leaders" of the race and their organizations, such as the churches, the NAACP and the NUL. Garvey therefore emerges as a much more colorful and effective organizer than membership figures alone would suggest. Viewed sociologically, the UNIA was a consequence of the migration of Negroes to the North and the attendant social disorganization coupled with mass frustration. (See Frazier, *op. cit.*, p. 540.)

class appeal of the UNIA. Though Communists were keenly disappointed in the shift in emphasis toward "Negro Zionism," they were sorry to see the movement die. On the eve of collapse, Robert Minor lamented:

> A breaking up of this Negro association would be a calamity to the Negro people and to the working class as a whole... The organization itself represents the first and largest experience of the Negro masses in self-organization.... It is composed very largely, if not almost entirely, of Negro workers and impoverished farmers, although there is a sprinkling of small business men. In any case the proletarian elements constitute the vast majority of the organization.... We believe that the destruction of such an organization of the Negro masses, under the circumstances would be a calamity.[40]

The Garvey Movement was failing, the Communists maintained, because it had succumbed to the pressures of the bourgeoisie; it had deviated, from the basic policy laid down at its 1920 convention and was now placing its whole emphasis on a "Back to Africa" program. The UNIA, according to the Party, could be salvaged only by a concentration of its energies around the fight for equality for Negroes within the United States. While Party members within the UNIA were under orders to force acceptance of this latter program, they were so few in number as to be ineffective. Lacking any decisive influence, they could do little more than protest the sorry turn of events. Had they been able to "capture" the UNIA, and especially Garvey himself, they could have had much more to show for their "Negro work" during this period.

While Communists even before 1928 were anxious for the development of race consciousness among Negroes, they at this time did not want this new self-consciousness to find expression in the "separate nation" idea—either in Africa or in the United States.[41] However, after 1928 they were to take a position similar to that of Garvey, because of the program of "self-determination for Negroes in the Black Belt" laid down by the Sixth World Congress. The fact that Negroes had responded to the Garvey program helped to change the Communist mind in the United States and in the Kremlin.

Just how much Garvey's success impressed them is difficult to measure. The Programme of the Communist International in 1928 stated:

Garveyism which was formerly the ideology of the masses, like Gandhism, has become a hindrance to the revolutionisation of the Negro masses. Originally advocating social equality for Negroes, Garveyism subsequently developed into a peculiar form of Negro "Zionism" which, instead of fighting American imperialism, advanced the slogan: "Back to Africa!" This dangerous ideology, which bears not a single genuine democratic trait, and which toys with the aristocratic attributes of a non-existent "Negro kingdom," must be strongly resisted, for it is not a help but a hindrance to the mass Negro struggle for liberation against American imperialism.[42]

But it is significant that, in spite of this criticism, the self-determination and black republic programs adopted by the Comintern and the Communist Party in 1928 had the Garvey look. Like the UNIA, the new Communist view held that Negroes had a distinct culture of their own; that common racial features were the basis for a national state; and that Negroes had a "natural area" for the location of such a state: in Africa according to the Garveyites; in the Black Belt of the United States according to the Communists. And both the UNIA and the Communist Party in advancing this program ultimately were defeated by a basic Negro American attitude which Bunche has well described:

It is conceivable that conditions might become so intolerable for Negroes in the United States that the black man would seek refuge on other shores. It is extremely doubtful that any significant support for a colonization or repatriation movement could be developed among Negroes under present conditions. However, the glamour of a black state, either here as a 49th state or in Africa, as an independent nation, has not caught the imagination of the Negro—either of the Negro intellectual or the Negro in the mass. The Negro in his customs, in his thinking, and in his aspirations is an American, and he regards America as his home. He lacks even those religious ties which would attract the Jewish refugee to Palestine. If the Negro is to be gotten out of America he will have to be driven out. Only when racial persecution becomes so efficiently brutal, so thoroughly institutionalized that life for the Negro will become impossible here, will there be any likelihood that the black American will seek refuge elsewhere.[43]

Although the UNIA was the largest of Negro protest and betterment movements during the 1920's, other organizations became quite active. Among them were the African Blood Brotherhood, the Equal Rights League, and the Friends of Negro Freedom. These organizations were frequently antagonistic toward each other, competing for followers and dissipating meager resources in duplicative programs. None could be said to have had a national structure or any wide influence. Nevertheless, they were among the protest agencies to which Negroes in the North might turn. Like the Garvey movement, they were a product of the great migration, their principal branches functioning in those cities to which large numbers of southern Negroes had recently moved.

In February, 1924, the Negro Sanhedrin was convened in Chicago—largely as a result of the efforts of Professor Kelly Miller. It was hoped by Miller and other sponsors that a greater degree of unity of action might be achieved among various protest and betterment organizations. It represented also an effort on the part of the NAACP to place itself in the leadership of a unified Negro movement. While the delegates to the Sanhedrin knew what they were *against*—Garvey and the Communists—they were not at all sure of just what they were *for*. Consequently the deliberations were largely consumed with talk and maneuvering.

Miller's appeal, like that of DuBois fifteen years earlier, was primarily to the Negro intellectuals and the "talented tenth." Lacking contact with the lower and less fortunate strata of black America, he could not appreciate the importance of organization at the grass roots level; rather, he would have used the "influence" of Negro "leaders" in advancing the general interests of the race. This was the only meeting of the Negro Sanhedrin. The idea of uniting varied Negro organizations around a minimum action program was not new even at this time. However, the Negro Sanhedrin failed to achieve its purpose. It was similar in some respects to the National Negro Congress, which was organized in Chicago some twelve years later. But the Sanhedrin differed from the NNC in that the former had little or no labor and radical participation.

Neither in the Sanhedrin nor in the other protest movements did the Communist Party have any significant influence. Having set itself in opposition to the Negro "reformist" organizations, and having rejected the militant nationalism of the Garveyites, it found itself posed against both the major trends in Negro protest. Miller and DuBois and Garvey, all were listed in the Party's books as "betrayers of the Negro people."

The Communists' rejection of the general program of the Socialist Party carried over, of course, into a rejection of the latter's stand on the Negro question. Taking its cues from the earlier declaration of the Comintern that:

The Third International once forever breaks with the traditon of the Second International which in reality only recognized the white race. The Communist International makes it its task to emancipate the workers of the entire world. The ranks of the Communist Internationale fraternally invite men of all color; white, yellow and black—the toilers of the entire world.[44]

the American section proceeded to flail away at the followers of Debs and Thomas. The latter were denounced as "petty-bourgeois reformers," and "segregationists," who followed the lead of the southern white ruling class in their projected program and within their own party.

Although the Socialist Party was never able to claim any large Negro following, it commanded the interest and loyalty of a number of Negro intellectuals during the post-World War I period and even earlier. Outstanding among the Negro socialists were A. Philip Randolph and Chandler Owen, editors of the *Messenger*. Later a number of Negro Socialists left the organization and joined the Communist Party. Among them were Otto Huiswood, Lovett Fort Whiteman, Richard B. Moore and Cyril Briggs. Huiswood subsequently went to Hamburg, Germany, as Executive Secretary of the Comintern-controlled International Trade Union Committee of Negro Workers. Lovett Fort Whiteman was one of the principal organizers and participants in the first American Negro Labor Congress in 1925. Moore and Briggs served in the capacities of journalists and organizers. Only Randolph, Owen and a few others among the prominent Negro socialists steered clear of later identification with the Communist Party. Randolph focused on the organization of the Brotherhood of Sleeping Car Porters, while Owen turned to conservativism.

One of the principal reasons for the Socialist Party's failure among Negroes during the middle and late 1920's was its inability to attract Negro intellectuals to carry out agitational and propaganda work or to draw undifferentiated Negro radicals into day-to-day organizational activity. It not only failed to attract new blood and talent; it failed also to keep even what it had. The fact that the Communist Party was successful in winning over a number of socialist Negro intellectuals during this period is a further indication of the misgivings with which these and other Negroes viewed the Debs philosophy of "nothing special to offer."

Any organization that proposes to include in its membership both Negroes and whites in the United States confronts the question of race relations within its own group. It may be a religious, fraternal, business, professional, trade union, political, or other type of institution. It must decide how the organization is to relate itself to the rest of the community and how its members are to relate themselves to each other. The decisions and practices may take many forms. Negroes may be organized into separate branches or sections, with inevitable subordination. They may be admitted formally on an equal basis, but with the tacit understanding and practice of second-class participation; or they may be admitted on an equal basis with a corresponding practice of genuine equality. In any event some decision must be made.

From the outset, the Communist Party in the United States had to take a position on the role of the Negro within the Party. It was obvious that its formal policy could be nothing less than one of complete equality, for theoretically it recognized no difference on account of race. But many of its white adherents during this period frequently committed the sin of "white chauvinism." Spero and Harris cite cases in Detroit, New York, Seattle and Norfolk in which the policy of equality was flagrantly violated.[45] While many whites were willing to join in a struggle for the overthrow of the existing social and economic order, they did not necessarily include in their target the existing practices of discrimination and segregation.

This, of course, was not the first instance in which a politically radical organization in the United States was threatened by the racial conservativism of its own members. Even the ardent abolitionists saw themselves as doing something *for* inferior blacks rather than *with* colored men who were their equals. The National Labor Union, although economically radical for its day, was essentially conservative in its outlook on the race question. The Socialist Party never came to grips with the problem of anti-Negro prejudice within its own ranks. The Communists took a much more positive attitude. In view of the role they projected for Negroes, they had much more reason to do so.*

There was still a tendency to carry over the biracial pattern into the day-to-day operations of the Party apparatus, especially at the local branch levels. The Party had been cautioned that:

Any projected Communist work among American Negroes must take as a concrete basis the general social grievances of the race. The slow growth of Marxism among Negroes has been wholly due to the inability of both the social democrats and the Communists to approach the negro on his own mental grounds, and to interpret his peculiar social situation in terms of the class struggle. To-day the American negro has evolved his own bourgeoisie, even though as yet but petty. And more and more the lines sharpen between the white and black bourgeoisies. The Negro petty bourgeoisie rallies the negro masses to him in his struggle against the more powerful white bourgeoisie, and the negro masses are permeated with the belief that their social degradation flows from the mere fact that they are markedly of a different race, and are not white. It is a mere waste of time to circulate the same Communist literature among negroes that you would among white workers, or to make the same speech before an audience of the negro workers that you would before that of white workers. The negro evinces no militant opposition towards Communism, but he wants to know how it can improve his social status, what bearing does it have on the common practice of lynching, political disfranchisement, segregation, industrial discrimina-

* The continuation of the phenomenon of internal race prejudice in an organization as ardently committed to equality as the Communist Party has been during certain periods of its history is well worth exploring in detail. A study on a historical and comparative basis, with an emphasis on sociological factors, would without doubt prove very fruitful. While we shall have occasion to refer to the matter again during the course of this discussion, we shall not be able to give it the treatment which it merits.

tion, etc. The negro is revolutionary enough in a racial sense, and it devolves upon the American Communist Party to manipulate this revolutionary sentiment to the advantage of the class struggle.[46]

But it proceeded to act in many instances as if its tasks were much more simple. The difficulty was evidenced, not in the revolutionary program itself, but in the failure to use the proper methods for its realization. The failure of methods lay in two areas: a lack of understanding of the "Negro problem" and "white chauvinism" among Party members and functionaries.

The task that confronts the American Workers (Communist) Party in organizing the Negro workers and rallying them for the daily class struggle and the final overthrow of Capitalism, side by side with the white workers is no light one. On the contrary it is a difficult and dangerous job.

No one who does not appreciate this fact should be allowed to come within a thousand miles of the work. It is something that cannot be expedited by undue optimism nor can the work be furthered by magnifying to Negro comrades the mistakes of the party and exaggerating its present strength and abilities.

Ill balanced comrades who know little of the role of the Negro in American industry and less of the labor movement, comrades who think that the whole problem centers around the right of the races to intermarry, whose utterances give one the impression that they believe the labor movement, a product as it is of historical conditions in America, is a conscious conspiracy against the Negro workers, comrades who without thought of possible consequences would have the party begin immediately the organization of dual independent Negro unions, such comrades as these are useless in this work.[47]

The Party did make a constant effort to re-educate its white members to an acceptance of the Negro as an equal, and it tried to place Negroes in positions of responsibility. "White chauvinism" was considered grounds for disciplinary action; some of those found guilty of practicing or condoning it were expelled. But progress was, apparently, slow and the director of organization in 1928 pointed out:

It is necessary that this work [among Negroes] shall not be confined merely to the Negro comrades. That is nonsensical. Such a conception is a wrong conception. Likewise we must not merely limit the

Negro comrades to Negro work, but they must be drawn into actual leadership and leading committees of our Party in all fields of Party work. I would like to see some districts with Negro Agitprop directors and industrial organizers and we must see to it to have district organizers to demonstrate that Negro work does not mean carrying on work among Negroes, that the Party must carry on work among Negroes and Negro comrades work in the Party.[48]

The Communist Party believed that by emphasizing the socially equal role of the Negro within the organization it would have another basis for securing Negro support of a revolutionary political program. White Party members were urged to cultivate prospective Negro members on this basis. To what extent it was actually done, and with what success, are factors which the present study does not attempt to measure. No accurate judgment can be made on the basis of documentary material now available. It is the opinion of the author, and only an opinion, that the chance to participate on an equal basis in the tight, closed society of the organization was not a significant factor in the Negro's joining. A few individuals might have been so motivated, but it was not a primary determinant in many cases. A definitive answer would have to be based on a much closer psychological and sociological examination of the Negro's role in the Party.

It is also the opinion of the author that Negro-white equality within the organization was emphasized out of all proportion by the Party as a propaganda technique, and by certain of its critics for the same reason.*

The Party was thought of frequently as one of the leading advocates of racial intermarriage. And this charge gained wide acceptability in the South, where the fear of race "contamination" had a strong hold.[49] Again it is the opinion of the author that intermarriage among Negro and white Communists occurred on an extremely small scale. Drake and Cayton make some references to the matter, and although their conclusions are not emphatic, they tend to support the above opinion.[50]

* For example: A super-patriotic organization, American Women Against Communism, with headquarters in New York City and for a number of years active on the lunatic fringe of American reaction, made the advocacy and practice of "social" equality among Negroes and whites by the Party one of its principal points of attack.

Obviously the Party took no position against interracial marriage; but the amount and kind of acceptance was another matter. Again it is difficult to make any sound judgments on the basis of available material. It would seem that the specific decisions here, as elsewhere, were influenced primarily by the tactical consideration of whether or not interracial marriage among Party members would contribute to the advancement of the "line" at any given time. Certainly during the united front period, for example, the Party had little to say on the subject and probably discouraged members anxious to form such unions. The extent to which this "discouragement" was carried is, of course, not known.

As already stated, one of the primary aims of the Party during the twenties was to develop Negro leaders not only for the proletarian revolution in the United States but also for the national liberation movements in the colonies. A number of Negro journalists, intellectuals, and trade unionists were sent to Moscow for training in Marxist dogma and revolutionary strategies.[51] Among them were James W. Ford, vice-presidential candidate in 1932; Eugene Gordon, a Negro journalist; and William L. Patterson, who became Secretary of the International Labor Defense. Young Negro trade unionists were particularly sought after by the Trade Union Educational League, and one of the proposed functions of the American Negro Labor Congress was to select and provide training for radical Negro unionists.

During this period, however, Negroes did not occupy the positions of leadership within the Party that they have held since. James W. Ford entered the Party in 1926 and was a delegate to the Fourth World Congress of the Red International of Labor Unions. In 1928 he was a delegate to the Sixth World Congress of the Communist International. Shortly afterward he assumed the post of Negro Organizer for the Trade Union Unity League. In 1930 he went to Hamburg, Germany, as Secretary of the Communist-affiliated International Trade Union Committee of Negro Workers. However, it was not until 1932 that he became the vice-presidential nominee or played any important role in the American Party. With the exception of Ford, no Negro Communists during that period attained positions of leadership comparable to those held by Benjamin Davis, Henry Winston,

Edward E. Strong, and Doxey A. Wilkerson at the present time.

A number of Negro intellectuals, but surprisingly few, did join the Party during this period. However, they functioned primarily as writers and propagandists and occupied no positions of political power. The Party made no sustained effort to win over Negro writers and artists, much of whose audience consisted of "white-bourgeois elements." Frequently the Party was extremely critical of this group and tended to identify them with the Negro middle class, to which most of them belonged both economically and ideologically. For example, William L. Patterson in criticizing Negro poets declared:

> There is little in recent Negro poetry that would lead one to believe that the poets are conscious of the existence of the Negro masses. There is no challenge in their poetry, no revolt. They do not echo the lamentations of the downtrodden masses. Millions of blacks are suffering from poverty and cruelty, and black poets shut their eyes! There is no race more desperate in this country than the black race, and Negro poets play with pale emotions!
>
> We can be frank. Our Negro poets voice the aspirations of a rising petty bourgeoisie. Occasionally they express the viciousness of black decadents. And that is all. They are sensationalists, flirting with popularity and huge royalties. They are cowards. Instead of leading heroically in the march of the world's workers, they are whimpering in the parlors of white and black idlers and decadents. . . .
>
> Let us sound the bugle-call for militancy. Let us have strong vital criticism, Marxian criticism. Let us have the poetry of the masses. Let us have an international poetry.[52]

Negro academicians were extremely slow in responding to the Party's appeals. Most of them were in the small denominational schools of the South. These were on the whole thoroughly conservative institutions, largely dependent on acceptance by the local white community and northern philanthropy for their continued existence. The tenure of radical teachers, particularly those looking with favor upon Communism, would have been short. In addition, Negro intellectuals were economically and socially identified with the Negro middle class.[53] And the Negro middle class was scorned by the Negro Communists, whose program centered around Negro laborers. The Party later set out to cultivate a following among Negro intellectuals and academicians, but during the period from 1919 to 1928 it could regard these groups as nothing more than the "lackeys of the southern ruling class."

Even before 1928 it was apparent that the early hopes of the American Communists to build a mass revolutionary movement of any kind were almost completely unrealized. The Trade Union Educational League was an irritant, not a force of consequence, in the labor movement. It had failed to penetrate any of the really important unions, although experiencing some success in those organizations whose memberships were composed largely of foreign language groups; for example, the needle trades unions in Chicago and New York. It had organized relatively few separate unions on an industrial basis. At best it reached only a few thousand Negro workers, winning these through default of the conservative craft organizations in the American Federation of Labor. Though the craft unions in a few instances had removed some of their more discriminatory practices against Negroes, these developments could not be attributed to the TUEL's influence.

In summarizing the 1921-1928 period, it may be said that for all practical purposes, the American Negro Labor Congress, after three years of organizational activity, existed only on paper, an example of sweeping promises unmatched by performance. Only a few local committees or councils had been established; these were isolated in local communities, failing to reach even the Negro trade unions, failing also to establish any working relationships with non-labor Negro groups. The International Labor Defense remained weak and ineffectual. It had failed to become identified with symbolic and dramatic court cases involving Negroes; it functioned primarily as a propaganda agency.

The Garvey Movement continued on its "Back to Africa" trail in spite of the Party's efforts to steer it along a different course. It was broken to pieces by the jailing of Garvey and by internal conflicts; the Party was unable to pick up the fragments and glue them onto its own apparatus. The NAACP and the NUL had remained impervious to Communist admonitions to change their ways; the Party's effort to penetrate these moderate organizations had fared as badly as the TUEL's effort in the trade union sphere. The attempt to secure the Negro vote for radical political parties or coalitions backed by the Communists was almost farcical in its results. Negroes in the urban-industrial centers such as Chicago, New York, Detroit, Pittsburgh, and Cleveland were tied to the old political machines; colored voters were not willing to trade the patronage crumbs from the capitalist political table for the pie-in-the-sky promises of the vociferous radicals.

The Party had not yet realized that the Negro churches were agencies through which it might work; Communists identified these basic institutions as their sworn enemies and fought them accordingly. The churches still preached salvation in another world; political radicalism was at worst a major sin and at best a dangerous thought. Nowhere was the Party's misunderstanding of the Negro past or of the psychological needs of the colored masses more apparent than in the position it took on religion. Like the Socialist Party and other radical movements, the Communist Party failed to appreciate the focal role of the store-front church in Harlem or Bronzeville.

Further evidence of the Communist failure is found in membership figures. Even by 1928 there were probably less than two hundred Negro Communists in the United States. Membership drives were periodically launched with great fanfare and high hopes only to conclude with a few score Negro recruits—these of doubtful value. The Communist ideology had failed to capture the attention of the Negro masses, even at a time when there was a bewildered groping for new ideas and new movements, even when the great migration had broken down many of the traditional ties and habits.

It was now obvious that the "boring from within" strategy, on which Foster, Lovestone, Gitlow, and Stachel had placed so much reliance, was an ineffectual strategy for building a revolutionary movement. No one was more aware of this than the men in the Kremlin who directed the activities of the Communist International and of the American section. While the Party in the United States had followed faithfully the various directives of the Executive Committe of the Comintern in its Negro work, it was apparent that something more than a failure to use the "correct" detailed methods was involved. The problem demanded a thorough rethinking.

A short time prior to the Sixth World Congress of the Comintern in 1928 the Negro program was brought under review. It was evident that a number of changes in the general strategy of the American Communist Party would be handed down; the most important one perhaps concerned the Negro question. These changes were formalized and made explicit as a new "line" adopted at the 1928 meeting. What were these changes? How were they introduced? What were their implications for Communist strategy in the United States? How did they affect the Communist position on the Negro question? What new ideology was promulgated? What specific practices resulted? What organizations did the Party attempt to build among Negroes? How did these organizations attempt to carry out the Communist program? These and other questions we will consider in the next chapter.

# III

# THE KREMLIN SOCIOLOGISTS AND THE
# BLACK REPUBLIC, 1928-1935

THE Negro Question in the United States was not brought before the Communist International until the Fourth World Congress in 1922. While there was considerable discussion at the time, no definite decisions altering the previous formulation were reached. It is significant that prior to Lenin's death and Stalin's successful bid to obtain control of the Party apparatus through the elimination of Trotsky and his followers, no special analysis of the Negro question was advanced. The Fourth World Congress did establish a special Commission on the American Negro to study the race issue. However, it apparently was not contemplated that it would eventually produce the "Theses" that were circulated and recommended for adoption in early 1928.

Prior to the Sixth World Congress the American Communist Party's basic position on the Negro question did not differ substantially from that of the hated Socialists'. While the Communists proposed a different tactical role for Negroes, they did not view the group in other than economic class terms. Both in the United States and in the Kremlin Communist bureaucrats completely misread labor and race unrest in America during the immediate post-war years, identifying discontent with radicalism, strikes with revolutionary manifestations, and unfocused Negro protest with race consciousness. They had expected the lower, unorganized elements of the American working class, including Negroes, to rally to the Russian Revolution and organize similar movements of its own. They were deeply disappointed in the failure of the Party to make headway under what appeared to be exceptionally favorable conditions. It became apparent that unless something was done, the Communist Party in the United States was destined to play a minor and ineffectual role in the overthrow of the world's strongest capitalist power.

A new line was definitely in order. "Boring from within" tactics, which the Party had followed between 1923 and 1928 partly as a result of Foster's influence, were to be abandoned. In their place was substituted a policy of dual organization, and the Trade Union Educational League was ordered to transform itself into the Trade Union Unity League as the principal instrument of this program.[1] The Negro question was extensively reviewed on the basis of the report of the special Negro Commission and the "Theses" circulated by the Executive Committee of the Communist International for "pre-Congress discussion." The Negro question was redefined as that of an *oppressed nation,* and the doctrine of self-determination was declared to be the core of the program of the Communist Party of the United States. It is this doctrine and its application that we wish now to examine.

As early as 1924 the Communist International had expressed its disappointment with the failure of the American section to make greater headway among Negroes, the Executive Committee declaring: "By ignoring the question of racial antagonism our Party has allowed the negro liberation movement in America to take a wrong path and to get into the hands of the Negro bourgeoisie which has launched the nationalist slogan—'Back to Africa.' "[2] However, there was no hint of the things that were to come in 1928. For in 1924 the Executive Committee concluded:

... the main task of our American comrades as to this question must consist in fighting against these prejudices, and in energetic action for full equality of rights regardless of race as well as for the extirpation of all humiliating customs which draw a dividing line between whites and blacks. It is only under such conditions that it will be possible to draw the negro masses in America into a general fight for the dictatorship of the proletariat.[3]

The "Theses" circulated prior to the Sixth World Congress of 1928 declared that the Negro question in the United States was a "national problem," one aspect of the pattern of imperialism, and that its solution should follow the line laid down by Lenin on the national question. Negroes in the United States were a separate and distinct nation. They were under the heel of an imperialist power. They met all the requirements of a nation as defined by Stalin, being a historically evolved, stable entity, defined by language, territory, economic life, and psychological make-up, and manifested in a community of culture. They should therefore be approached, declared this Comintern edict, in the same terms and with the same program as any other oppressed colonial nation. The doctrine of self-determination, with the right to secession and the establishment of an independent Negro nation, was declared applicable to Negroes in the southern United States.[4]

There was some disagreement with the proposals set forth in the "Theses," and a number of Communists in the United States and England took exception to this new "line." Among them was A. Shiek, who maintained that Lenin's concept of national-colonial exploitation under imperialism was never intended to be applied to the Jewish question or the Negro question in the United States:

For when we speak of the oppression of colonial or other subject nations, we have in mind not social groups, formed on the basis of general secondary peculiarities, having no practical importance, but groups consolidated by the real bonds of common territory, economic system, language and culture, and striving toward an independent economic existence.[5]

The Communist Parties, Shiek continued, were in danger of being "ensnared" by such movements among Negroes and Jews. The former should put forth their demands for the Negro on the basis of race alone and in the United States should demand full social, economic, and political equality. The basic strategy of the Communist Party in the United States, he declared, should be to:

... safeguard the hegemony of the proletariat in the emancipation movement of the race, consolidating the great masses of the oppressed racial minority around the Party in the form of a non-Party mass racial organization under the leadership of Communists. To this end it is necessary to ensure the confidence of the negro masses in the Party. And this cannot be achieved otherwise than by way of bringing certain activities to the forefront as part of the militant tasks of the Party.[6]

But in spite of the opposition of Shiek and others, the resolutions adopted were the same as the "Theses" with a few minor modifications.[7] It is significant that there was no strenuous opposition voiced by the American delegation. Its members should have been aware of the limitations of this "line" and of the difficulties, both tactical and long range, in applying the self-determination doctrine in the United States. They should have known, as they were to realize soon afterward, that it would antagonize both Negro and white workers. And yet the members of the American delegation to the Sixth World Congress gave their approval to the draft resolution without exception.

Three factors help to explain this. First, a number of the delegates were top leaders of the Party in the United States. There was in process at the time a bitter internal fight for control of the organization. Victory would come to the faction which could secure the nod of approval from leaders of the Russian section, who in turn controlled the Communist International. Each delegate was therefore reluctant to take exception to proposals which had been made by the Executive Committee of that body. Second, American leaders had been severely castigated for their failure to secure a following among Negroes and could point to no success with alternative programs. Finally, they had been much impressed by the growth of race and national feeling among Negroes during the 1920's and believed that such sentiment might be turned to account if a Negro nationalist movement under Communist Party control were launched.

The Sixth World Congress continued the Special Negro Commission, one of whose next duties was to submit a final draft of Communist Party strategy and tactics on the Negro question in the United States within the framework of the new line. A few weeks after the adjournment of the Congress the report of the Commission was approved and released by the Executive Committee. It declared:

The Negro question in the United States must be considered in relation to the Negro question and struggles in other parts of the world. The Negro is an oppressed race. Whether he is in a minority (U.S.A., etc.), majority (South Africa), or inhabits a so-called independent state (Liberia, etc.), the Negroes are oppressed by imperialism. Thus, a common tie of interest is established for the revolutionary struggle of race and national liberation from imperialist domination of Negroes in various parts of the world. A strong Negro Revolutionary movement in the U.S.A. will be able to influence and direct the revolutionary movements in all those parts of the world where the Negroes are oppressed by imperialism.[8]

The immediate significance of the resolution for the Communist Party in the United States was interpreted by Jay Lovestone, then one of its principal leaders, in these terms:

For the American Party the Negro question assumes ever growing importance. The especially intense exploitation and heavy oppression to which the millions of Negroes in America are subject make it imperative for the Party to devote its best energies and its maximum resources towards becoming the recognized leader and champion of the interests of Negroes as an oppressed people. Our objective, of course, here is to have the Negro proletariat assume the hegemony in the entire national Negro movement.[9]

While the earlier analysis of the Negro question in the United States had emphasized the specific class characteristics of the problem, the new position taken by the Communist International required the development of theoretical rationalizations for the changed line. Accordingly, there began within the Party a continuous effort to reinterpret the Negro problem in terms of the new program. "John Pepper," a representative of the Communist International, assumed the principal responsibility. He declared:

The Negro question in the United States must be treated in its relation to the liberation struggle of the proletariat against American imperialism. *The struggle against white oppression of the Negro masses is a part of the proletarian revolution in America against capitalism.* The American working class cannot free itself from capitalist exploitation without freeing the Negro race from white oppression.

*At the same time the Negro question in the United States of America must be treated in its relations to the huge Negro masses of farmers and workers oppressed and exploited by white imperialism in Africa and South America.*[10]

According to Pepper, whose statements reflected the official position of the Communist International, industrialization created a potential organizing base among Negroes. It made possible a new working-class leadership for all Negro race movements, and offered the opportunity for Negro workers, under the leadership of the Communist Party, to assume "hegemony of the Negro liberation movement."

In addition, it increased the importance of the Negro question for the revolutionary struggle of the American proletariat.

The racial caste system was seen as a "fundamental feature of the social, industrial and political organization of the United States." It therefore became the duty of the American Communist Party to develop all the revolutionary potentialities of the Negro race. The Communist Party, Pepper said, must consider itself not only the Party of the working class generally, but also the champion of the Negro as an oppressed race and, especially, the organizer of the Negro working-class movement.

Because Negroes were still in virtual economic and political slavery, he continued, they constituted a "colony within the body of the United States of America." The disintegration within the Negro farm group meant the "proletarization" of the Negro masses. Realizing that Negro workers and farmers might make common cause with the white working class, the bourgeoisie made every effort to promote racial prejudice and thus drive a dividing wedge in the revolutionary forces. The Communist Party would not only struggle for immediate social, economic, and political equality of Negroes in the United States, but at the same time would advance the program of full national self-determination.

Then followed a brief definition of the separate nation:

*. . . In the economic and social conditions and class relations of the Negro people there are increasing forces which serve as a basis for the development of a Negro nation* (a compact mass of farmers on a contiguous territory, semi-feudal conditions, complete segregation, common traditions of slavery, the development of distinct class and economic ties, etc. etc.).[11]

The compact Negro farming masses of the Black Belt were, according to this official view, a potential base for the national liberation movement and the basic elements of the self-determination program. The Negro national liberation movement had tremendous potentialities. It must first take the form of a bourgeois-nationalist movement, but as it progressed, the Negro proletariat would play an increasingly important role and ultimately obtain control of it. "*It would be a major mistake to believe that there can be any other revolution in imperialist America, in a country of the most powerful, most centralized, and concentrated industry, than a proletarian revolution. . . .* The American Communists should emphasize in their propaganda the establishment of a Negro Soviet Republic." [12]

It remained for later writers such as James S. Allen and Harry Haywood to supply the more "scientific" rationalizations of the self-determination theory.[13] The similarity between the program laid down for the Communist Party of the United States and the earlier doctrines of Lenin and Stalin on the national and colonial questions is readily apparent; and the connection is a direct one, through the Sixth World Congress of the Communist International. Not only were the general ideas taken over; they were advocated in precisely the same terms, down to the slogans, and even to the sentences and phrases, employed by the Communist International.

The new analysis of the Negro question in the United States was a part of a sweeping reorientation of the whole revolutionary program of the Communist International. It can be understood as a manifestation of the changed line that followed the less revolutionary period from 1923 to 1928. The self-determination doctrine has had its ups and downs. Sometimes the American Party has pushed it; at other times, shelved it. It was strongly advocated from 1928 through most of 1934. But when at the end of this period the Communist International ordered its affiliates to organize and support united front movements in opposition to Fascism, particularly in France, the Party in the United States dropped the self-determination demand and made little use of it in propaganda work. In 1939, following the signing of the Stalin-Hitler pact, the doctrine was revived but not seriously advanced, because the Party's efforts were concentrated on rallying the Negroes in opposition to the "imperialist war." After the German attack on Russia in 1941, agitation for the program was gradually dropped; following Teheran, it was renounced completely. After the Duclos letter of April, 1945 and the "reconstitution" of the American Communist Party in July of that year, the self-determination theory was again revived and made the central plank of the program on the Negro question. The uses to which the theory of self-determination is put are a remarkably accurate index of the Party "line" at any given time. And it should be added that the Party's position on self-determination vacillates, not in response to innovations in the Negro question but in response to the momentary needs of Soviet foreign policy. The new line on the Negro question apparently took most American Communists by surprise in 1928. The Party spokesmen, however, dutifully recovered and fell into line, turning out a voluminous amount of material reinterpreting the Negro question and the Party's future role.* That the faithful, with a few exceptions, were anxious to abide by these pronouncements from on high was indicated, for example, in Browder's statement before the Twelfth Central Committee Plenum in 1930, when he asserted:

*The work of this plenum is a continuation of the line of the Comintern laid down at the Sixth World Congress, the line that was further developed in the tenth plenum of the ECCI* [Executive Committee of the Communist International], *which was established as the line of the American Party in the Seventh convention last June.*[14]

Having imbibed freely of this Kremlin-concocted patent medicine, he continued:

* As late as May, 1928, the American Communist Party declared: "*The Negro question is a race question and the Communist Party must be the champion of the oppressed Negro race.*" (Resolution of the May, 1928, Plenum of the Communist Party Central Executive Committee: *Communist*, VII, No. 7 (July, 1928), 418.) However, following the change in line, the new definition was offered: "... *To contend that the Negro question in the United States is a race question in contradistinction to a national question is to contend that Negroes are oppressed because they are black!* The real economic and social essence of the Negro question consists in the difference between economic and cultural developments of Negro and white peoples in this country under a capitalist imperialist social order." (Harry Haywood, "The Theoretical Defenders of White Chauvinism in the Labor Movement," *Communist*, X, No. 6 (June, 1931), 505-506.)

We have taken steps [in Negro work] which will have tremendous political results in the breaking down of the old separation between white and black workers, we have shown the Negro masses the meaning of our main political slogans, and especially the slogan of self-determination which has received an instantaneous response from the Negro masses. They understand our slogans now as something that touches their daily life and that are quite different from the slogans of any other political party in the United States.[15]

The Communist Party in 1930 did not have more than a thousand Negro members. The General Secretary did not make himself clear on how the establishment of a separate Negro state was to break down "the old separation between white and black workers," or how the slogan of self-determination touched the daily life of Negroes. He presented no evidence of the "instantaneous response from the Negro masses." We must grant, however, that the Communist program was indeed "different."

The Comintern's position on the Negro question was given a more detailed expression in the form of a resolution adopted some two years after the adjournment of the Sixth World Congress. While it contained nothing new by way of general theory, it did provide a more specific analysis and program of action for the American section. This document is worth examining in some detail. It declared first that the Party had always acted openly and energetically on the Negro question, and, as a consequence, Communists had won wide respect among Negroes. The Party had succeeded in purging its own ranks of "white chauvinism and the grass roots opportunism of the Lovestone renegades," the resolution continued. (Lovestone and others had insisted that industrialization of the South and migration of Negroes would destroy any potential base for a "Black Republic.")

But because of the Lovestone influence, the resolution charged, the Party has not yet succeeded "in overcoming in its own ranks all underestimation of the struggle for the slogan of the right of self-determination and still less succeeded in doing away with all lack of clarity on the Negro question." The problem in the United States was that of an oppressed nation which found itself in an "extraordinarily distressing situation of national oppression" because of the racial distinctions and social antagonisms which were remnants of the slavery period.

Because Negroes were an oppressed people with a common background and tradition and were situated in a relatively contiguous geographic area, they were, the resolution declared, "a nation within the United States." While advancing the slogan of "Equal Rights" it was incumbent on the Party to demand "self-determination for Negroes in the Black Belt." "The struggle for equal rights of Negroes does not in any way exclude recognition and support of their rights to their own special schools, government organs, etc." It was not anticipated that Negroes outside the "Black Belt" would make such demands; among them the Party was to advance the "full equality" slogan.

In the struggle for Negro rights, the resolution insisted, it was the duty of the white workers to march in the forefront. The white vanguard everywhere was to make a break in the Jim Crow citadels which had been erected on the bourgeois "slave market morality." One of the primary duties of the Party was to expose the "false" bourgeois friends of the Negro who were "only interested in siphoning off revolutionary aspirations of the Negro masses into reformist channels."

Upon the revolutionary Negro workers, said the resolution, fell the job of carrying on "tireless activity among the Negro working masses to free them from their distrust of the white proletariat and draw them into the common front of the revolutionary struggle against the bourgeoisie." The Party should place great emphasis on the immediate, every-day needs of the Negro. However, the basic program should demand the confiscation of the large farms of the South and the establishment of the state and territorial unity of the Black Belt under Negro control. Self-determination meant "the complete and unlimited right of the Negro majority to exercise governmental authority in the entire territory of the Black Belt as well as to decide on the relations between their territory and other nations."

The resolution further stated that the Communist Party could not make its stand for self-determination dependent on any specified conditions, even on the hegemony of the proletariat in the national Negro revolutionary movement. The establishment of a separate Negro republic was not required by the Party, but Negroes should be free to erect such a state if they so desired, and it was the responsibility of the Party to see that this choice was possible. The resolution added, however, that Negroes probably would not want to secede in the event a proletarian dictatorship was established in the United States. Actually the Party should advocate separation only so long as capitalism continued its rule. Although Communists should associate themselves with separatist movements, the resolution warned that such support should be accorded only to "genuine" nationalist programs.*

In order to implement this policy the Party was to undertake the following seven-point program:

1. Link immediate demands for alleviation of the Negro's condition with the ultimate goal of self-determination.

2. Bring the wide masses of the Negro people into "at least partial struggle" by adopting the kind of immediate goals which the Negro could understand.

3. Select such immediate demands as would be in keeping with the revolutionary slogans, "with no fixed type or number" to be advanced.

4. Fight in the forefront of the Negro mass liberation movement, and completely dissociate the Party from "reformist" and "bourgeois" elements in the field of race relations.

5. Develop a solid Communist Party and a revolutionary trade union movement among workers, Negro and white, in the South.

6. Expose and criticize bourgeois Negro leaders and brand them as apologists of white reaction.

7. Link the struggle for Negro rights in the North with the national liberation movement in the South, giving national scope to the Negro struggle.

While such a program may sound fantastic to the student of race relations in the United States, it must be remembered that it was taken quite seriously by the Comintern and by the Communist Party. Although such theoretical gerrymandering and

* Resolution on the Negro Question in the United States (Final Text Confirmed by the Political Secretariat of the Executive Committee of the Communist International, October 26, 1930) *Communist International*, Vol. VII, No. 2, January 15, 1931, 65-74.

sloganizing were a distinct handicap to the Party, as its subsequent efforts to apply the self-determination program indicated, this continued to be the Communist policy—at least officially—until the dissolution of the Party in 1944. It was revived following the Duclos letter in 1945 and is currently in vogue.

In its publications, particularly the theoretical and educational organs, the Party placed great emphasis on the self-determination doctrine, but in its more practical day-to-day work among Negroes, it was obscured, even consciously played down. Party functionaries were frequently taken to task for their failure to apply a "Leninist conception" and a "Marxist understanding" to the Negro question; i. e., their failure to preach salvation through self-determination. Winestone, writing in the *Communist International*, declared, for example: "The slogan of the right of self-determination of the Negroes has not at all been taken up by the Party. There is opportunistic resistance to this slogan as well as a lack of clarity both of which must be quickly overcome." [16] Actually, American Communist leaders were attempting to find some middle path which would (1) pacify the Marxist "sociologists" in the Kremlin, and at the same time (2) make an effective appeal to Negroes. Since these two goals were largely incompatible, it is not surprising that the over-all results were meager.

The Communist Party's self-determination program was widely criticized; it was construed by many Negroes to be an ideological red-winged Jim Crow.[17] *The Crisis*, for example, declared editorially:

They [Communists] swear by all that's holy that such a plan of plain segregation is *not* segregation, but who can predict what they will say tomorrow or next week? Anyway, we maintain that the mere existence of the proposal proves that the idea of separateness is uppermost in the minds of the Red brain-trust and not the idea of oneness. And in advancing this theory of separation, the Communists are hand in hand with the southern ruling class which they so delight to lambast. But since their Moscow masters are opportunist in the matter of war profits [in Ethiopia], who would dare criticise the American followers for opportunism in a little thing like race segregation? Who, indeed, except the segregated American Negro? [18]

The Socialist journalist Berenberg, discussing the "bankruptcy" of the American Communist Party, suggested:

> This [self-determination doctrine] smells much of the desire to exploit to Communist advantages the vexed question of the Southern race question. It enables the Communist Party to appear to the Negro as the champion of his racial rights. It enables it also to seem to say to the Southern whites, in effect, that in the event of revolution the Negroes will be segregated, herded into a separate area, given "self-determination." What is the theory that the Negro is a "separate nation," whose cultural development has been retarded, but the old theory of Negro inferiority in a new form.[19]

Even among the Communists themselves there were certain manifestations of doubt and "incorrect" tendencies. Doubtful members were assured, however, that once they "really understood" what self-determination meant, they would have no hesitation in accepting it as the only solution to the Negro question.

It was particularly difficult for the Communists to secure acceptance of the idea of the "Black Belt" as a potential national state. It was also difficult to explain just what role the southern white workers were to play in the revolution or what their status would be once Negroes had been given absolute jurisdiction over the region. James S. Allen vaguely stated that the cultural, economic and territorial unity of the area of Negro majority was a fact (apparently a self-evident one since he was not at pains to prove it).

The Party also took the position that there was no conflict of interest between the demands for a Negro nation and the demands for the emancipation of the white working class in the South. One Party functionary put it this way:

> Every revolutionary white worker will understand that to demand the right of self-determination, the right to separate, does not mean to advocate separation of Negro workers from white workers. On the contrary, our aim is complete unity and fusion of Negro and white toilers. Ours is not a general cry for unity on the condition that the Negro toilers "forget about" peonage, lynching, and the system of white supremacy as the Lovestoneites propose. But inasmuch as American imperialism retains *by force* within its state boundaries the Black Belt with its oppressed majority of Negro population, we stand for

their right to separate. . . . In other words, we understand that any lasting unity between the white and Negro toilers must be voluntary, on the basis of mutual confidence of both races and not upon the basis of force.[20]

Comrade Haywood and the Party were apparently determined to have their self-determination cake and eat it too. If they suffered ideological indigestion in the process, there was always some Stalinist bicarbonate on the shelf. But all their "explanations" remained unsatisfactory; they continued to gloss over the basic desire of Negroes to be accepted as equals in the whole of American society and failed to designate a specific role for southern white workers.[21]

The belief that Negroes in the southern United States represented an agrarian culture comparable to a number of those in Czarist Russia undergirded the Party's new theory of the Negro question. Stalin had specified that one of the characteristics of a nation was a common language. In order to fit this definition to the American Negro, Party spokesmen were forced into an insistence that the requirement was fulfilled because all Negroes spoke English! The Party also misread into Negro ideology aspirations for small-scale land ownership, which, though significant, were not as strong as among the peasants of the European countries. The Party also glossed over the fact that American Negroes of the 1930's had no separate culture of their own, leaving little foundation for a separatist movement which the self-determination doctrine required.[22] A systematic effort on the part of the Communists to uncover African survivals, even with the unsolicited help of certain American anthropologists, produced few additional props for the self-determination theory.

How were the struggles for the national liberation of Negroes and the establishment of the black republic to be carried on by the Party? According to the Communist tacticians, the effort would be concentrated in the area consisting of east Virginia, North Carolina, South Carolina, central Georgia, Alabama, the delta regions of Mississippi and Louisiana, and the coastal regions of Texas. It was in these areas that a large number of counties, frequently contiguous, had Negro majority populations. (Apparently it would have been necessary to redraw the map of the

Negro nation after each census. And with the continual migration of Negroes from the Deep South, the counties having a colored majority would have decreased in number. This little item of statistics, however, made no dent in Party thought.)

The continuing crisis in southern agriculture, the Party maintained, would force many of the small farmers off the land, reducing most of them to the status of day laborers. Negroes would become increasingly impoverished; they would attempt to protest and would meet with increased violence. But this would merely strengthen their protest, which would in turn become the base for the national liberation movement. The landless Negroes would realize that their plight was hopeless in the framework of the plantation system; their only alternative would be revolution, and this the Communists proposed to lead.[23]

However, the "Draft Program for Negro Laborers in the Southern States" emphasized that in order to rally Negroes for ultimate revolutionary action, it would first be necessary to concentrate on a series of immediate demands. In the process, the Communists would emerge in positions of leadership. Among the demands the Party proposed to make were: immediate relief for destitute farmers, sharecroppers, and day laborers; written contracts to replace verbal agreements between landlords and tenants; revision of the credit system, with landowners providing cash advances rather than "furnish" for their tenants; and ultimate confiscation and redistribution of the large plantations among the landless Negro and white farmers.[24]

Prior to undertaking large-scale organization in the rural areas, the Party proposed to develop in Birmingham a revolutionary industrial union movement that would be the hub from which successive efforts among the sharecroppers and tenant farmers would radiate. From the industrial union base in the steel and coal industries in and around Birmingham would come the material resources and the leadership required for organization in the countryside. With these goals realized, the Party would be in a position to press not merely for immediate demands but for the ultimate items on its revolutionary agenda, including self-determination for Negroes and the establishment of the black republic.[25]

The new line demanded a substantially different conception of the American Negro. The depression beginning in 1929 (but affecting southern agriculture for a number of years previously) coincided with the adoption of the self-determination theory. By placing progressively greater emphasis on such problems as relief, employment, welfare and housing—matters of growing importance for Negroes because the economic débacle bore most heavily upon them as a group—the Party made some rather impressive gains among the race, even in the South. By some curious bit of logic, perhaps with no logic at all, these advances were attributed to the soundness of the self-determination line.[26]

According to the Communists, the most significant developments in the Negro question as a consequence of the depression were the growing impoverishment of the Negro masses, the widening split between the black working class and the black bourgeoisie, and the development of a revolutionary psychology among the distressed masses. As Robert Minor put it:

> Against this background, and as a result of the drastic wage cuts, speed-up and unemployment, entirely without real measures of relief, there is a fast increasing will on the part of the proletarian Negro masses, and to a considerable degree also amongst the landless Negro farmers, to militant action against exploitation as proletarians and peasants, and also against exploitation as a suppressed and persecuted race (national minority).[27]

Though the Negro bourgeoisie in a few instances had taken militant action in defense of race rights, its principal function according to the Party, had been to quell protest among working-class elements, or else direct it to the benefit of Negro shop-keepers through "do business with your own race" campaigns. The reformist organizations, Communists declared, sought to frustrate the revolutionary aspirations of the Negro people; and "the deepening crisis and rising temper of the Negro masses against the increasing yoke of oppression, [make] necessary greater demagogy on the part of the Negro bourgeoisie." [28] Negro protest in the 1920's was betrayed by the "Back To Africa" program of the Garvey Movement; the Party considered itself properly, and successfully, channeling the ferment of the 1930's toward the "hegemony of working class elements."

Industrialization and migration, the Party admitted, had resulted in the enlargement of the Negro middle class, but the latter was no longer capable of assuming race leadership. On the contrary, it was the enemy of the Negro masses:

> It is clear that the segregational interests of the Negro bourgeoisie are reflected in the Jim Crow nationalism of this group (Negro insurance companies). Interpreting its own interests as the interests of the Negro people as a whole it attempts to rally the Negro masses in support of its class interest through such slogans as "race loyalty," "race solidarity," etc., etc.[29]

The function of the Party, then, was quite clear. It must wage a continual campaign against the Negro middle class. It must show to the Negro people the reactionary character of the NAACP, the National Urban League, and other reformist organizations. It must assume leadership of the protest among lower-class Negroes, and it must channel this protest along revolutionary lines in terms of the general strategy of the Party. For now the Negro people found themselves "unable even to fight for the lives of their innocent children against the habitual murderers of the ruling class, without associating themselves with the revolutionary movement which will overthrow our common oppressors." [30]

In the Communist view, those Negroes who pretended to see some hope in the New Deal program were doomed to disappointment. Some relief had been furnished to the most depressed elements in the Negro population, and a few Negroes received jobs of some consequence in the Administration; but fundamentally the New Deal was the

> ... aggressive effort of the bankers and trusts to find a way out of the crisis at the expense of the millions of toilers. Under cover of the most shameless demagoguery, Roosevelt and the capitalists carry through drastic attacks upon the living standards of the masses, increased terrorism against the Negro masses, increased political oppression and systematic denial of existing civil rights, and are strengthening the control of the big monopolists over the economic and political life of the country.[31]

Having analyzed the Negro question in terms of an "oppressed nation," and having rejected the reformist policies of the Negro middle class (and the early New Deal), how did the Communist Party of the United States propose to implement its program? One of the first steps was to place greater emphasis on organization of Negroes in the South. The Party's general position was briefly outlined earlier in the present chapter. Revolutionary organizations were to be built among industrial workers and among Negro farmers in the Black Belt. Foster had previously suggested the method and expressed the Party's determination to carry it through. Writing immediately after the Sixth World Congress, he declared:

The role of the Left-Wing as organizer and leader of the working class of the South is further emphasized by the increasing importance of the Negro workers in southern industry which stresses our need to organize them. Our Party is the only one that can organize and lead the Negro masses in real struggle. . . .

The situation in the South in addition to offering constantly more favorable opportunities for our party to come forward as the leader of the working class, also progressively facilitates its activities as organizer and defender of the Negro race. . . . It is the historical task of our party to lead the fight against this organized persecution of Negroes. This is a revolutionary struggle. . . .

The fight around the race issue will be a hard and bitter one, especially in the South. The reactionary advocates of "white supremacy" will meet the assault of our party on their caste system with armed force as well as legal terrorism. They will seek to crush our organizations with violence. Of this we may be sure when our party gets its work well under way, but our party will be equal to the situation. Overground or underground in the South it will successfully carry on its activities. . . .

The decisive factor in all our work in the South is our policy on the Negro question. We must realize from the outset that it is the basic task of our party to lead a militant struggle for and with the Negroes. All our activities there, all our success and failures will turn around this central fact. In the South we must be vigilantly on guard to combat all tendencies in our party to soft pedal the Negro question and to compromise with Jim Crowism. This has not been done sufficiently. . . . Those workers who are not willing to join a common branch with Negroes and participate with them in Communist Party activities are not yet ready for membership in the Workers (Communist) Party.[32]

Immediately after the Sixth World Congress of the Communist International it was apparent that considerable resources of the Party would be directed toward organization in the South, particularly among Negroes. But it was not until 1931 that the Party made any serious attempts to reach white or Negro workers there. The deepening depression, bearing heavily on southern workers and farmers, afforded an opportunity the Party would not otherwise have had.

Four fairly distinct, but closely related, types of organization were undertaken by the Communists:

1. Branches of the Party itself, composed of a select number of industrial workers, intellectuals, and sharecroppers.

2. Revolutionary industrial unions in the steel, coal, and textile industries, which were affiliated with the Trade Union Unity League.

3. Unions of sharecroppers and tenant farmers, primarily in Alabama and Louisiana, composed of both Negroes and whites, but concentrating on Negroes.

4. Organizations of the unemployed in various urban centers such as Atlanta, Birmingham, and New Orleans.

No statistical data are available on the actual branches of the Party itself in the South during the period from 1928 to 1934. In all probability its principal units were in the industrial area around Birmingham and in some of the textile manufacturing towns. The Party did not place emphasis on direct recruitment but preferred to exercise its influence through organizations set up to meet specific needs of different groups. Even some Negroes and whites who under no circumstances would embrace the revolutionary goals of the Party were not too hesitant to join front organizations whose immediate purpose was raising wages, increasing relief payments, or obtaining better terms under tenancy agreements. Although Party membership remained small, the influence it exercised in the working-class protest of the South was of some significance.

The Sharecroppers Union was organized in Tallapoosa, Alabama in 1931. Direction of the movement came from Party headquarters in Birmingham. Violent efforts were made to stamp out the organization, white vigilantes joining with the regular law enforcement officials to suppress the "Yankee-led rebellion" of Negro tenants and sharecroppers. The Union was driven underground but continued its work in Tallapoosa and Chambers counties. In 1932 mob action on an even larger scale was directed at the Union, but the latter succeeded in holding on; and by 1933 it claimed 3,000 members, including a few white sharecroppers. In 1934, with a more favorable administration in Washington and with the aid of grants from the Garland Fund, the Union undertook its first strike in Tallapoosa County. Cotton pickers in some areas were given the seventy cents per hundred-weight asked by the Union.

The Sharecroppers Union was dissolved in 1936 and its members were directed to affiliate with other organizations.[33] Had there not been a shift in the Party line from a revolutionary to a united front approach in 1935, and had not the Communists been in positions of influence in the emerging CIO movement, the organization probably would have continued, though how effective it would have become is problematical.

The revolutionary industrial unions which had been organized around Birmingham likewise met with violent opposition from police and employers. Meetings were broken up; organizers were arrested and frequently convicted under hastily enacted laws designed to "stamp out subversive influences." Racial prejudice was systematically invoked in an effort to forestall organization of black and white workers.[34] The unions organized by the Communists, however, managed to survive. With the national administration encouraging the organization of labor, and later with the formation of the CIO, industrial unionism of both Negro and white workers grew by rapid strides, even behind the moonlight and magnolia curtain. With the dissolution of the Trade Union Unity League and the adoption of a new set of "boring from within" tactics by the Party in 1935, the members of the Communist unions around Birmingham were directed to join regular labor organizations. Frequently these workers became the core around which the new unions were built.

The Party usually carried out organization among jobless workers through local Committees of the Unemployed. During most of this period there was no central organization outside the

Party giving direction to these movements. The extent of Party influence on their programs and tactics is difficult to measure. Greatest gains were made in the larger urban-industrial centers, where relief problems were more acute and the concentrated numbers of unemployed provided a more solid organizing base.[35]

The Party's role in the organization of jobless workers in the South during this period has been greatly overestimated. Local law enforcement officials and business interests in southern communities reacted on a hysterical basis to even the slightest manifestations of mass discontent. As a result, small protest movements were emphasized out of all proportion to their real importance. The violent handling of Communist organizers, and the publicity surrounding it, gave the impression that their program and influence were far more pervasive than they actually were.

In its practical organizing work in the South, the Party, particularly after 1932, placed little emphasis on the doctrine of self-determination. It was realized, as Browder later admitted, that the Negro masses were not yet ready to carry through the struggle for self-determination, but were willing to fight against Jim Crow and other abuses.[36] The job of publicizing the self-determination aspect of the Party program fell largely to the conservative white press of the South, which made it one of the principal points of attack on the Communists.

Outside the South the Party attempted to reach Negroes through three types of organization: (1) the revolutionary industrial unions affiliated with the Trade Union Unity League, (2) the local organizations of the unemployed, and (3) the committees and councils of the League of Struggle for Negro Rights. The Sixth World Congress, and later the Red International of Labor Unions, had directed that the Trade Union Educational League be transformed into the Trade Union Unity League and embark on a program of revolutionary dualism. The Fourth Congress of the RILU held in Moscow in April, 1928, declared:

> Further appeals to the bureaucracy and dependence upon the so-called progressives in the reactionary unions is useless and wrong. The Trade Union Educational League must itself become the basis [sic] organization for the organization of the unorganized.[37]

At the time the TUEL met to comply with the directive from Moscow a letter from Lozovsky, Secretary of the Executive Committee of the RILU, further outlined the tasks of the Party in the trade union field. "It is your task," he said, "to create a trade union center uniting all revolutionary unions, minority groups and individual militants. The new center must become the organizer of the masses of unorganized workers, as well as direct the work of minorities in the reformist unions against the A. F. L. bureaucracy." [38] These and other directives were dutifully complied with by the American section.

The TUUL took the position that under no circumstances would concessions be made to the biracial pattern in the organization of revolutionary unions. Negroes were to be admitted on an equal basis, and the League was to fight for their rights both on and off the job. While emphasis was to be placed on the building of new, "militant" workers organizations, the Party functionaries in existing unions were to continue their fight for the equitable admission of Negroes. The establishment of the new radical unions was to be characterized by the formation of Negro shop committees whose function it would be to win over all Negroes in the plants. To facilitate closer cooperation with white workers, these committees would then be meshed with larger groups including white militants, which would in turn assume over-all responsibility.[39] This program's parallel with that of the later-established International Trade Union Committee of Negro Workers was readily apparent.[40] In order to facilitate its approach to colored workers, the TUUL established a special Negro section, with James W. Ford as Negro Organizer.

The major TUUL affiliates shortly after its formation were the National Miners Union, Needle Trades Workers Industrial Union, and National Textile Workers Union. The Metal Trades group of the old TUEL became the Metal Workers Industrial Union; it included a substantial number of Negroes in the steel industry. The Marine Workers League was the TUUL instrument through which an effort was made to organize Negro longshoremen. Among the other affiliates of the TUUL by 1930 were the Office Workers Union of New York City, Sugar Beet Workers of Colorado, Building Trades Industrial League, Auto

Workers Union, Printers and Publishers Industrial League and the Railroad Amalgamation Committee.[41] A number of other organizations were added during the next year, including the Food and Packinghouse Workers Industrial Union. With the exception of the Metal Workers Industrial Union, the Marine Workers League, and the Food and Packinghouse Workers Industrial Union, the TUUL affiliates had few Negro members.

One should not get the impression, however, that the above organizations were mass unions; they were not. Almost without exception they were small and weak, frequently involved in unsuccessful strikes and lacking any over-all integration. The TUUL was in fact proving about as ineffective as the TUEL. The Executive Bureau of the Red International of Labor Unions complained in early 1931 that the TUUL was isolated from the masses, employed poor strike strategy, displayed a tendency toward formalism, and exhibited weakness in boring from within the old-line unions. "The fundamental weakness of the Trade Union Unity League," declared the Secretariat, "is that at a time so favorable for revolutionary work it is still failing to organize the workers in struggle for their daily demands and needs." [42]

However, as the depression deepened and as the plight of industrial workers and farm laborers became worse, the TUUL was in a position to expand its influence. In many cases it had a wide-open field largely through default of the conservative craft unions in the American Federation of Labor, to whom organization on an industrial basis was anathema. The latter preferred to keep what little they had, play it safe, and let the unorganized be lost. Neglected by the established unions, pushed around by management, with their plight becoming increasingly worse, workers in the mass production industries in many cases found that only the TUUL was ready to organize them. This was especially true of Negro workers; the craft exclusiveness and race prejudice of the AFL affiliates made it doubly hard for colored laborers to secure admittance.

The TUUL was thus able to expand its existing organizations and to establish a number of new ones—in the mass production industries and among the argricultural workers. The Sharecroppers Union in Alabama and Louisiana was almost exclusively

Negro. It was organized under the most unfavorable circumstances with illegal violence systematically employed against it. The fact that it made any headway at all reflected the desperate plight of the Negro sharecroppers and laborers in the rural South. The TUUL also organized the Cannery and Agricultural Workers Industrial Union in California, which was in the forefront of the farm labor strikes that swept the Golden State in the early 1930's.[43] It, too, was met by large-scale illegal force. The CAWIU included in its membership individuals belonging to various ethnic and racial minorities—Mexicans, Japanese, Chinese, Filipinos, and Negroes. While its diversity in composition and its revolutionary ideology were distinct handicaps, they were not the underlying causes of ultimate failure. The CAWIU merely duplicated the failure of previous organizations—and for the same reasons.

In the mass production industries the TUUL had more to show for its efforts. However, it faced the same dilemma as had the IWW: how to build a revolutionary working-class movement and at the same time stabilize its organization through assumption of collective bargaining responsibilities. The success which the Committee for Industrial Organization later experienced among the Negro workers in the automobile, steel, meatpacking, rubber and longshore industries was due in part to two factors—the use of the TUUL affiliates as the core of the new unions, and the use of former TUUL organizers who had gained experience in organizing Negroes in the early 1930's. Had the Comintern not laid down the united front line for the American Communist Party in 1934, and had the Committee for Industrial Organization not been formed, the TUUL in all probability would have continued to function. The united front line called for abandonment of revolutionary dualism in the labor movement, and the CIO provided an opportunity to carry out the Party's new industrial organization program. The Communists and not John L. Lewis made the most of it. Negro workers, nevertheless, benefited in the process.

While the TUUL and the Councils of Unemployed served as the principal instruments for organizing Negro workers under Communist control during the 1928-34 period, the League of

Struggle for Negro Rights was established for purposes of developing a wider race movement and bringing various classes of Negroes under Party direction. The Party had been instructed to transform the then almost dormant American Negro Labor Congress into "an intermediary mass organization, as a medium through which the Party can extend its work among the Negro masses and mobilize the Negro workers under its leadership." [44]

This directive the American Party duly complied with, establishing in November, 1930 the LSNR. This new organization, for which many sweeping gains were predicted, proposed to unite a wide range of Negro groups around a broad, and frequently contradictory, program. Party control was complete from the outset, so obvious that it could not escape the attention of even the most naive. Langston Hughes was elected President. The policy-making body, the National Council, was under the firm hand of the Communists. Elanor Henderson, an organizer for the TUUL-affiliated Agricultural Workers Union; Clarence Hathaway, a Party journalist; William Z. Foster, Secretary of the TUUL; Robert Dunn, Director of the Labor Research Association, also a journalist and Editor of *Labor Unity,* the TUUL organ; Irving Potash of the Needle Trades section of the TUUL; Henry Shepherd, Trade Union Unity Council of New York; B. D. Amis, an old Party functionary; Earl Browder, General Secretary of the Communist Party of the United States; Gil Green, Director of the Young Communist League; and Harry Haywood, another Party journalist—all held positions on the National Council; this gave the Party a direct and decisive majority.

James W. Ford; William L. Patterson, Secretary of the International Labor Defense; Robert Minor, an old Party hatchetman; and Benjamin J. Davis, Jr. were among the vice-presidents. Other officers in most instances were closely identified with the Party or its front organizations. This heavy loading of the LSNR with Communists was without doubt responsible for the fact that the organization throughout its existence tended to be "sectarian."

The League's program was a sweeping one. It proposed to correct all the wrongs of all the Negroes in the United States—and to do it immediately. It called for the abolition of Jim Crowism in every field, abolition of all forms of forced labor, peonage, and chain gangs. The "white supremacy ideology," with its attendant instruments of terror against Negroes, were to be eliminated. This meant the outlawing of the Ku Klux Klan and other terroristic organizations, with a mandatory death penalty for those who indulged in the illegal use of force against Negroes. In the South all Negroes were to be given immediately the right to bear arms in their self-defense. Past injustices were to be corrected by the immediate liberation of "all victims of white ruling-class frameups." Negroes were to be accorded the unqualified right to vote, hold office, and sit on juries.

The League demanded, further, that Negroes be given full rights to trade union membership, to relief, to relief work, and to jobs in industry. "Debt slavery" was to be abolished, and the right of the Negro sharecropper to sell his crops directly was to be guaranteed. Evictions from the land were to be challenged by "mass resistance," while immediate cash relief was to be furnished to small farmers and tenants. All residential segregation was to be abolished, with restrictive covenants outlawed. Free, universal, and compulsory education was to be provided in both private and public schools without discrimination; in the South modern secondary schools were to be constructed and all textbooks presenting a "distorted" version of the Negro were to be banned.

Widening the program still further, the LSNR proposed the mass boycott of newspapers, radio stations, and other agencies portraying the Negro in a derogatory way. All forms of discrimination against Negro artists and intellectuals were to be abolished; this meant that professional people would be accorded the full right to pursue their callings regardless of race. In the government service and in private industry discrimination in employment was to be outlawed. Negro small business men were to be given relief from high taxes and rents. For Negro women complete economic, political and social equality was demanded— this to be realized through abolition of employment and wage differentials, repeal of all laws against intermarriage, legalization of all the offspring of Negro women, and, finally, the establishment of equal female property rights.

For Negro youth the LSNR likewise called for full equality. Segregation in the armed forces was to be eliminated, and Negro soldiers were to be given opportunities to qualify for higher skills and for officer positions. In final emphasis, the League demanded "equal protection of Negroes in all walks of life," with a guarantee of freedom of speech, press, assembly and petition.*

Such a program, the Party thought, would accomplish two general aims: first, it would enable Communists to reach Negroes who had no organized means of protesting against those special forms of discrimination which bore most directly on them as members of a social or economic sub-group within the Negro society; second, it would bring under the influence of the Party those Negroes who had theretofore turned to the moderate Negro organizations such as the NAACP and the NUL for aid. This latter purpose was clearly indicated in the League's official declaration that:

To realize this program the Negro masses must disown the dallying, hesitant, grovelling methods of those who have been in the past and are today hailed by the powers-that-be as the leaders of the race. Booker T. Washington, who has been followed by a whole line of betrayers of the best interests of the Negro people, can be no source of inspiration for the tremendous tasks that face the people today. His scraping before the ante-rooms of the mighty is faithfully aped today by the leaders of the National Association for the Advancement of Colored People, the Whites, the DuBoises, the Pickenses, by his disciples at Tuskegee and other Negro institutions of higher learning. The efforts of present-day "leaders of the race" to chain the Negro people to the chariot of American imperialism, to perpetuate and build further

---

*We are aware of the repetitive character of many of the items in this summary. However, it is a highly condensed version of the points actually listed in the LSNR program. It must be borne in mind that the League was attempting to formulate a series of demands in which practically any Negro might find some reference to his individual needs. It is interesting to note that the program even provided for assistance to the Negro small business man, whom, presumably, the Communists, even at the time, regarded as a "traitorous" element in the black community. It was one thing to enumerate the myriad grievances of the race; it was something else to focus action on even a few of them, as the LSNR was soon to find out. For a full statement of the program see League of Struggle for Negro Rights, *Equality, Land and Freedom: A Program For Negro Liberation* (New York: League of Struggle for Negro Rights, 1933), *passim*.

the distrust and antagonism towards white workers of the country, must be smashed.[45] *

But while the LSNR was extremely critical of the Negro middle class and its bourgeois aspirations—to put it mildly—it was not above making a bid for bourgeois support, as a number of items in the program suggest. The Negro middle class, for example, might be responsive to a genuine program of improved education, aid to Negro business, and the abolition of discrimination in the artistic and professional occupations. However, the LSNR apparently did not intend to push its proposals in behalf of this group. Any real intent in this direction would have been inconsistent with its screaming and irresponsible attacks on the "black bourgeoisie."

That the LSNR embraced the whole of the Party's Negro program—that the organization amounted to nothing more than an appendage of the Communist apparatus—was evident in the adoption by the LSNR of the self-determination theory. In its program the League incorporated the analysis of the Negro question laid down at the Sixth World Congress of the Comintern. While it made immediate demands for the realization of specific Negro rights within the framework of the existing order, its ultimate goal was declared to be the establishment of a black republic in America.

"We proclaim before the whole world," said the official program, "that the American Negroes are a nation—a nation striving to manhood but whose growth is violently retarded and which is viciously oppressed by American imperialism." [46] Further:

The League of Struggle for Negro Rights declares that the territorial unity of this continuous stretch of land [Black Belt] must be proclaimed and established. It declares that upon this territory must arise that

* It is perhaps advisable here to remind the reader before he consults the footnotes in the back that the above statement was made in 1933 and not in 1950. The Party's attitude toward the NAACP, the NUL and other moderate betterment organizations has shifted frequently during the past seventeen years. Now it has made the full circle back to the position indicated in the above quote. Just when a new cycle will start is anyone's guess. Of course, DuBois is no longer included on the list of traitors, since he has become a contributing editor of *Masses and Mainstream* and a prominent figure in the "Partisans for Peace."

political state over which the Negro majority will have governmental authority.

The Negro nation cannot be free as a people until they have the complete right to set up their own government.

*The League of Struggle for Negro Rights stands for the complete right of self-determination for the Negro people in the Black Belt with full rights for the toiling white minority.*[47]

The LSNR, of course, made little headway with this ambitious program. Most Negroes would have agreed that many of its goals were desirable. But the organization was ill-prepared to lead a fight for the immediate needs of the various Negro groups in whose behalf it proposed to act. It had few resources; these were spread over a wide range of activities and little was accomplished, even in the more important areas of action. The local committees and councils, patterned in a number of respects on those of its predecessor, the American Negro Labor Congress, never really got going. A local committee would be established in New York or Chicago, and the formality—"ritual" would be a better term—of organization gone through. But the result all too frequently was merely a convening of the Party faithful under a new name.

The moderate organizations—the NAACP, the NUL, and others—steered clear of the LSNR. They warned their memberships against this latest Communist device and systematically exposed the Party affiliations of the top officials of the League. Black intellectuals were conspicuous by their absence. "Whom do we have among the Negro intellegentsia except Langston Hughes?" lamented one Party official. He received no reply. Toward the Negro church the League took the same attitude as had the ANLC. In short, Negroes generally were not inclined to hook up with the Communists, either in the Party itself or in a satellite organization, particularly when there was so much talk of high-flown sentiments and so little action on jobs and relief.

The Party itself was later to recognize and admit the limitations of the League. Writing during the united front period, after the establishment of the National Negro Congress, James W. Ford observed:

Such a program [of the LSNR] prevented the development of a broad movement. The masses did not understand this full program. Furthermore the L.S.N.R. fell into the same sectarian methods of work as the A.N.L.C. It did not base its activity sufficiently on immediate, daily needs of the people. Naturally this narrowed down the L.S.N.R. . . .

The organizational weaknesses of the L.S.N.R. were identical with those of the American Negro Labor Congress. Calling for affiliation on the basis of the complete program, the L.S.N.R. tended to make existing organizations suspicious. The by-laws provided for the leadership of the Struggle for the L.S.N.R. program of immediate and general demands. But many organizations could not be drawn into united front struggle on the basis of the full program of the L.S.N.R.[48] *

Ford's last observation in this instance is entirely misleading. The League did not propose a "United Front" program. It formulated its own program independently of other organizations and invited their participation on a "take it or leave it" basis. By the time it had finished castigating groups to whom a "United Front" program might have appealed, only the LSNR itself remained unspanked and acceptable.

While the League continued a formal existence for a number of years, it never became a force in any of the Negro communities it entered. It became largely a paper organization, issuing paper on which it proclaimed the virtues of the race-and-minorities program of the U.S.S.R. For example, it declared:

The Soviet union offers the shining example of the correctness of this program [self-determination]. There nations and races who, under the old Czarist regime, suffered oppression equal to that of the Negroes of the United States, are now, under the new Soviet government of the workers and farmers, enjoying complete freedom, equality, and the right of self-determination: there the workers and the farmers of the varied nationalities have united in fraternal and harmonious union in the work of building up a Soviet society.[49]

---

* It should be emphasized that Ford was writing after the change in the line of the American Communist Party in 1935. With shifts in the line there are correlative shifts in the Party's interpretation of its past activity. An evaluation of the same organization by the same man at the present time would probably be quite different than that indicated above.

However, something more than admiration for things Russian was needed to build an effective Negro protest movement in the United States.

During this same period the Comintern sponsored an international revolutionary movement among Negroes through the International Trade Union Committee of Negro Workers. This agency, which was under the direction of the Red International of Labor Unions, was organized in 1930 with headquarters at Hamburg, Germany. Its declared purposes were: (1) to carry on propaganda and agitation work among Negro workers, organizing them around immediate demands while positing long-range revolutionary goals; (2) to foster the development of unemployed councils among Negro workers and support programs for more relief, free rent, and non-payment of taxes; (3) to organize Negro workers in opposition to the "approaching imperialist war" or to intervention in the Soviet Union; (4) to develop a spirit of international solidarity between workers of all colors and nationalities, "calling upon them to support the Soviet Union which fights for the freedom of the working class and all oppressed peoples, as well as the Chinese, Indian, South African and all other revolutionary liberation movements of the colonial toilers"; and (5) to fight against "white chauvinism," social reform movements, and the "reformist programs of the Negro capitalist misleaders." [50]

George Padmore, an American Negro journalist who in the early 1930's broke with the Party, was for a time Executive Secretary of the International Committee and Editor-in-Chief of its official organ, the *Negro Worker*. James W. Ford, Cyril Briggs, and B. D. Amis, Communist functionaries in the United States, were among the contributing editors and advisors to Padmore. The prominence of American Negro Communists in the Committee reflected the Communist International's desire to provide this group with special training in international revolutionary movements, the aim still being to equip them to lead colonial liberation movements in Africa and elsewhere.

In 1935, after he had left the Party, Padmore charged that the ITUCNW had been liquidated in 1933 by the RILU and the Comintern without consulting the Secretary or the staff.

This move, he claimed, was the result of a Comintern decision to placate the British government, which had strongly protested the Committee's agitation among English colonies in Africa and the West Indies. The interests of Negroes in the colonial areas, Padmore continued, had been sacrificed by the Politburo, which was attempting to come to terms with the imperialist states in launching its united front program following Hitler's rise to power.[51]

Browder, the Communist Party Secretary in the United States, replied to Padmore, asserting that the latter had been dismissed for arguing that the Emperor of Japan was the legitimate protector of the world's darker races. Padmore, said Browder, was removed not by the Comintern but by his Negro associates in the Committee whom he [Padmore] had ignored and attacked. Browder denied that the Committee had been abolished, pointing out that Otto Huiswood had succeeded Padmore as Executive Secretary and editor of the official organ.[52]

While the ITUCNW was not disbanded at the time of Padmore's dismissal, and while Huiswood did function for a time as its Executive Secretary, the former's underlying charge was basically true. During the united front period Communist parties all over the world were toning down their revolutionary programs in an effort to secure joint action among anti-fascist elements. The U.S.S.R. was anxious to come to terms—at least temporarily —with the "imperialist" western powers. One way of facilitating this was to halt the "national liberation" agitation of Communists in the colonies. This did lead to the disbanding of the ITUCNW. The Committee had been formed as a result of the actions of the Sixth World Congress; it was abandoned for all practical purposes in 1935, when the Comintern concluded that it was no longer an asset in advancing the interest of the U.S.S.R. If the exploited colonial Negroes suffered as a result, the Communists could always explain that in the long run, it was really for the former's best interest. The life span of the ITUCNW covered the period roughly between the Sixth and Seventh World Congresses of the Comintern. It was the instrument of a specific line; when the line changed, it was no longer needed.

The ITUCNW, when it was functioning as a revolutionary

agitation and propaganda bureau, carried on its program in Africa, Liberia, Haiti, the British West Indies, British Guiana, and Central and South America. It vehemently attacked non-revolutionary Negro leaders in all these colonial areas. It recruited Negroes in a number of the industrial centers and was instrumental in organizing several national protest movements and strikes. It gave world-wide publicity to working conditions in the colonies, and its propaganda instruments were widely employed by American Communists in publicizing the American Scottsboro case. Had the Committee been permitted to continue its work, it might have been instrumental in the further development of revolutionary movements among colonial Negroes.

Perhaps the most effective instrument employed by the Party in its Negro program during the 1928-34 period was the International Labor Defense. This organization had not been widely known among Negroes or whites until its participation in the famed Scottsboro cases, beginning in 1931. The Scottsboro trials grew out of the indictment of nine Negro youths for the alleged rape of two white women (who were later shown to be of unsavory repute) on a freight train bound from Chattanooga to Huntsville, Alabama, in late March of 1931.

The chances for a fair trial, always slim for Negroes in Alabama, in this instance were practically non-existent. The NAACP quickly intervened in the case, and its attorneys were assigned to handle the defense. During the first trial the Party and the ILD carried on an intensive propaganda campaign in which southern injustice and the ineptness of the NAACP defense were the principal themes. As the trial neared its close the ILD in New York addressed a telegram to the presiding judge in which it advised him that he would be held "personally responsible unless the defendants were immediately released." [53] The boys were summarily convicted, and eight were given the death sentence. Then began the first of a long series of appeals to the higher courts.

While the appeals were pending the ILD sent its representatives to the parents of the condemned boys and persuaded them that the ILD rather than the NAACP should thereafter handle the cases. This maneuver, perhaps more than any other act of the

Communists, indicated the contempt in which they held the moderate organizations; it indicated also the extent to which the Party was willing to go in obtaining participation in trials of such obvious propagandistic value. "It was a sorry spectacle," said Henry Lee Moon—

—the scramble of the Communists to wrest the defense of the hapless boys from the control of the NAACP. To accomplish this end the whole propaganda machinery of the party was turned loose in a campaign to discredit the Association's leadership. Stunned by the violence of this attack, not only upon the principles and policies of their organization, but also upon their personal integrity, the leaders of the NAACP were bewildered and in the end relinquished the defense to the ILD. The Communists maintained that legal defense had to be supplemented by international propaganda. American consulates, legations and embassies were picketed and stoned in many parts of the world. Mass meetings of protest were held in the capitals of Europe and Latin America at which resolutions demanding the freedom of the Scottsboro boys were passed. Letters, telegrams and cablegrams poured in upon the President of the United States, the governor of Alabama, the presiding judge, and other state officials, demanding the immediate release of the boys. This propaganda was effective in exposing the hypocrisy of American justice, but it did not gain the freedom of the boys. Only after it had ceased was a compromise effected which resulted in the release of four of the accused.[54]

Having withdrawn from the case, the NAACP had nothing further to do with the Scottsboro matter until 1935. At this time, with the ILD facing failure in its efforts to obtain the freedom of the defendants, and with the new line of cooperation having been laid down to the Party and the ILD by the Communist International, the Communists agreed to share the case with the NAACP and other organizations; out of this grew a new Scottsboro defense committee. Among the participating organizations were the American Civil Liberties Union, Methodist Federation for Social Service, League for Industrial Democracy, Church League for Industrial Democracy, and the National Urban League, the latter in an advisory capacity.

During some four years in which the ILD had almost exclusive control of the Scottsboro defense, it widely employed the technique of "mass pressure" described in the previous chapter. The general position of the Party among Negroes was undoubtedly strengthened as a result, although it is highly doubtful whether its efforts were of any direct benefit to the defendants in the case. Scottsboro was not only publicized by the Communists among Negroes in the United States but, because of the ILD's connections with Communist agencies throughout the world, it became a global *cause célèbre*. In the fund-raising campaigns and at the protest rallies staged from San Francisco to New York, the ILD had an excellent opportunity to explain its larger program and the Communist cause to Negroes. "To the Communists," said Henry Lee Moon,

the whole campaign was much more than a defense of nine unfortunate lads. It was an attack upon the system which had exploited them, fostered the poverty and ignorance in which they were reared, and finally victimized them by legal proceedings which were a mockery of justice. It was a case made to order for the Communists and well worth the scramble they made for the privilege of representing the defendants. They made the most of it.[55]

For the Communist Party no intrinsic issues of justice were involved. It viewed the Negroes as victims of a capitalist economic order and the courts as one of its institutional extensions. The Scottsboro victims could be liberated only by an effective challenge to the economic order outside the limits of the regular judicial process. It is significant, however, that the ILD retained exceptionally able lawyers to handle the actual court proceedings. But basically, the Communists regarded Scottsboro as only a steppingstone for organizing the unemployed, recruiting Negro workers and sharecroppers, and building a mass Communist organization among colored Americans.*

* Ford, for example, as late as 1935 declared: "Properly brought forward not by liberal humanitarian methods, but as a support to the struggles of the working class, the correctness of our fight for Scottsboro can be shown to even the most backward worker. Similarly, among liberal groups who still believe in democracy and civil rights, support will be gained when the fight for Scottsboro is presented as inseparably bound up with the rights of the Negro people and the maintenance of civil rights. Scottsboro is bound up with the national liberation of the Negro people and with the struggle of the entire American working class for the dictatorship of the proletariat—Soviet Power." (James W. Ford, "The United Front in the Field of Negro

Scottsboro had values for the Party outside the general propaganda field; one of these values could be expressed in cash. How many of the thousands of dollars raised by the ILD, the Communist Party, and other Communist organizations in the name of the Scottsboro defendants actually went for defense purposes we have no way of knowing. The Party's ideological bookkeeping was frequently confused with the more regular forms of financial accounting. A thousand dollars raised for the Scottsboro boys' defense could be just as legitimately spent for pamphlets advocating self-determination for Negroes in the Black Belt as for the payment of lawyers' fees. And we have no way of estimating how much of these funds were used for activities having an even remoter connection with the Scottsboro case.

The Party also reaped an organizational windfall from the case. It attempted to follow up protest and fund-raising meetings with the building of local branches of the Communist Party and the Young Communist League. Party functionaries were instructed to employ the Scottsboro trials as a means for building Communist strength in the various communities. It was possible to get a hearing in the name of Scottsboro when a reference to self-determination would have been hooted down or tolerated in stony silence. The Party was aware of the organizational implications of the case, even if few other organizations were.

In trying to pass final judgment on the role of the Communists and the ILD in the Scottsboro case from the standpoint of their effectiveness in obtaining legal justice for the defendants, we are involved largely in speculation. It is not possible to predict what would have happened had the ILD not intervened, or, having intervened, if it had not attempted to employ the technique of mass pressure. The extremes of complete exoneration or the death penalty were possible; where the verdict would have to come to rest between these two poles is a conjectural matter. How effective the propaganda campaign of the Party was in influencing the courts we have no way of knowing. We can only describe the

---

Work," *Communist,* Vol. XIV, No. 2, February, 1935, 174.) Such statements as the above indicated also the confusion within Party ranks concerning the pursuit of revolutionary as opposed to united front objectives during the first phase of the 1934-1939 period.

propaganda techniques and the way they served Party purposes. We have no way of weighing the ILD's role in the changes which have occurred in the southern jury selection system or other procedural results growing out of Scottsboro.

The over-all judgment which one makes in matters of this kind is necessarily moral in dimension. One's convictions rest on what one conceives to be the worth of the individual and the character of justice. This question was posed and answered by the NAACP in an editorial some fifteen years ago. "To the aid of the defendants [Scottsboro]," said the writer,

rushed avowed Communists from the North who saw not only a chance to fight a dramatic case, but to make the welkin ring for Communism. For almost five years the welkin has been ringing. The exploitation of Negroes by the South has been pitilessly exposed to the world. An important legal victory has been won against the lily-white jury system. As far as propaganda is concerned the whole Negro race is far ahead of where it would have been had the Communists not fought the case in the way they did. . . .

It is not a question of whether the Communists have done a good job in exposing and fighting the evils under which Negroes live. They have. The question is: did they have the right to use the lives of nine youths, who, unlike Angelo Herndon, did not know what it was all about to make a propaganda battle in behalf of the Negro race or the theories of Communism? *The Crisis* does not believe they had that right.[56]

With the concluding statement the writer is in agreement.*

During the remainder of the 1928-1935 period the ILD participated in a number of other cases involving Negroes, not only in the South but in other sections of the nation. It was discovering that discrimination against Negroes in the courts was not a monopoly of the states below the Mason-Dixon line. None of these cases, however, was as significant or as dramatic as Scotts-

---

* A Negro sociologist in Chicago with whom I was discussing the Scottsboro case in 1940 held a different view. "The frying of nine Negro boys in Alabama would be a small price to pay for the right of Negroes to sit on juries in the South," he said. "If they didn't win that right, in all probability a great many more Negroes would become victims of southern justice in the long-run." "Have you ever been in an Alabama jail and charged with raping a white woman," I asked. "No," he replied, "I have never been in the South, and what's more I am never going there."

boro. None caught the imagination of the Negro communities as did the attempted legal lynching of these nine innocent black boys. None lent itself as readily to propaganda and organizational exploitation.

Like the League of Struggle for Negro Rights, the International Labor Defense adopted the self-determination theory promulgated by the Communist International. It held that the fight for the civil rights of Negroes could be regarded only as an immediate duty, worthwhile only insofar as it contributed to the radical reorganization of American society and the establishment of a self-determined Negro republic in the Black Belt.[57]

As we have indicated throughout this chapter, the Party's attitude toward the moderate Negro betterment organizations during this period was even more hostile than before. At the risk of some repetition, it would be well to examine the Communist attitude in more detail. Dual organization in the Negro and trade union fields was the order of the day for Communists after 1928. The Party's aim was to crush the NAACP, the NUL and any other Negro agencies which it could not capture outright or indirectly control. According to the Communists, the NAACP was a mere "reformist" conglomeration of reactionary Negro intellectuals and their white sympathizers. One Party hatchet-man went so far as to assert that the Association was, among other things, a lickspittle of the capitalist class, and a group of professional, conscious servants of the southern ruling class, engaged in "soliciting a further consolidation of the white capitalist class for the perpetuation of this slavery of the Negro people." While the NAACP might pretend to be interested in Negro rights, he said, the real purpose was to stifle "the growing revolutionary sentiment," of the "Negro masses." [58]

The Communists looked upon the National Urban League in much the same terms, bitterly attacking its program of cooperation with industrial management in the training and placing of Negro workers. The old charge of "strikebreaker" levelled against the NUL in the mid-1920's was revived and played for all it was worth.[59] There was some slight shifting of Communist criticism when the NUL later established a program of Workers Councils designed to acquaint Negroes with the trade union movement and the respective programs of the AFL and CIO. The NUL's Workers Councils lent themselves, in some instances readily, to Party penetration.

Even as late as 1934 the Communists continued condemning these and other moderate Negro organizations, not anticipating that the time would soon be at hand when the Party would invite these "sincere spokesmen of the Negro people" to join with it in building a "united Negro front." A draft resolution proposed for the Eighth Convention of the American Communist Party thus proclaimed:

Among the Negro masses, the Negro reformists are being revealed more and more as the chief social supports of imperialist reaction (White, Pickens, DuBois, etc.). They have supported the Roosevelt New Deal as a "New Deal" for the Negroes. They carried through treacherous activities in connection with the Scottsboro campaign, and sabotaged the mass movements of the Negroes against the Scottsboro verdicts.[60] *

What basis was there for the Party charges against these organizations and their leaders? Passing over, for the time being, the invective heaped on them by the Communists, was there a fundamental failure on the part of the NAACP, the NUL and other moderate organizations to carry out their programs and fulfill their responsibilities to the Negro community? The answers are both yes and no. The NAACP was not a mass organization; its top leadership as well as the membership in the numerous branches was primarily middle-class. Few lower-class Negroes—laborers and sharecroppers—participated in its activities. Even after several years of depression, the "talented tenth" psychology was still dominant within the NAACP leadership. And this was reflected in its program. Like all other large-scale organizations, the NAACP developed its own bureaucracy, a group of professionals who in time tended to identify the interests and needs of the organization and its membership with their own continuation in control. There was a reluctance on the part of leadership to

---

* Just to keep the record straight, let it be borne in mind that in the following year the ILD, the Party's instrument in the legal field, joined with the NAACP and the NUL in an effort to free the Scottsboro boys. Let it also be recalled that in 1935 Browder was not hesitant about inviting the NAACP to join with the Party in acting on "our common problems."

co-optate promising younger men and women, and even greater hesitancy to broaden the base of the organization by admitting new elements, who might or might not fit into the existing structure. This was evident, for example, in the reluctance with which the NAACP identified itself with the emerging industrial union movement.

The depression led to an almost fatal crisis in the Negro middle class, threatening to wipe out the slow, painfully won gains it had made through a long period of time, threatening to reduce its members to the status of indigent poor. But like the white middle class, it would not accept a radical alternative, preferring to hold on desperately to the continuously diminishing resources that remained, and always hoping for the best. This attitude found expression in the programs of the betterment organizations which they supported, particularly the NAACP. This organization at the time was an embodiment of the Negro middle-class mind, reflecting the tensions, the confusions, the uncertainties characteristic of a marginal, racially differentiated group. It might win court cases, but these were the shadows, not the substance, of victory.

Tradition, albeit a short one, had a profound hold on the NAACP leadership during the period of the early 1930's. Since its formation in 1910 the organization had worked out a fairly well defined strategy with corollary methods of fighting for Negro rights. As long as it focused on court cases and attempted to use the judicial machinery for effecting social change, or as long as it carried out educational and propaganda work among Negroes, such methods produced tangible results. However, the deepening crisis in all areas of Negro life emanating from the débâcle of 1929 required a different set of goals and new forms of action. For literally millions of Negroes in the United States the pressing problem was not securing the franchise, justice in the courts, or admission to the colleges on an equal basis. It was one of sheer physical survival. Man did not live by bread alone, but it was hard to survive in Harlem on a dissenting opinion of Mr. Justice Brandeis. For these critical problems the older methods of the NAACP were not sufficient.

Only later—only after the Communists, among others, had

demonstrated that Negroes could be organized on a much wider basis than the NAACP had attempted—was the latter's leadership able to grasp the new idea. In subsequent years this idea found specific expression in the changed organizational structure of the NAACP and in its ever-widening program. Much, however, remains to be done. It is to the credit of the leaders of the NAACP that they have developed an imagination and flexibility which have facilitated the adaptation of their program to the shifting needs of the colored people in the United States. This was a condition of survival during the past decade and a half.

During the 1928-1934 period, the NAACP criticism of the Communist Party was pitched on a liberal, intellectual level. Within this context it was sound. However, the great majority of Negroes were not thinking or acting in these terms. (It is hard to be a liberal when you are hungry; it is even harder if you are black and hungry; and there were a lot of hungry black men and women in the United States in 1933.) Negroes were sometimes attracted to the Party or to the organizations which it controlled, not because they favored a radical ideology or a revolutionary movement; they joined because Communists were frequently the only ones who were attempting to do something immediately about jobs, relief, and general welfare. Criticism of the Party by the moderates frequently made no sense to the unemployed Negro worker, or to the housewife facing eviction, or to the relief client being dropped from the rolls. In this connection the observations of Drake and Cayton in Chicago are pertinent. "There has been much loose talk," they said,

about Negroes going Red. A few hundred Negroes in Midwest Metropolis did "join the Party," some of them becoming prominent officials in the American Communist movement. They studied Marxism and became ideologically committed to the extension of World Socialism. But the Negro masses "who could not hate Reds" were not Marxian Socialists dreaming of a Socialist society—they were hungry, frustrated, angry people looking for a program of action. And the Reds had a plan. Negroes joined the parades, attended the picnics, and fought bailiffs and policemen.

"The Reds" won the admiration of the Negro masses by default. They were the only white people who seemed to really care what happened to the Negro. . . . Negroes are realists. They take "friends" and allies where they can find them.[61]

The National Urban League was placed in an even more difficult position than the NAACP during this period. Primarily it was an agency aiming at the extension of job opportunities in industry for Negroes. It could function effectively only when relatively full employment reduced the competition for available jobs. During the depression employers were under no economic compulsion to introduce Negro workers in their plants; and moral persuasion has never been a notably effective device to use with industrial management. Consequently the NUL encountered mounting difficulties in attempting to carry out this principal item in its program. Party criticism directed against it, however, was misplaced. The NUL had never visualized itself as a political organization; it never sought a mass base; it rarely undertook action outside the educational, training and placement fields. It could not be legitimately castigated for failing to do what it never proposed to do in the first place. Like the NAACP, it was not instrumentally or ideologically equipped to tackle the bigger problems of employment, housing and welfare in the Negro community.

The Communists were likewise critical of the various interracial organizations, composed usually of liberals. The most prominent of these during the early 1930's was the Commission on Interracial Cooperation, founded in 1919 for the purpose of alleviating the tensions in Negro-white relations which came with the post-World War I reaction. The agency's policies were set primarily by southern white liberals. It proposed no drastic changes in the pattern of race relations in the South; it sought, rather, to improve the economic and educational opportunities of Negroes within that framework. It was opposed, of course, to the Communist program; the Party's radical doctrines, it thought, were confusing the issues and providing for the white supremacists of the region an opportunity to stigmatize all racial betterment programs as Red-inspired. Party criticism of the CIC during this period was further evidence of the former's inability to regard any liberal-humanitarian race program as anything more than a calculated effort on the part of the "Wall Street bankers" and the "Southern landlords" to keep the Negro in his same old place under the guise of "mutual cooperation." [62]

Although the Party was anxious to develop a national consciousness among Negroes during this period, it wanted to be certain of its revolutionary orientation around the self-determination program. The depression and consequent suffering of Negroes throughout the country produced in the urban-industrial centers a number of nationalist and separatist groups similar to the Garvey Movement. These efforts to establish a national homeland for American blacks outside the United States were bitterly fought by the Communists after it became apparent that they could not be steered toward a self-determination program in the Black Belt.

In 1932 the Ethiopian Peace Movement was organized in Chicago. Its purpose was to support the Bilbo repatriation bill, which provided for the use of Federal funds in the colonization of American Negroes in Africa. The movement was extremely chauvinistic, holding that Africa was the national home of the Negro and seeing a completely separate Negro state as the only solution for the Negro question in the United States. It petitioned President Roosevelt for the use of relief funds to aid Negroes who desired to acquire land in Liberia and to finance their colonization. [63]

Another organization was the National Movement for the Establishment of a 49th State. Organized in Chicago in January of 1934, it set as its goal the creation of a separate Negro government in one of the less densely populated areas of the United States. It held that Negroes could never secure social or economic justice in a white-dominated society and regarded campaigns directed toward full equality as futile. [64] Its leadership was drawn primarily from the Negro middle-class, particularly businessmen and lawyers. It never had the large following or elicited the response from the Negro lower classes that characterized the Garvey Movement. [65] The Communists, of course, opposed this organization. They maintained that its purpose was to divert attention from the immediate problems of obtaining more employment and organizing the Negro workers. The Communists also offered objections on the grounds that it was essentially a "bourgeois" movement and did not regard the "natural" state of the Negro as the Black Belt.

It should be noted that these separatist movements were opposed by the non-Communist organizations such as the NAACP and the NUL. The programs of the latter were drawn in terms of ultimate full equality for the Negro in American society. It was therefore logical that they would oppose the separate state idea, not only as advanced by the Communist Party but as advocated by the conservative Negro groups as well. Their opposition to the latter, in fact, was much more effective than that of the Party because they were unencumbered with any self-determination baggage or revolutionary ideology.*

During the 1928-1935 period, then, the Communists with their revolutionary self-determination program stood in opposition to practically all the Negro betterment, interracial and nationalist organizations. The Party failed to see merit in any of their programs; rather, it lumped them together as conscious conspiracies to defeat the potentially radical Negro masses. The Party alone was right; the Party alone had the correct theory; the Party alone had a program of action—according to the Party. Communists blessed only those extensions of themselves: the League of Struggle for Negro Rights, the International Labor Defense and the Trade Union Unity League.

The Communist Party displayed an attitude of complete hostility toward the Socialist Party during this period, much of the former's criticism being centered around the Socialists' Negro program. After 1928 the Communists intensified their efforts to destroy the social-democratic movement in the United States. The theory of social fascism which grew out of the Fifth and Sixth World Congresses of the Comintern became the determinant of the Party's approach to the non-revolutionary socialist movements. In line with this theory, the Socialist Party in the United States was viewed as a totalitarian organization, more dangerous, however, than open fascist movements because it was

* For a rapid fire criticism of Negro nationalist movements of both the conservative and Communist varieties see: George S. Schuyler, "The Separate State Hokum," *Crisis*, Vol. XLII, No. 4, April, 1935, 135, 148.

clothed in a progressive mantle. So far as the race question was concerned, "Social fascism (Norman Thomas and the Socialist Party) [tends] to concentration in the effort to head off the rising movement of the Negro masses under the mask of the economic crisis and the race persecution that [goes] with it." [66]

The Socialist Party, the Communists maintained, was in league with the Ku Klux Klan, National Association of Manufacturers, NAACP, NUL, Carnegie Foundation, Rosenwald Fund, Young Men's Christian Association, and Negro fraternal organizations, all of whom were conspiring to vitiate the protests of the potentially radical Negro lower classes. Differences in composition, ideology, and programs of these groups were nothing more than superficial formalities. There was no essential distinction between the Socialist Party, the Black Shirts, the southern politicians, and the "Lovestone renegades," where the Negro question was concerned, the Party maintained.[67]

Even the new and more radical program adopted by the Socialists at their 1934 convention constituted, according to the Communists, "a danger to the workers, farmers, and intellectuals of this country." And, the charge continued:

> Eloquent testimony to that danger may be found in the graves, the prisons, the concentration camps of Fascist Austria. There "left" social-democracy succeeded in befogging the working masses with radical "Marxist" phrases and thus led them step by step on the path of compromise with capitalism to surrender to fascism, to the bloody defeat of February. The recent history of the international Social-Democracy, both "left" and right demonstrates that there is no middle road between reform and revolution, that Communism, the Communism of the Communist International and its sections throughout the world, offers the only way out of the ghastly blind-alley of capitalism for all producers of hand and brain.[68]

More specifically, and among other things, the Communist Party alleged that the Socialist program made no provision for large-scale mass action among Negroes in the South. The stand on the whole race question, it continued, was weak and ineffectual, merely reiterating the sentimental phrases of Debs. The persistent view that the Negro question was one of class rather than of nation was to be condemned.[69]

While the Communist Party made such charges out of one side of its mouth, it proposed to the American Socialists in 1934 a "United Front" program out of the other. The Communists declared that they were willing to work on a basis of mutual cooperation with the Socialists to increase wages, reduce hours of work, secure unemployment insurance, obtain relief for farmers and sharecroppers, extend Negro rights, and oppose war and fascism.[70] The Socialist Party, of course, rejected these proposals. It was not easy to grasp this left hand of fellowship proffered by an organization that with its right was attempting to insert a knife between social-democratic ribs. It was difficult, even for a forgiving Socialist, to accept the friendship of one who on the day previously had accused him of ideological cohabitation with Wall Street bankers and robed Klansmen.

With the failure of the Socialist Party leaders to accept the "United Front" proposals of the Communists, the latter attempted to appeal directly to individual socialists. While many dissidents displayed an understandable skepticism, a number of them did shift over to the Communist Party. The Communists knew all along that this offer of "unity" would be officially rejected, but they reasoned that it would lead to the withdrawal of extreme left-wing elements from the socialist ranks and create further splits in the organization. Subsequent events bore them out. But a more important reason behind this "United Front" offer was Adolph Hitler. He was not the ninety-day wonder whom the German Communists could permit to come to power and then crush at will. He was becoming a continually more serious threat to the Soviet Union. Neither the Comintern nor the American Communists were sure just how far the ex-paperhanger would force them to go in forming alliances with social-democratic elements. The Communists wanted to make no real commitments to the Socialists, but they wanted to be in a position to use these "social fascists" if necessary. Hence the curious combination of proposals for unity and screaming criticism of those with whom they proposed joint action. Later, of course, the Communists were to speak of unity with even more eloquence than the 1948 Republican presidential candidate.

While there was a grain, perhaps several grains, of truth in the

Communist criticism of the Negro program of the Socialist Party, the bulk of the charges were without foundation. The Socialists did make a number of mistakes in their work among Negroes during the early and middle 1930's. They did not understand the psychology of Negro workers; they failed to appreciate the immediate problems that Negroes confronted as a racial minority rather than as an economic class. While the Socialist Party, and particularly Norman Thomas, exposed the deplorable plight of the Negro sharecroppers in the South and the unemployed in the urban North, this was not followed up by effective organization. The Socialists did not sharpen their tactics and focus specifically on the special needs of Negroes, which, though similar to those of distressed whites, bore on the black American with a special intensity. All this is not to say that the Socialists ignored the Negro question or mishandled it completely.

As the depression deepened the Socialist Party's Negro following dwindled, in many cases going over to the Communists. At the same time the Party was unable to attract the young Negro intellectual as it had in earlier days. Much of the Socialist strength was among the trade unions, particularly the needle trades organizations. It did not have and could not secure a following among the unorganized workers in the heavy mass-production industries where the great majority of Negroes were employed—when they were employed at all. The attempts to organize the unemployed in the early 1930's did not come off well. Had they succeeded, the Socialist Party would have been able to reach literally thousands of destitute Negroes whom it might have rallied around immediate demands, if not the general Socialist program. In the South the Socialist influence, never strong among whites or Negroes, and never focused especially on the Negro question, was further weakened.

The leaders of the Socialist Party were not blind to these developments. By 1933 leading Socialists were proposing a more systematic and extensive approach to the Negro question. They argued that the Party should intensify its efforts in the industrial union field, since this offered the best means for bringing white and Negro workers together in united economic action. Renewed efforts to break down the traditional race barriers within the

AFL organizations should be made. Socialists should "convince growing Negro radicals that their only hope lies in joining hands with the democratic Party of the workers for curtailment and abolition of the exploitation of all workers." In the South, among the Negro and white tenants and sharecroppers, the Socialist Party should achieve a unity of action around common problems that would break "the artificial barriers of race." [71]

The Socialist Party, however, did not propose, on its own initiative, to embark on a program of radical industrial unionism in those fields where the old-line craft organizations might claim jurisdiction. Rather, it hoped that these unions might be persuaded to do the job themselves. There was a wide opportunity for pioneering organization among the unemployed, the farm laborers and the sharecroppers of the South. Large numbers of Negroes were to be found in each of these groups. Even before 1933 the Communists were moving into these fields, building their organizations and conducting strikes, protest demonstrations and political pressure activities. The Socialists were soon to follow.

However, the tactics employed by the Socialists, in spite of the criticism voiced by Doerfler, Mrs. Lamont and others, were mere extensions of old practices, slightly altered to fit new problems. So far as concerned the Negro question, the Socialist perspective remained essentially the same. Even the Declaration of Principles, adopted at the 1934 convention over the objections of the old-line, right-wing elements, was couched in language reminiscent of Debs:

The Socialist Party is the party of the workers regardless of race, color, creed. In mill and mine, shop and farm, office and school, the workers can assert their united power, and through the Socialist Party establish a cooperative commonwealth forever free from human exploitation and class rule.[72]

The Negro problem was still a class problem; the strategy for handling it was still the strategy of working-class organization.

This did not, however, prevent the Socialist Party from attempting to organize among groups composed primarily of Negroes. In 1934 Socialists were instrumental in the establishment of the Southern Tenant Farmers Union, a relatively short-lived but very dramatic and highly publicized effort to form an organization of small farmers, sharecroppers and laborers— Negro and white—in the Delta areas of Tennessee and Arkansas, and later in eastern portions of Texas and Oklahoma. Probably half of the STFU membership was Negro. Colored organizers, usually part-time ministers, served on its staff. The union disregarded state and county laws and conducted its meetings on an interracial basis, usually in small out-of-the-way churches or in country schools. Many of its organizers were beaten and jailed; its members were thrown off the land, denied relief, and frequently driven from the community. Its strikes were met with the combined violence of the local deputy sheriffs and the plantation "ride bosses." *

Such outside aid as the STFU was able to obtain came largely as a result of the fund-raising activities of Socialists in the North. A number of the old-line unions, having a strong socialist tradition and recovering their strength under the labor policies of the New Deal, contributed to the cause of the sharecroppers. Norman Thomas, perhaps more than any other man, publicized their cause and focused the attention of the whole nation on the misery and starvation of these people.

The road of the STFU was not easy and its burden was never light. Facing the organized violence of the planter element on the one hand and the poverty, ignorance and suspicion of the

---

* The hatred with which the sharecroppers regarded the plantation ride bosses is illustrated in the following incident. In 1936 the Religion and Labor Foundation with the cooperation of the STFU and the Socialist Party established near Clarksdale, Mississippi, a cooperative-type farm on which it hoped to rehabilitate sharecroppers thrown off the land in the STFU Arkansas strikes. An administrative council on which these former sharecroppers had representation was set up to supervise the farming program. The council designated one man to coordinate the activities of the field workers who were engaged in a variety of jobs. This required that the man cover many of the 2,000 acres on the farm each day. The question of the coordinator's travel came up at one of the council meetings which I attended as a guest. The former sharecroppers contended that he should walk, since "he was no better than anyone else, and besides he would look like a ride boss even if he didn't carry a gun." The farm's general director pointed out that unless the coordinator could move about quickly from place to place, he could not perform his duties. He suggested that the coordinator be permitted to use a horse since that would be much less expensive than a car. The former sharecroppers finally agreed, but only on the condition (1) that the man not be permitted to carry even a quirt or a stick, and (2) that he dismount from the horse when talking with any of the field workers.

sharecroppers on the other, it was involved in an insurmountable task. And in the background was the crisis of southern agriculture, the failure of the one-crop system, the collapse of the whole cotton economy, remedied in part through the AAA program, but largely at the expense of the sharecroppers, who were either completely dispossessed or ground down to even lower levels of poverty—if that were possible.

The STFU probably never had more than 30,000 members at any one time. And these were dispersed over a relatively wide area. It was never possible to mobilize the entire resources of the organization in a concerted move. Membership participation was sporadic. Frequently there were divergent aims as between the small farmers and the sharecroppers and between the sharecroppers and the laborers. But the Negro question was not a divisive factor. And it was here that the Socialists made one of their most significant contributions. To get lower-class Negroes and whites in the South to unite in the same organization for a more or less common set of goals is always a major accomplishment.*

While the Socialists could point to the STFU as a significant beginning in the joint organization of Negroes and whites in the South, it had less to show for its program in the regular trade union sphere. Margaret I. Lamont in reviewing the Socialist Party's Negro work in 1935 observed:

> It must be recognized . . . that many individual Socialists in the American Federation of Labor have remained passive or criminally indifferent in the face of open or veiled discrimination against Negroes. Such passivity or indifference cannot be pardoned or justified. Furthermore, in view of the extent and acute nature of discrimination in the A.F. of L., the militant socialist must raise the question of whether the Party's agitation on this issue has been adequate to the situation. An honest answer must be in the negative.[73]

Socialists, she maintained, should examine carefully the program and strategies of the Communist Party on the Negro question and then undertake a specialized approach of their own rather

---

* For a summary of the history of the STFU see: Stuart Jamieson, *Labor Unionism in American Agriculture* (Washington, D. C.: U. S. Government Printing Office, 1945), pp. 302-327.

than rely on a deceptively "simple formula." The militant Socialist, she continued, should make no reservations on full legal, political, social and economic rights for the Negro as immediate issues, emphasizing at the same time that these goals were attainable in complete form only under Socialism. "While he participates in the struggle for the rights of the Negro before the law and under the constitution, seeing an inch painfully gained here and there," she continued,

the militant socialist is also involved in the essential job of educating white workers to overcome their unreasoning bouregois-fostered prejudices against the Negro; he is trying to build up the trust of Negro and white workers in each other through common action in meetings, demonstrations, and strikes where the results of solidarity will be unmistakable even to politically naive workers.[74]

The difficulty with the Socialist Negro program was that there weren't enough militant Socialists in the trade unions or in the Party itself to carry it out.

To what extent Socialists within such unions as the International Ladies Garment Workers and the Amalgamated Clothing Workers considered the possibility of carrying out the organization of Negro workers as a part of the Socialist program in splitting from the AFL and helping to form the CIO in 1935 is difficult to measure. Racial discrimination within these two unions was at a minimum and their leaders were, without doubt, anxious to extend the non-discriminatory pattern among existing labor organizations as well as to establish it in any new bodies that might be formed. However, it would appear that strict industrial union strategies rather than ethical considerations or socialist ideology were the major determinants of CIO action in the organization of ethnic and racially differentiated groups.

While the Socialists in the early 1930's did not have much to show for their Negro program, they were quite sure that the Communists had nothing to offer. In attacking the Communists the social-democrats focused on the Kremlin-dictated self-determination theory. (This was a vulnerable point, but the Communists made gains in spite of it.) Norman Thomas, writing in 1932, declared:

The Communist demand for self-determination in the "black belt" implies Negro and white governed counties and states. It is based on a false analogy with conditions in Russia where different races, *speaking different languages,* occupy different geographic areas. At best it suggests segregation for the Negro tenth of our population, at worst it invites race war. It is not what the Negroes want. They want to be treated on a level with whites. We who seek to capture political power to use it for the workers cannot complicate the building of a working class party by trying to build a racial party of government, white in one country or state and black in another, according to the chance numerical preponderance of one race or another.[75]

The removal of exploitation of workers—white and colored—said Doerfler, "cannot be done by crackbrained slogans of self-determination which serve in fact to disunite and retard the growing solidarity of Negro and white workers." [76]

These ideological and programmatic distinctions between the Socialist and Communist parties, however, made an impression only upon the intellectual and more politically conscious Negroes; they did not influence the mass of lower-class blacks. To the latter, esoteric theories and ultimate goals enunciated by the two parties were far removed from the immediate needs of destitute colored people. While a Negro family in Black Metropolis facing eviction for non-payment of rent might cry "Go get the Reds," the latter were summoned only to fight the bailiff and the landlord—not to preach salvation by self-determination. While a Negro relief client in Harlem whose grocery allowance had been cut might decide to call Frank Crosswaith and "those socialist fellows," it was only for purposes of getting the original amount restored—not for being informed about the basic contradictions of the capitalist system.

In one important area the Communists were far ahead of the Socialists during this period; this was in the development of Negro leadership and its integration in the larger party apparatus. While the Communist Party had always emphasized placing Negroes in positions of leadership, this was not done on a significant or dramatic scale until after the Sixth World Congress of the Comintern in 1928. Several considerations governed Communist policy on this matter. The Party was aware that Negroes would base their judgments of the organization partially on the leadership role played by members of their race. It believed that Negroes' holding high positions in the formal structure would be good propaganda, while at the same time such persons would be essential for the successful prosecution of the special Party work among colored people.

The symbolic and propagandistic uses which the Party made of Negro leadership is indicated, for example, in a speech by Clarence Hathaway at the 1932 Communist convention. Hathaway, a member of the Communist Election Campaign National Committee, in discussing the nomination of Ford for vice-president on the Communist ticket, declared:

> The Communist Party has decided to recommend an action by this convention never before taken by any national political party. We propose as candidate for vice-president of the United States a Negro worker, a leader of the oppressed Negro people. We make this proposal not with a vote catching motive. We do it because it corresponds to the fundamental position of the Communist Party and of those who support the Communist Party on the Negro question . . . we stand for complete unconditional equality for Negroes . . . not equality in some narrow limited sense, but for complete economic, social and political equality. . . . We stand for a solid fighting front of all toilers, Negro and white, to force the granting of such equality now . . . to march forward to the emancipation of all those oppressed by the yoke of capitalist rule.[77]

For the next several years the Party made few appeals to Negroes without somewhere along the line reminding them that "our 1932 vice-presidential candidate was a Negro, a Negro worker." Emphasis of this type on the Party's Negro leadership became a characteristic device.

The Party developed a number of organizations which, if not composed almost exclusively of Negroes, were primarily concerned with Negro problems and nominally under Negro leadership. The Party pointed to itself as an example of complete racial equality in action. It emphasized continually among Negroes that there was no discrimination of any kind in the Party, the League of Struggle for Negro Rights, the Trade Union Unity League, the International Labor Defense, or in any other Communist-led organizations. Such claims were only partially true. The Party never succeeded in "stamping out the 'virus of white chauvinism' " even in its own structure; it was even less successful in those satellite organizations which it built or captured from time to time. Negro leadership of such organizations was probably of some importance in the recruitment of colored members; just how important is difficult to judge. The Negro Communists were probably more effective than whites in recruiting among the race, but they were always forced to operate within the framework of the general Party line. This stifled their imagination—as it did in the case of white Communists—and limited whatever natural leadership abilities they might have had.

To what extent high intelligence and strong personality traits were responsible for the rise to leadership in the Party apparatus of such Negroes as James W. Ford, William L. Patterson, Benjamin Davis, Jr., Eugene Gordon, and Harry Haywood is not easily measured. Ford was an ex-postal clerk, Patterson and Davis, lawyers; Gordon, a writer; and Haywood, a sort of professional radical. Only Patterson and Davis had much to show in the way of occupational accomplishment prior to joining the Party. The Party's effort to build up Ford never came off, and his docility toward Foster and Browder was more responsible than anything else for his being hailed by Communists as "an outstanding leader of the Negro people."

Regardless of individual capabilities, a number of Negroes would have held—formally and publicly at any rate—positions of responsibility in the Communist apparatus. These were institutionalized leadership roles which only a Negro could fill. What the role of Negro leadership was at the all-important informal level of policy determination (insofar as American Communists could determine the program of their organization) is difficult to judge. The true picture could be reported only by a person who was a part of the apparatus itself or had access to such persons. Unfortunately, the varied "confessions" of both Negro and white ex-Communists who at one time or another were high in the Party bureaucracy are of little help in this connection.

Within subsidiary organizations of the Party, too, Negroes held numerous leadership positions. The executive secretary of the International Labor Defense was a Negro. The various special committees which the ILD established from time to time for propaganda and fund-raising purposes were frequently headed by black Communists. In the League of Struggle for Negro Rights, of course, the top positions were held by Negroes, practically all of whom were members of the Communist Party. In addition, Negroes usually led such local councils as the LSNR was able to establish. The Trade Union Unity League, with a special Negro department, employed colored organizers, while in a number of cases the top elective positions of its affiliates were filled by Negroes. Negroes served as organizers for the Unemployed Councils and in a number of fairly important elective positions. A number of colored organizers worked with the Sharecroppers Union and a black tenant farmer was at one time its president.

None of this leadership, however, was independent. The Negro Communist leaders, like their white counterparts, could function only insofar as they rigidly conformed to the general line of the Party. The Communist bureaucracy would have been no more hesitant in bouncing a Ford or a Patterson than in getting rid of a Gitlow or Chaplin. Hughes would have been as roundly denounced as Lovestone if the Negro poet had been considered guilty of "revisionism" or "American exceptionalism." The Communist "leader"—Negro or white—can lead only if he is willing slavishly to follow.

While the Party's effort to build up Negro leadership during the period from 1928 to 1935 met with considerable success, certainly more than that experienced by the Socialists, it failed in one important respect. The aim of building up among the Negroes in the industrial North a revolutionary race cadre was not realized. It was the Party's intention to train Negro industrial workers to head the organization of the colored sharecroppers and laborers in the South and to direct the Negro national liberation movements in the colonies. The Negro Communists from the urban North proved very ineffective in work below the Mason-Dixon line. Handicapped from the outset with a revolutionary program, they were further limited by ignorance of the history and psychology of the people among whom they proposed to work. Linked with these liabilities was their unfamiliarity with the etiquette, the "do's" and "don't's," of race relations in the South, violation of which frequently resulted in their being jailed before they got started on the more important job at hand.*

The Party's effort to train American Negroes for leadership roles in the colonial liberation movements proved even more ineffective. While a number of black Communists had been schooled in Moscow, they were shipped to the United States rather than assigned organization jobs in the colonies. George Padmore, Otto Huiswood and James W. Ford did stints with the International Trade Union Committee of Negro Workers, but they operated from the relatively safe Committee Headquarters in pre-Hitler Hamburg, Germany. Outside of attendance at a few Comintern-sponsored conferences on colonial movements, few American Negroes saw action in this area of world revolutionary focus.**

While the Party concentrated on training and placing promising Negroes in responsible organizational positions, it did not neglect another important group—the artists and intellectuals—whose creative energies it hoped to tap for political purposes. Prior to 1928 the Communists had displayed a singularly hostile attitude toward this focal group, identifying them with the "black bourgeoisie" and criticizing them accordingly. The Party became aware, haltingly to be sure, that Negro novelists, painters, musicians, poets and dramatists might, through their respective mediums, create the kind of nationalist consciousness appropriate for the self-determination theory. However, these artists would first need the "proper orientation" and the correct "perspective." These the Communists volunteered to supply.

* A good illustration of this was found in the efforts of a Chicago Negro to assist in the organization of the Sharecroppers Union in Alabama. To announce a meeting he prepared a leaflet containing a quotation from Lenin on the minorities question. He then circulated the leaflet among Negroes in the local community. The only person besides the Negro organizer who appeared at the meeting site was the white sheriff of the county. The latter came with a warrant for the arrest of "Leenine" on a sedition charge.

** An examination of Negro leadership is almost completely lacking in the voluminous amount of material on the Negro that has appeared in the past two decades. Myrdal's study contains some very suggestive observations. Bunche's unpublished studies represent a beginning in what I would regard as the right direction. However, neither of these sources contains anything on Socialist-oriented Negro leaders. A study of the latter, employing the methodology of both political science and sociology, is much needed.

First it would be necessary for the Negro artists to become aware of the "peculiar national culture of American Negroes." And what were the sources of this culture? "The birth and death of generations of blacks, who passed from the status of indentured servants to the status of slaves," explained one Moscow-trained Negro writer, "effected profound changes in the mass psychology of blacks. The factors of slavery," he continued,

had already so welded these diverse peoples that long before 1863 they had been forced into the category of an incipient nation. Differences in physical characteristics were less sharply apparent; a common tongue (English) had been developed; they all lived compactly together under the evolving aegis of slavery. Here lay a condition fallow for the birth of a national psychology.[78]

It was with the struggle of this Negro nation to achieve its "manhood" that the Negro artists and intellectuals were to be concerned. Its trials, its tribulations, its suffering—these were to be the major themes of novels, of music, of other creative forms. To select other themes was tantamount to betrayal of the race. What the Party in effect demanded was that Negro artists develop an aesthetic extension of Stalin's definition of a nation, as applied to the American Negro by the Sixth World Congress of the Comintern.

The Party was especially concerned with Negro music, seeing in it not only a striking manifestation of the black's "peculiar national culture" but an immediate resource for propaganda purposes. "When the American Revolutionary Movement finds expression in Negro music," said Richard Frank in the *New Masses,*

it is expressing itself in a medium capable of arousing not only the twelve or fifteen million Negroes of America, but also all the toiling masses of America, who for generations in one form or another have made Negro music their own.[79]

Anticipating Paul Robeson by some fifteen years, Mr. Frank then cited as examples of revolutionary music a number of Negro spirituals—with the lyrics supplied, however, by members of a local Communist unit in Richmond, Virginia. Pointing to the more immediate political value of such music, he continued, among the Negroes, it will be to a great extent through singing that recruiting will be done, for the masses of Negro workers are held at illiteracy. Leaflets cannot appeal to them. But singing is their great form of artistic expression. In order to win the Negro people most effectively, the revolutionary movement will have to make use of this instrument.[80]

Negro music—or any music—contained no intrinsic value; the Communist could listen only with an ideological ear.

As for the Negro actors, the Communists could find little that was hopeful during this period. The contemporary theatre, they maintained, presented nothing but derogatory stereotypes of the American Negro. The Negro actor was afforded no serious roles. Protest and revolutionary themes were absent from the works of Negro dramatists. It was the responsibility of both Negro playwrights and actors to cease catering to the wider white audience and the Negro middle class with their bourgeois sense of artistic values. The dominant themes of the Negro drama, according to the Party, should be those of national and racial awakening, of protest and struggle. The hero should be the radical Negro worker (preferably a Communist). The villains should be the southern planters and the Wall Street bankers. The plots should be simple and clear, with the issues not obscured by psychological subtleties. They should conclude on a note of triumph, the victory of the black proletarian over his white oppressors. One hopeful development was the recent creation of a Negro Peoples' Theatre out of which would come "something positive, cleansing and illuminating," a movement that would "develop a body of actors and playwrights who [were] building a revolutionary drama movement—a creative part of the renaissance of Negro consciousness which has been nourished on the waters of revolutionary thought." [81]

The Negro novelists were taken to task for their unawareness of the revolutionary traditions of the Negro people and their failure to make protest plots central in their works. Gordon criticized them for catering to the white critics and for mocking the lower classes in Negro society. Among the creative Negro writers in 1933 he found only one exception—Langston Hughes, President of the League of Struggle for Negro Rights, whose later works had shown vast improvement because of "his recent political development." [82] The Negro creative writers, another Party critic maintained, continued to play the role of the "Meek Moses" and the "Black Hamlet," shunning protest plots and dealing with bourgeois stereotypes. Negro writers were urged to "become cognizant of the social reasons for these conditions [destitution among Negroes] and, with the Negro and white masses, take up the tasks which confront us as the inheritors of the revolutionary traditions of our people." [83]

And as heirs to these traditions, the specific task of the Negro writers was to "eradicate the distorted stereotypes of the Negro people prevalent in American literature and drama; to create literature dealing with the struggle of the Negro masses for liberation; to portray the disintegration of the Negro petty bourgeoisie. . . ." [84]

To remain passive was to enhance the terrors faced by the Negro people. The Negro writer should take his place in the struggle against the "foes of culture and progress." This need could best be filled by the writer's identification with the Communist Party and its program of national liberation for Negroes.

Turning on the Negro intellectuals, James W. Ford charged them as individuals with treachery and their organizations with betrayal of the Negro people. The current crop of Negro intellectuals, he said, had too close a social and occupational identity with the middle class; they could not accept a genuine revolutionary philosophy because they feared the radical potentials of the working class. Political and ideological differences among them, he continued, were superficial. As a group they stood together, a black aristocracy of privilege, talent and conservatism. They were not a resource for the Negro revolutionary movement. But, said Ford,

among the Negro proletariat [we will] discover those talents necessary for building up the intellectual opposition to the traitorous leadership of the National Association for the Advancement of Colored People and similar groups. Many honest intellectuals among the Negroes do not yet recognize the role of the Pickens, Whites, DuBoises, the McKinneys, Millers, Calvins and Schuylers. True, the Scottsboro case has been the beginning of the end for these turncoats; but they still possess great potentialities for misleadership.[85]

While there was during the early 1930's considerable discontent with the leadership of the intellectuals in Negro protest and betterment movements,* such Communist accusations as the above were extremely overdrawn. Party criticism, coupled with the inroads made by the Communists in a number of areas of Negro protest, without doubt had some bearing on changes in the attitudes and programs of the established Negro intellectuals. Just how much is difficult to say. While the latter might dismiss many of the Party's accusations on the basis of their source, this did not completely vindicate their leadership.

It is important to keep in mind, however, that Communist criticism of Negro intellectuals and their moderate organizations was merely another manifestation of the line being followed during the period from 1928 to 1935. If the Party had honestly regarded this group as "traitors" it would not have attempted to work with them on a "United Front" basis a few years later, or hailed its members then as "responsible spokesmen of the Negro people."

Communist criticism of the Negro intellectuals during this period stemmed also from the Party's failure to win over many of the black intelligentsia for its own organizations. Nowhere was the failure of its Negro work more apparent than among this group. Neither the carrot of praise nor the stick of criticism, the latter being employed most, produced any significant results. Party tactics in this respect were self-defeating. Negro intellectuals, like other members of the race, were looking for a way out. They were far from being unreceptive to new ideas and movements. But the Communists, for example in the League of Struggle for Negro Rights, offered them only a doctrinaire revolutionary program on a "take it or leave it" basis. While many

* The Communist ideology, if not its specific program, seemed to have considerable appeal for a number of younger intellectuals. The Second Amenia Conference (the first was held in 1916) convened at the Spingarn estate near Amenia, New York, in 1932 was made up largely of Negro intellectuals. They had been called together to discuss ways and means of carrying on Negro protest during the depression period. Many points of view were represented. It was notable that such Negro leaders as DuBois, White, Pickens, and Wilkins were attacked openly and directly by the younger radicals, not all of whom were by any means Communists. (Bunche, *Programs, Ideologies, Tactics and Achievements of Negro Betterment and Interracial Organizations,* pp. 209-210).

white intellectuals were willing to go the whole fish and swallow this line completely, their Negro counterparts displayed considerably more independence.

The Party's failure in this connection is explained further by the fact that not only the mass of Negroes but also the black intellectuals were attracted to Roosevelt and the New Deal program. The New Deal meant a new deal for the American Negro as well as for the working class as a whole. The black intellectuals found that the Administration would go much further than merely handing out a few patronage plums to Negro politicians. The leaders of the NAACP, the National Urban League and other Negro organizations found themselves being ask to participate in the formulation and administration of government policies that embodied some of the measures that they had long advocated. In such agencies as the Department of Agriculture, the Department of Interior, and in a host of newly created planning and administrative bureaus, Negroes were assigned important posts. These were not mere jobs, but responsible positions in the prosecution of programs which the Negro intellectual could honestly support, Communist claims to the contrary.

How much the Administration's general idealism on the one hand and its sensitivity to the demands of practical politics—the Negro vote—on the other was responsible for this turn of affairs is a moot point. The New Deal had a lot of both. In any event the result was that Negroes were presented with and accepted a reformist alternative; the Communist Party was the loser. The Negro intellectuals were keenly aware, as they had been all along, that the interests of the race could not be realized except in conjunction with the genuinely liberal white elements in American society. They did not want to be separated from these elements —by the Communist Party or any other spokesman of an alien tyranny.

While the Party failed to win the support of many of the black intelligentsia, and while the New Deal siphoned off much of the potentially radical ferment among the mass of Negroes, Communists did exert something more than an inconsequential influence on the Negro question during this period. It widely publicized the varied injustices suffered by American blacks—in the courts, the schools, the trade unions, the government services, and in all areas of life in the South; there can be no doubt about this. Along with the moderate organizations it exposed the hypocricy of a nation that *spoke* with the Constitution and the Bill of Rights and *acted* with the restrictive covenant, the segregated street car, the poll tax, the lynch rope and the faggot. And it publicized these injustices not only in America, but throughout the world. It did not succeed, however, in turning such matter to organizational account among Negroes.

The Communist Party was also instrumental in heaping further discredit on the compromising philosophy of Booker T. Washington, a tendency that had its beginning with the Niagara Movement in 1905 and had been strengthened steadily by the NAACP since 1910. The Communists were a source of ferment among many of the younger Negroes, articulating and expanding their discontent, if not channeling it behind the Party organizations. Among the tenant farmers and the sharecroppers of the South the Communists set the example of organization, albeit an ineffectual one. It provided some organizational outlets for the unemployed Negroes who frequently lacked any means of expression except through the Party-controlled councils. Further, the Communists without doubt provided a stimulus for the alteration of some of the encrusted habits of the moderate organizations, although at the same time they deflected the energies of the latter by forcing them to defend themselves from demagogic and irresponsible attacks. The Communists must also be credited with a special effort to develop a political consciousness among Negro women during this period, again an effort that was not to pay off in organizational profits.

From the standpoint of numerical growth from 1928 through 1934, Communist gains were not especially significant, among either whites or Negroes. The increase in Party membership itself is difficult to pin down because of the contradictory figures supplied by official sources. It was claimed by one spokesman that total Party membership in 1928 was 7,000; by another it was put at 14,000. According to Joseph North, who had access to the Party's membership lists, the organization had 7,500 members in 1930; 9,275 in 1931; 14,475 in 1932; 19,164 in 1933; and 24,536 in 1934.[86]

These figures were released at the Eighth convention of the Communist Party in 1934. North reported further that the convention was attended by 470 delegates, 233 of whom had voting rights. Of the latter, 145 were native born. Thirty-eight of the delegates came from AFL affiliates and eighteen from independent (TUUL) unions. Sixty-four per cent of all delegates carried union cards, while almost two-thirds were between the ages of 26 and 30. North omitted all references to the sex and racial breakdown of the convention delegates. However, he gave considerable attention to the role of several representatives of the Sharecroppers Union and other primarily Negro organizations.[87]

Had there been any significant proportional growth of Negro membership in the Party, this fact would have been widely publicized by the Communists themselves. Taking the above figures and considering other indices of Negro membership in the Party proper, meager as the data are, it seems safe to conclude that there were not more than 2,500 Negroes in the organization as the revolutionary dualism period drew to a close. This was a small figure indeed for an organization that proclaimed itself the "responsible spokesman for the Negro masses." It must also be borne in mind that there was a rapid turnover in Communist Party membership during this period. Since the figures were not carefully explained, it is not clear whether they represented existing membership or the total traffic of Negroes in and out of the Party during any particular year. It must also be remembered that Party spokesmen would have been inclined to exaggerate rather than minimize the figures released to the public.

Figures on Negro membership in the Trade Union Unity League, the labor arm of the Party during this period, are not available. However, in view of the fact that the TUUL had few important affiliates representing workers in the heavy mass production industries, where the bulk of Negro industrial workers were to be found, it seems safe to conclude that the TUUL was not an important source of Communist strength among Negroes. The black membership in the Sharecroppers Union probably never exceeded 3,000, although a delegate at the 1934 Party convention claimed that the number had been increased to 6,000 within the preceding year. This may have been another case of clocking total traffic rather than counting permanent membership cards.

Negro participation in the various Committees and Councils of the Unemployed, which the Party had been instrumental in organizing, was probably greater than in all the other organizations combined. However, not all of these Negroes were by any stretch of the imagination Communists. The Party attempted to recruit among them, of course, and this was one of the sources from which the Party itself drew members. The Party could influence these organizations only as long as it focused on the immediate needs of the black and white unemployed. It therefore failed to turn the Unemployed Councils to account for its larger revolutionary aims.

Perhaps the less said about the League of Struggle for Negro Rights, the better—from the Party point of view. As Ford in one of his more forthright statements later indicated, this organization was almost a complete failure, being unable to supply leadership to any Negroes except the few who were already identified with the Party. Narrow, hidebound, dogmatic, and self-righteous, it could not activate the black radicals, much less the mass of non-political Negroes. While we have no figures on membership of the LSNR, it seems safe to conclude that it never exceeded a few hundred. It did serve some propaganda aims of the Party, but poorly so.

The significance of the International Labor Defense is not indicated by any kind of membership figures. Its purpose was not to build up a mass organization among Negroes around a civil rights program. Primarily, it was a propaganda and fund-raising agency whose influence was established through the Scottsboro and Herndon cases. It reached wide numbers of Negroes through mass protest and money-raising meetings, through its own propaganda, and through the Negro press. It dealt with matters close to the hearts of all Negroes; but the latter responded to the pleas for Scottsboro and not to the self-determination program, not even to the idea of justice by "mass pressure."

From an over-all view, then, the Communist Party and its

satellite agencies made only limited gains among Negroes, although allowance must be made for their "influence" among Negroes as opposed to organizational growth during this period. The Party failed to build any mass organizations with sustaining possibilities among American blacks. It did not succeed in appreciably weakening those "reformist" organizations to which it was bitterly opposed. It drew only a few Negroes into Communist-sponsored trade unions. Its special Negro organizations made very limited headway. Its widely-heralded efforts to build up a radical Negro leadership did not come off. It alienated the bulk of the Negro intellectuals; it insulted rather than persuaded the Negro artists, by demanding that they conduct themselves as Negroes, and Communist Negroes at that, rather than as creative human beings.

The Party failed to understand that Negroes, perhaps more than whites, were fundamentally American in the sense that they aspired to equality, or at least to getting ahead within the existing institutional structure rather than through any radical reorganization of society. Had a Bilbo or a Talmadge drafted the general program of the Communist Party on the Negro question during this period, they could have not served their own purposes better than by including the self-determination theory. No proposal more antagonized the whites or promoted the distrust of Negroes than this Kremlin edict. The Party made gains among Negroes only when it acted like any other political party: when it courted support on immediate issues stripped of any ideological claptrap.

But the dedicated Communists had what they always had, what other groups in the field of Negro rights lacked—the illusion that they and they alone were right, and that they were right all the time. They believed in the ultimate triumph of their cause, whatever the Comintern might declare that cause to be. They displayed those peculiar impulses—religious, perhaps mystical—that impel some men to fight and die for the inevitable. Clothed in the full Stalin-designed armor of Marx they did battle with the deputy sheriffs and vigilante mobs of the South, with the ruling-class courts, with the "traitorous" leaders of the Negro people, with the corrupt "misleaders of labor," and with the bourgeois-inspired intellectuals; most of all, with the "Social fascists" in the American Socialist Party. However, dogmatism did not mean right; complete faith was not understanding; bravery was not always good sense. Though five years of preaching self-determination and theorizing about the revolution had gleaned less than 3,000 black converts, the Communists still insisted that they had the "correct" approach to the Negro question. If there was any fallacy in the situation it lay in the minds of the Negroes who failed to agree with them.

It was not an intensive and critical searching of their program that forced them to change their ways, beginning in 1934. The major causes were (1) an ex-Austrian Army corporal named Adolph Hitler, who called himself an anti-Communist and a National Socialist, and (2) another edict from the Kremlin, one of those wonder-performing documents that struck momentarily blind the Communists on the road to revolution, revealing the errors of their ways and pointing to the new path of salvation.

# IV

# "BUILD THE NEGRO PEOPLE'S
# UNITED FRONT," 1935–1939

WHY did the Communist International direct its affiliated
sections to change their general program from "world
proletarian revolution" to "united front against reaction," beginning in 1933? What was the significance of this change for the
general line of the Communist Party in the United States? How
was the Party's program on the Negro question affected? What
altered conceptions governed its approach to the Negro question?
What new strategical and tactical devices did it employ in its
Negro work? What new organizations did it attempt to build
among Negroes? How did it attempt to relate itself to the non-
Communist Negro protest and betterment organizations? How
successful was it in building a Negro Communist following? And
what was the result of its over-all effort during this period, which
ended with the Stalin-Hitler pact in August, 1939? These are
the questions with which we shall be concerned in the present
chapter.

The Party's change to the united front line was not as abrupt
as either the preceding or the subsequent shifts in its program.
Although the united front period could be said to have its
beginning in 1933, it was not until 1935 that the full program
got underway. The united front period had two phases: the first
was introduced by the resolution of the Comintern Executive
Committee, adopted on March 18, 1933; the second, by the
Seventh World Congress which met in Moscow in late July and
early August, 1935.

The first period was characterized by confusion in program and action among American Communists, the second by a much clearer line and corollary operations. During the first period the Party was not certain (because the Comintern itself was not certain) whether it should continue its revolutionary dualism or embark on joint action with "reformist elements" on some kind of united front effort. It did not know whether it should continue building separate revolutionary unions or return to "boring from within" the old-line crafts. It was not certain whether to build up its own organization or to cooperate with other groups in the formation of "mass" agencies in which the Party would have influence but not complete control. It could not decide whether to attempt reaching an agreement with the Socialists or try to destroy the latter's organizations. It was not clear about the New Deal—was it a Wall Street dictatorship or a liberal coalition representing the interests of the common man? It could not make up its mind whether the "reformist" Negro organizations were extensions of the southern ruling class or the "bearers of the great aspirations of the Negro people."

The Communist Party in the United States could not fathom the role it was to play in this next act of the Comintern-directed drama. So it attempted a little bit of everything. It talked in shrill tones about betrayal in one instance, and in syrupy phrases about joint action in the next; it orated about the evils of reformism in the first speech and purred the virtues of moderation in the second; it donned the tattered pants of revolution in one appearance, only to do a quick-change and emerge with a pressed-trousers compromise. Few people could grasp just what role the Party was playing; not even the Communists themselves knew.

Behind this initial confusion lay the indecisiveness of the Comintern. The need for a general overhaul and redirection of the revolutionary apparatus was apparent immediately following the successful establishment of the National Socialist régime in Germany, after it was clear that Adolph Hitler and Hermann Goering, not Wilhelm Pieck and Ernest Thälmann, would probably use the military and political resources of Germany to set up a series of totalitarian puppet dictatorships throughout Europe. This need was underscored by mounting evidence that the U.S.S.R., the "socialist fatherland," would be the country at whose expense the Nazis would expand their power. Coupled with this was the fact that the Communist revolutionary movements in France, Great Britain, the United States, and other "capitalist-imperialist" nations had failed—even during a prolonged economic crisis—to seize power, or even exert an appreciable influence on the course of events.

Even before the Nazi régime was firmly in the saddle, the Executive Committee of the Communist International, hedging against its wager that Hitler was a ninety-day wonder, proposed united front action with social-democratic elements and non-revolutionary trade unions for purposes of stopping "reaction and fascism." On March 18, 1933 the Committee declared that its affiliated sections had always been willing to undertake such a program, stating further that renewed efforts were now imperative due to the violent capitalist offensive in militant totalitarian form.[1]

The Committee asked that the various working-class political parties and other labor organizations now unite to stop destruction of the cooperatives, to ward off attacks on the trade unions, and to strengthen labor's political power. It proposed that Communists and Socialists jointly conduct strikes and protest demonstrations for higher wages, shorter hours, better working conditions, extended social security, and against "fascism and war." In this resolution the Comintern was offering bogus money for a political insurance policy in the event its life expectancy tables for the Nazi régime contained errors. If Hitler collapsed, the Communists in Germany would seize power, destroying his movement and that of the social democrats as well. If he retained power, growing as a threat to the U.S.S.R., then the Comintern and its affiliates would have the resolution as a basis of appeal for joint action against fascism. Hitler didn't last a thousand years; but neither did he collapse in ninety days.

The 1933 resolution of the Comintern Executive Committee was a curious document. At the moment of its release the Communists in Germany working hand in glove with the Nazis, were digging the grave of social democracy. Thorez, Cachin and

Duclos in France were grasping for the jugular vein of Léon Blum and the French Socialist Party. In the United States Browder, Foster, Ford and Minor were denouncing Norman Thomas and the Socialists because the latter refused to commit political suicide and let the Communist Party pick up the remains. The various sections of the Communist International had never been willing to form a united front with any of the social-democratic and reformist elements—except on the Communists' own terms. In practice they were not inclined to do so now, the Comintern resolution notwithstanding. The Comintern during 1933 and 1934 hoped that fascism in Germany, Italy and Japan would collapse or be overthrown; it did not want to act jointly with social-democratic elements, or abandon its own bid for power through its affiliated sections in various countries until it became absolutely necessary. This waiting and hoping was reflected in the program of the Communist Party of the United States.

While the united front line was not laid down in complete and binding form until the latter part of 1935, a number of Communist parties took action on the 1933 directive, meeting with some success in France and other European countries. In the United States the Party was slower to act and less effective. Its strategy was obvious, its efforts piecemeal and half-hearted. The memories of the non-Communist elements—the Socialists, the trade unions, the liberals—would not blank out overnight. The Socialists, for example, could not forget that in 1933, even in 1934, the Kremlin spokesmen who now offered the limp-fish hand of unity had denounced them as "Social Fascists" and "Wall Street collaborators." They suspected—rightly—that the new Comintern strategy, even when enunciated with a Kansas twang, was the same as that outlined by Karl Radek at the Fourth World Congress when he declared:

> The road to the United Front is a much harder one than our tactical motto of 1919, "smash everything up"; it is much easier and pleasanter to smash everything up, but if one is not strong enough to do so, and if this road (that is, the United Front) is necessary, we must walk along it . . . in the firm belief that this road will not lead us but the Socialists to perdition . . . with the conviction that we shall be able to stifle them in our embrace.[2]

Laboring against its background of violent opposition to practically every non-revolutionary Socialist, trade union, and minority group organization on the American scene, and lacking any clear conception of what it was to do or where it was to go, the Party rode off in all directions during this preliminary phase of the united front period. It was not until late 1933 that any action at all was taken on the Comintern directive. And these steps were slow and halting, dragging from one side of the road to the other, and frequently landing in the ditch. During the latter part of 1934, the Communists moved a little faster, though no doubt wishing that the Comintern would put up more sign posts and an occasional policeman to guide them on their way. A few months prior to the Seventh World Congress they began to discern more clearly the road they were to travel during the next four years.

In late 1934 the Communists proposed cooperation with the Socialists on a series of specific issues.[3] These overtures, discussed in the previous chapter,* received no direct reply from the Socialists, who charged that they had been advanced for the purpose of splitting the latter's organization and destroying its independence of action while committing its members to an indorsement of the Communist dictatorship in the U.S.S.R. Communists retaliated with the charge that the social-democratic leaders had betrayed the working class, and called for raids on the Socialist Party with the aim of drawing off the more radical dissident elements. This last maneuver met with some success. However, while the Socialist Party declined during this period, it was not primarily a result of defections to the Communist ranks. And "Social Fascism" remained in the Communists' vocabulary of invective, although they were a bit more circumspect in its use.

In late 1934 the Party also attempted to bring together various organizations of the unemployed behind a national political and legislative program. It succeeded in the partial unification of these groups in the National Congress for Unemployment and Social Insurance.[4] It noted that a greater measure of success would have been realized but for the presence of Trotskyite "disrupters"

* See pp. 97-105.

and certain "honest and sincere, but misled" elements. The Party was convinced that the program adopted by the Congress did not go far enough, and expressed the hope that the latter would devise a program which Communists could whole-heartedly support.

A new program for the penetration of the AFL unions was worked out—or more correctly, the old Foster tactics used by the Trade Union Educational League were dusted off. Organizing "opposition caucuses" in locals of the old-line crafts, the Communists carried their demands for more militant action to the union meetings. In some cases they succeeded in taking over local affiliates; in others, they forced a change of policy.[5] At the same time the Party continued its program of revolutionary dualism through the TUUL. It also tried to push the Gompers-gazing AFL leaders into large-scale political action on a permanent basis, the goal being a farmer-labor party with the trade unions as its core. But at the same time, Communist leaders warned against political involvement with the "reactionary trade union politicians."

Some effort was made to bring farmers and farm-laborers into a program of action on immediate issues in late 1934 and early 1935. Some penetration of existing farm organizations was attempted. At other times the Party proposed joint action with such organizations as the Farmers League and the Farmers National Committee for Action. The organization of farm laborers under the revolutionary banners of the Sharecroppers Union and the Cannery and Agricultural Workers Industrial Union was continued. The difficulties involved in trying to combine the "boring-from-within" and the "dual-organization" tactics were illustrated in the complaint of one organizer who said:

By arbitrarily demanding that the militant farmers of the countryside be organized in our left-wing locals we have isolated them from their more backward neighbors and lost contact with the masses of farmers still affiliated to the reformist and capitalist-controlled groups. Party comrades in agrarian work have not yet learned how to go among farmers in the right-wing organizations and carry on revolutionary work, how to adopt our tactics to win the not yet class-conscious farmers.[6]

The Party was one of the guiding spirits at the first American Youth Congress. Its representatives played an important role in the proceedings. Well prepared beforehand and disciplined in committee-room maneuvers, the young—and some not so young —Communists built what Browder termed an "anti-fascist bloc." Using this group, the Party subsequently captured the national organization and still later succeeded in taking over some of the AYC's state conferences.[7] During the several years of its always-stormy existence, the AYC never succeeded in breaking this Communist grip. Its program embodied many of the Party's demands, which shifted more and more to the moderate side in the second stage of the united front period.

In the South an effort was made to promote a united front between the Southern Tenant Farmers Union and the Sharecroppers Union. Discussions were held between leaders of the two organizations. The STFU was reluctant to merge on the basis proposed by the Communists, who were still clinging to the self-determination doctrine though not insisting on its acceptance as a condition for unification. The STFU backed away, suspecting what it later found to be true when it affiliated with the CIO's Communist-led United Cannery, Agricultural, Packing and Allied Workers of America—that it would be swallowed up by ex-Columbia University farmers.

While the Party deplored the failure of the SU-STFU merger, it did not regard it as an important setback. It was now concentrating its efforts among the industrial workers in the steel and coal industries in the Birmingham area. Here the Communists claimed credit for "the growing militancy among larger sections of the trade union membership and lower secondary officials who are clamoring for united action against the capitalist attacks let loose following the N.R.A. decision." [8] * While there was grow-

---

* This same Party official, who in October, 1935, was proposing united action among the AFL unions, the farmers organizations, the NAACP, and "progressive" political elements in the South, in January, 1935—six months prior to the Seventh World Congress of the Comintern—had this to say: "Between the bureaucrats in the A.F. of L. and the Socialist Party and the reformist leaders of the N.A.A.C.P. there is an unholy division of labor. The white bureaucrats try to prevent the white workers from solidarizing with the Negroes, while the Negro misleaders sow mistrust in the minds of the Negro masses against the white workers. Some of the 'left' reformists

ing unrest among the industrial workers—black and white—of the area, it would be going too far to attribute even a substantial portion of it to the Party. The stirrings of the mine workers and the steel workers were part of the general labor resurgence under the New Deal. Their subsequent militancy was to be attributed to the great organizing drives staged by the United Mine Workers and the Steel Workers Organizing Committe in the vast domains of the Tennessee Coal and Iron Company, which was the Birmingham arm of United States Steel. The early united front efforts of the Party, however widely publicized and dramatic, were not the principal ferment.

The Party's approach to the NAACP, the NUL and other protest and betterment organizations among Negroes was characterized by a high degree of confusion and inconsistency. It visualized some form of joint action with them as early as 1934. However, when the selection of specific issues came up, the Communists were willing to participate only on their own terms. While the Party applauded the "changes" in the programs of these organizations, even claiming some credit for them, it continued to criticize and berate their leaders in an unmerciful fashion.[9] While it at times looked with approval on their gains, it continued to try to infiltrate and "capture" their local branches; for example, it wrecked a number of the Workers Councils organized by the National Urban League in 1934. That the Communist overtures were viewed with a jaundiced eye, by moderate Negro leaders is not difficult to understand.[10] They had learned the score during the decade and a half in which they had to ward off the Communist attacks while trying to carry on the normal functions of their organizations.

As limited and piecemeal as these preliminary efforts by the

---

speak about economic and political equality, but not social equality. Others claim to be for 'social equality' but against self-determination. Linked up with this tendency of the reformists in the South is their emphasis that better conditions can be won, not through revolutionary struggle, but by currying favor with the ruling class. The Negro reformists who are concentrating their attack against the I.L.D. in its fight for the freedom of the Scottsboro boys, are trying to cement an alliance with the liberal bourgeoisie elements in the South, who in practice try to sugarcoat the lynch and hunger program of the Southern ruling class." (Nat Ross, "Some Problems of the Class Struggle in the South," *Communist*, Vol. XIV, No. 1, January, 1935, 71-72.)

Communists had been, Browder in his speech before the Seventh World Congress of the Comintern pointed to them with pride as evidence of the American section's compliance with the earlier directives of the Executive Committee.[11]

The Seventh World Congress of the Communist International was convened in Moscow in late July, 1935, for purposes of transmitting a complete united front line to the various affiliated sections. This new line had been shaping up since early 1933, initiated by the resolution of the Executive Committee in March of that year. The Comintern had been waiting and hoping that the collapse or overthrow of Hitler and Mussolini would remove the fascist threat to the U.S.S.R., and thus enable the Party to return completely to the revolutionary line it had followed with a special zeal since 1928. However, its hopes did not materialize; it became apparent that the expansionist programs of Germany and Italy could be halted only through concerted diplomatic and economic action by Great Britain, France, the United States and the U.S.S.R., or by a display of military strength by such an alliance.

Effectively to counter the fascist threat, the Comintern recognized that it would be necessary to come to terms with the "imperialist" and "capitalist" powers against whom it had waged a program of violent revolution for more than a decade. And to come to terms required dropping—or more properly, holding in abeyance—the world revolutionary apparatus which was built by and centered in the Communist International. A new line was called for; the second phase of the united front program was introduced. Thus, the Seventh World Congress declared:

In face of the towering menace of fascism to the working class and all the gains it has made, to all toilers and their elementary rights, to the peace and liberty of the peoples, the Seventh Congress of the Communist International declares that at the present historical stage it is the main and immediate task of the international labor movement to re-establish the united fighting front of the working class. For a successful struggle against the offensive of capital, against the reactionary measures of the bourgeoisie, against fascism, the bitterest enemy of all the toilers, who, without distinction of political views, have been deprived of all rights and liberties, it is imperative that unity of action be established between all sections of the working class, irrespective of what organization they belong to, even before the majority of the working class unites on a common fighting platform for the overthrow of capitalism and the victory of the proletarian revolution. But it is precisely for this very reason that this task makes it the duty of the Communist Parties to take into consideration the changed circumstances and to apply the united front tactics in the new manner, by seeking to reach agreements with the organizations of the toilers of various political trends for joint action on a factory, local, district, national and international scale.[12]

The implications of this new strategy were numerous and quite at variance with past practices of most of the affiliated sections, even during the preliminary united front period. Henceforth, at least for the immediate future, the various Parties were to seek not the conquest of power by revolution but a sharing of power in reformist coalitions—and to accept the responsibilities which this implied. The ultimate aim of political revolution, however, was not renounced; it was postponed. The removal of the fascist threat would inevitably lead towards socialism, and, at the opportune time, the basic aim of a drastic reordering of capitalism and the establishment of the dictatorship of the proletariat would be realized.[13]

Social-democratic movements were to be opposed only within limitations, and the immediate aim of Communists was not to be the former's liquidation. On the contrary, social-democrats were to be sounded out with a view to reaching agreement on those immediate issues central to the defeat of reaction and the prevention of a war of conquest against the U.S.S.R. Left-wing Socialists were to be approached over the heads of their moderate leaders, but certain concessions were to be granted in an effort to take all Socialists into the united front camp.

Trade union movements were to be captured, not for purposes of revolutionizing the working class immediately, but for use in a common-front struggle centered around the immediate problems of the workers. If they could not be infiltrated, then Communists were to seek some working arrangement whereby labor organizations would be drawn into united front programs through agreement at the top. Where no trade unions existed, the Communists were to conduct intensive organizing drives, bringing the heretofore unorganized workers under Party leadership, but not emphasizing the overthrow of capitalism as an immediate aim. If other parties were active in this sphere, the Communists were to attempt to reach agreements on jurisdiction and programs.

Political parties of the extreme right, of course, were to be opposed. But "progressive" non-revolutionary movements were to be supported, especially where there was a possibility that "anti-fascist" coalitions or a "farmer-labor party" could strongly influence the conduct of government or even capture the administrative apparatus of the state. The middle classes, the balancing forces in such countries as France, Britain and the United States, were to be drawn into active political participation with the farm and labor groups. The lower middle classes were no longer to be viewed as lackeys of the respective ruling classes; they were to be approached as a significant political resource, large numbers of which could be turned against the monopoly capitalists who were grinding them down to even lower levels of poverty. Farmers and peasants were to be rallied around programs of land reform, relief from debt, and government assistance.

Sectarian dogma had admittedly hampered the parties in the capitalist countries in the past. It was to be dropped now, and rigid insistence on doctrinal purity as a condition of cooperation with other elements was to be abandoned.[14] In addition the Comintern proposed to allow a much greater degree of freedom to the various affiliates in developing their own programs of united action. The area of discretion allowed leaders of the Communist parties was to be widened, but warnings were issued against "incorrect" tendencies and unwarranted "deviations." [15]

The national liberation movements in the colonies were to be toned down. Their immediate aim was not to be the overthrow of their imperialist oppressors in conjunction with the revolutionary proletariat in their industrial centers. These movements were to continue their drive for liberation, but through more gradual means. The various racial minorities in the capitalist nations were to be rallied around programs designed to meet their more immediate needs, and at the same time directed into the general united front camp against "war and fascism." The techniques for accomplishing this aim were to be developed by the various affiliates themselves.

With these new guide posts supplied by the Comintern, the Communist Party in the United States was now in a position to map a much straighter course. What course did it outline, and how did it propose to travel? First, it was necessary to reformulate its general position, and second, to develop techniques and organizations for its application. The Party reanalyzed the American economic and political scene, viewing the major forces and groupings in a different light. Capitalism, it held, was in grave crisis, but partial remedies could be achieved through concerted action by the trade unions and progressive political forces. The establishment of a socialist society was not now the alternative. The extension of the trade union movement, the enactment of various types of social legislation, a more positive economic role by government—all these, it now argued, could produce positive, perhaps lasting, results.

The Republican and Democratic parties were no longer identical instruments of the capitalist class in America. The Democratic Party could serve a useful purpose, particularly if its liberal and labor wing could come to the fore. However, its limitations were many and the Party explored the possibility of joining with various dissident elements in the creation of a farmer-labor party. A little later the Communists for all practical purposes dropped the third party idea and put their canvassers and precinct workers at the disposal of the Democratic Party machines. The Republican Party, the Communists held, was dominated by big business and isolationists—the spearhead of native fascism. Little did the Party suspect that it would one day join these "native fascists" in an attempt to defeat the Roosevelt "warmongers." The Democratic Party, whose leaders appreciated the threat of totalitarianism abroad, the Communists argued, was an advocate of collective security. By 1936 the Party had dropped much of its criticism of Roosevelt and the New Deal, redirecting its vitriol almost exclusively toward Roosevelt's detractors.

The trade union movement, while criticized by the Communists for a number of past failures and current practices, was not now hampered with dual revolutionary movements. It was supported in those industries where it had a foothold, with "boring-from-within" tactics being employed to chart a "progressive" course. The Party was particularly insistent that the trade unions concern themselves with foreign policy and support the collective security measures of the Roosevelt administration. Where workers were unorganized the Party was to support the industrial form of organization, even though in some instances such movements were under the direction of long-time, anti-Communist leaders. If possible, it was to capture these new organizations and use them as a political and economic resource in extending the Party as a whole.

The great American middle class, politically powerful when it was aroused, was to be handled gently. The conjunction of its interests with those of the labor movement was to be emphasized; it was to be courted rather than fought as a collection of bourgeois incipient fascists. It was to be guided into the area of progressive political action, and the lower strata directed into the trade union movement.

The Party was to drop its doctrinaire and blanket criticism of religion, recognizing that the churches offered an opportunity for the further pursuit of its united front program. Party members were to display at least outward respect for the ideas of "progressive" ministers, although it was not incumbent that they join the church. (This policy was later to pay off handsomely when the Catholic Church and the Communist Party formed what amounted to a united front for organizing the CIO industrial unions in manufacturing centers of the North. Philip Murray and Harry Bridges shaking hands was an appropriate symbol.)

That the Party would have some difficulty in disposing of this new general line of imported goods, although it had a close similarity to native products, was anticipated at the outset. Its salesmen were warned that they would meet in the political market the competition of numerous organizations which the Party had bitterly fought for years. But they were cautioned about any lack of confidence in the latest brands, and urged to get rid of their old inventories of hostility, which in a potentially shared market would be a handicap. One of Browder's state-

THE NEGRO PEOPLE'S UNITED FRONT   133

ments is particularly revealing in this connection. "We have," he declared,

completely underestimated our potential allies in the S.P. [Socialist Party]. We have become the victims of spontaneity in this respect. We think we have no allies there because they don't spontaneously come forward and stand by us. But we have not understood our role in leading these elements in the S.P. If we but attempted to reach these friendly elements, we would have immediate results. But we don't even speak to them. We still have in our heads the idea expressed in our song books. When we were singing that song, "On the Picket Line," there was that line, "If you don't like thugs, and Socialists and scabs, come picket on the picket line." We have stopped singing that line of the song and cut it out of the book, but it still has much influence in our minds. We still think too often that there is something shameful in associating with Socialists.[16]

Along with the change in the Party's general program went a change on the Negro question. Neither the theory of self-determination nor the underlying conception of the Negro question as a "national problem" was formally dropped. However, these ideas, definitive for the Party since 1928, were abandoned for all practical purposes during the united front period. Communists continued to insist that the "ultimate" solution would have to be along the black republic line, but this insistence was confined mostly to their "theoretical organs" and to communications to the Communist International. The new line held that the self-determination theory did not contravene the demand for full equality; the Party now proposed to continue the latter with greater vigor, uniting "all segments" of the Negro community behind a minimum program for Negro rights. As Browder later explained:

Some people think that because we do not insist that the issue of the right to self-determination be adopted now by the National Negro Congress [an organization which the Party helped establish in 1936] our Party is abandoning its revolutionary demand for the right to self-determination in the Black Belt in the South. Nothing is further from the truth. Never was it more clear than it is today that the complete liberation of the people in the Black Belt will be accomplished only by the revolutionary overthrow of the white land lords and capitalists, the destruction of the semi-slave agricultural relations and the realization of the right to self-determination. But there is a problem which we must face. And how shall we face it? The problem is how to link up the daily struggles of the Negro masses in the Black Belt today for their economic and political demands with our revolutionary slogan of the right to self-determination. *It is clear that the Negro masses are not yet ready to carry through the revolution which would make possible the right to self-determination. But they are ready to fight against Jim Crowism and oppression, for democratic rights and other partial economic and political demands.*[16-a]

The new Negro program contained a different version of the black social structure and the role of its component groups. The Negro middle class, the hated "black bourgeoisie," was now viewed as a progressive element in the struggle for Negro rights. It was not the "natural" enemy of colored workers or the national liberation movement, as the Party had previously insisted. It was a potential ally. It was the most articulate of the Negro strata and could play a focal role in building the united front among American blacks. It was "more conscious of the race as a whole," more aware of its traditions and aspirations; so said the new Party directives. Criticism of its leaders was to be dropped except in the most unusual cases. It was to be welcomed, even invited or solicited, for the Negro mass movement.[17]

The colored working class was to be brought into the trade unions, either into the existing crafts or into the new industrial organizations. But its resources were to be deployed in conjunction with other Negro groupings, being joined with the middle-class organizations and progressive political elements who saw the struggle of the black workers as an important part of the advancement of the race. The old practice of placing the colored workers in separate revolutionary organizations or trying to develop them as the spearhead of a self-determination program was to be abandoned.

The Party was now to take a different attitude toward such protest and betterment organizations as the NAACP and the NUL. This was reflected, for example, in Browder's statement:

We know that the past struggles between us (NAACP, NUL, and Communist Party) have also had one bad effect upon our own forces, of making them too suspicious, too inclined to see enemies everywhere, sometimes even where they do not exist, and where they are potential friends. We ourselves must break loose from these self-appointed limitations, we must have greater confidence in those broad circles, not hitherto associated with us, who are taking up the struggle for Negro rights.[18]

No longer was Walter White to be characterized as a lickspittle of capitalism, or Lester Granger as a Judas of the race. The Communists now held that these men were among the foremost leaders of black America, deserving the good will and cooperation of Negroes in all walks of life, certainly deserving of the support of the Party. "We Communists," declared Ford, "desire to do everything possible in building and broadening the movement of the Negro people in cooperation with the N.A.A.C.P., the National Negro Congress, the Urban League and other organizations." [19]

While the Party bitterly opposed the Negro nationalist organizations during the preceding period, it was now to follow an entirely different course. "How do we approach the Garveyites, and other nationalistic elements. . . ?" asked Ford.

We approach them in a friendly manner, and Negro Communists say: "We Communists are defenders of our people, defenders of the Ethiopian people. . . ."

We welcome this friendly attitude and the possibility of working with all sections of the Negro people to consolidate the united front. We also appreciate the friendly attitude that governs the response of the Negro nationalists. We must say to our Negro Communists: "We have to stop using the word 'nationalist' too loosely and in a derogatory manner." [20]

Like the other Negro groups which the Party had fought bitterly and with a special intensity since 1928, the Negro nationalist organizations now were to be brought into the united front program. (And it was among these groups that some espousal of the self-determination theory continued.)

The Negro churches were no longer to be charged with misleadership and betrayal of the race. They, too, were to be approached in a "friendly" manner, and the aid of ministers "who were very close to the daily needs of their poor parishioners" was to be enlisted. Communists were to prove that they could work in "close harmony" and in mutual cooperation with a wide number of Negro churches and religious societies. Various Negro associations, fraternal and business, and Negro women's organizations were to be courted, not condemned. Thus the Party proposed to use practically all segments of Negro society and their various agencies for carrying out the new line on the Negro question.

What were the major items in the new program behind which the Communists proposed to rally the mass of American blacks? Dropping the demand for self-determination, foregoing, for the time being at any rate, the larger revolutionary goals, and abandoning much of the previous theoretical dogma, the Party now concentrated on a series of immediate issues of vital concern to the vast majority of Negroes in the United States. The program it now advocated was similar in many respects to those of a number of other organizations, Negro and interracial, long active in the field of race rights. While a number of these items had been included in previous Communist programs, they were now made more specific and tied in with the support of concrete measures. They were accorded major rather than incidental emphasis.

Among them were the following: (1) repeal of the poll-tax; (2) abolition of lynching through legislation; (3) abolition of discrimination in public services; (4) enactment of a comprehensive civil rights program; (5) equal treatment of Negroes by government administrative agencies; (6) equitable admission of Negroes into the trade unions; (7) fair employment opportunities in the government services and in private industry; (8) equal treatment of Negroes in the armed forces; (9) equality of colored people before the law; (10) relief and other forms of assistance to Negroes in the cities and to the sharecroppers and day laborers in the South; (11) equal educational opportunities at all levels of instruction; and (12) abolition of state and local laws of a racially discriminatory character. Its program included other measures related to these.

How did the Communist Party attempt to implement this new Negro program, and what were the results of its efforts? Before we consider the answers to these questions, it is necessary first to give considerable attention to a development that seriously limited the Party's Negro work at the very outset, that handicapped and haunted it throughout the united front period.

During the spring and summer of 1935 it became apparent that Italy would undertake a campaign to conquer Ethiopia and add that country to its African "Empire" unless the major powers, including the U.S.S.R. and the United States, offered strenuous opposition in the form of economic sanctions or more drastic measures. While discussions were in progress before the League of Nations, Mussolini was completing the necessary preparations for this newest African venture. The Soviet Union, which had been admitted to the League only a short time before, appeared to be the chief advocate of opposition to Italian imperialism, and Maxim Litvinov was its chief spokesman.

The American Communist Party, by this time travelling faster on the "broad highway of the united front," saw in the Ethiopian issue another opportunity to build its unity program among American Negroes. It assumed that all strata of the Negro population would readily identify with Haile Selassie's cause. The Party accordingly called for the mobilization of all Negro groups, ranging from the extreme nationalists to the trade unions, to cooperate with liberal and labor organizations in pressuring the American government to impose economic sanctions against the Italian aggressors.[21]

The Party's immediate program called for: (1) a united front organization to coordinate the work of all groups supporting Ethiopia; (2) an organization to raise funds and provide material aid to Ethiopia, with priorities assigned to medical supplies and munitions; and (3) united pressure from Negro, liberal, and labor organizations to halt the shipment of oil, wheat, and other items from the United States. At the same time the Party was careful to point out that the U.S.S.R., alone among the major powers, had taken a firm and unequivocal stand against Italian aggression and had refused to supply the Italian war machine with vitally-needed materials.[22]

While many groups in America were willing to take these claims at their face value, accepting Litvinov's assertions as an accurate reflection of Soviet policy, there were spokesmen, particularly among Negroes, who remained skeptical. For example, George Padmore, the former Executive Secretary of the International Trade Union Committee of Negro Workers, charged as early as May, 1935, that the Soviet Union would be quite willing to sacrifice Ethiopia to Mussolini if the interests of the "socialist fatherland" might be served. And such an act, he continued, would well fit into the pattern of desertion of colonial peoples which the U.S.S.R. had followed since Hitler's rise to power.[23]

Considerable criticism of Soviet policies also appeared in the Socialist organs and in the general Negro press. The Party at first attempted to ignore such charges. However, it became increasingly apparent that the U.S.S.R. was playing a strictly power politics game in much the same manner as France, Britain and the United States. The Party in August, 1935, made a strenuous effort to answer criticism of the Soviet role in the Ethiopian matter.[24] Editorials in the *Daily Worker* and lengthy articles in the *Communist*, however vitriolic and self-righteous, did not suffice. William L. Patterson, for example, called critics of the Soviet Union all the usual names in the Party's handbook of invective. He praised the minorities program of the Soviet republics. He bewailed the plight of Negroes in the United States —but he did not answer the charge that the U.S.S.R. was giving material assistance to Italy in its African invasion.[25]

As criticism of the U.S.S.R. mounted there was considerable tension within the Negro ranks of the Party itself, resulting in a number of defections. The most conspicuous case was that of Herman W. Mackawain, acting secretary of the still-functioning League of Struggle for Negro Rights. In his resignation, Mackawain charged that the U.S.S.R. had been instrumental in arming and equipping Mussolini's armies, thereby losing whatever claim it had as a champion of racial minority rights.[26]

The most damaging criticism of the Soviet Union's role, however, came in the form of a news item which appeared in the September 8, 1935, edition of the *New York Times*. This brief article revealed that while Litvinov had been arguing the Soviet position before the League of Nations, the U.S.S.R. had been shipping large quantities of oil, coal tar, and wheat to Mussolini, some of it going directly to Africa for immediate use in the Ethiopian campaign. It was disclosed further that the U.S.S.R. had insisted on payment in cash at prices substantially above the world market level.[27]

This latest exposure of U.S.S.R.'s double-dealing on the Ethiopian issue did not catch the American Communists completely by surprise, but it did involve them in some labored and anguished explanations. Just how labored these efforts were was indicated in an article by Harry Gannes which appeared in the *Daily Worker* as a reply to the *Times* story. After pointing out that the Soviet Union "had always expressed its willingness to trade with all capitalist countries," Gannes continued:

These contradictions of trade between a Socialist country and a capitalist land, even a Fascist regime, whose significance are now distorted by the boss press in relation to Ethiopia, arise inevitably out of the fact that a Socialist country striving for peace, deals with an imperialist nation plunging to war. But only a banker's sheet like the *New York Times* or agents of counter revolution such as the Trotskyites, or incorrigible enemies of the proletarian revolution in Russia such as the Socialist Old Guard, can try to twist this to mean the deliberate assistance of the Soviet Union to Italian Fascism's plans for war against Ethiopia.

The two systems, existing side by side, are forced to trade with each other, and find it mutually beneficial. That the imperialists at all times in the purchase of oil from the Soviet Union utilize it for their bombing planes, for preparation for war, for their armies oppressing the masses in their colonies was always well known. But intelligent honest people understood this contradiction. They saw, yes, gains to imperialism, but above all they saw greater gains to the bulwark of the world revolution, the Soviet Union, which became a greater and more powerful force for peace and for succor of the oppressed colonial masses in the colonies.[28]

Few American Negroes were willing to grant the major premise on which the whole of Gannes' and other Communist explanations rested—that whatever served the interests of the U.S.S.R. necessarily served the interests of colored peoples in Ethiopia and in the United States. The Party was confronted with a series of embarrassing questions. Why should a "Socialist country striving for peace" deal on a business basis with a "capitalist land plunging to war?" Did one have to be a banker, a Trotskyite, or an old-guard Socialist to see that Russian wheat and oil in Mussolini's hands (although at a higher price) was just as useful for the conquest of Ethiopia as American wheat and oil (at the regular market price)? In what way was the U.S.S.R. a "powerful force for peace and for succor of the oppressed colonial masses" when it provided an imperialist nation with the means for destroying such colonial masses? Were the people who failed to understand these contradictions lacking in either intelligence or honesty? If so, then many Negroes in the United States fell into these categories.

Negro defections from the Party and its satellite organizations continued. The Negro press devoted substantial space to discussion of the U.S.S.R.'s contributions to the Italian venture. An editorial in *The Crisis* probably summarized the feeling of most of the American Negroes who were acquainted with the matter. It declared:

Of course, close students of Soviet Russia discovered long ago that the great idealism of the so-called Communist nation was in reality hard-boiled opportunism, and opportunism as shameless as that of any nation not professing the high idealism preached by the Kremlin. Therefore it is only recording one more inconsistency and not one more surprise to set down that the Soviets are raking in good Capitalist profits selling wheat and coal tar to Italy for use in the war against Ethiopia.

We have little quarrel with the Soviet pursuit of profits—even imperialist war profits. Business men are business men whether their offices are on Red Square in Moscow or West [sic] street in New York. We do object to the pious flub-dub sported by Communists such as: "love for the downtrodden," "self-determination for small nations," "fight imperialist war," etc. They are always ranting about capitalist exploitation and robbery and drawing themselves up in their pet holier-than-thou attitude, but whenever the opportunity presents itself they are in the midst of the arms and munitions races, military alliances and in garnering of profits.[29]

The Communists would have liked to drop the whole Ethiopian question, but it was now impossible to do so. Explanations of the "contradictions" continued to flow from the Party press. In approaching Negro groups, however, the Party was cautious, not stressing the matter until it was brought up. Communists took the position now that the U.S.S.R. had always been willing to impose sanctions against Italy, but that it was prevented from doing so because the United States, Britain and France would not agree to a general embargo, the only measure that would have been effective. Negroes, the Communists argued, should join with the Party in demanding a general halt to all trade with Italy.[30]

This argument remained as unconvincing as the earlier ones. It was evident that the Party would make little headway among American Negroes by playing up the Ethiopian issue, particularly since there had been no halt to Russia's shipments of war materials. However, the Party was favored by the fact that the masses of American Negroes tended to be indifferent to the Ethiopian conquest. They retained practically no identity with African culture and did not consider themselves an immigrant minority whose homeland was being overrun by an aggressive outsider.*

The Communists were further favored by the fact that during this period most American Negroes—and whites in similar economic positions—were confronted with pressing problems of employment, welfare and housing. During this time Negroes who otherwise might have shown an active concern with foreign affairs, including the Ethiopian issue, were preoccupied with finding a job, a place to live, and providing minimum opportunities

---

* Melville J. Herskovits, the anthropologist, has placed great emphasis on the survival of African traits in American Negro culture. Alain Locke, the Negro philosopher and educator, has pointed out that such emphasis can lead to a growth of anti-Negro prejudice since it lends support to the idea that Negroes are an unassimilable racial minority. E. Franklin Frazier seems to have refuted Herskovits on strictly empirical grounds by showing that African survivals are indeed few and insignificant, and explaining further the disappearance of earlier traits. At any rate, it is apparent that Negroes in the United States do not identify with the colored peoples of Africa on the basis of a common cultural heritage. There are only loose and sporadic ties of a political character. The Negro's struggle for acceptance in American society has led to continuous emphasis on the singularly American origins of his character and ideology. This will account in part for the general failure of American Negroes to act as if their own status, as Negroes, was threatened in the Italian invasion of Ethiopia. See: Melville J. Herskovits, *The Myth of the Negro Past* (New York: Harper and Brothers, 1941), Alain Locke, "Who and What is a Negro," *Opportunity*, March, 1942, and E. Franklin Frazier, *op. cit.*, pp. 3-21.

for their children. In their work among this group the Communists could emphasize the latter problems without being called to account on the Soviet role in Ethiopia.

The Party did make an attempt to approach the Negro nationalist movements on the Ethiopian issue. It was anticipated that the Party's program would meet with a wide response among those Negroes who visualized their emancipation in terms of the establishment of a separate Negro state in Africa. The Party argued that the conquest of Ethiopia would jeopardize the chances of a Negro nationalist state in Africa or in the United States, insisting that it was logically incumbent on the Negro nationalists to join with the Communists in pushing for a general embargo on shipments of materials to Italy.[31]

The nationalist movements among American Negroes during this period, however, were extremely weak. They had no mass base and only elementary organizational structures, with few resources, political or financial. They were extremely mistrustful of outside groups, including the Communists. They did display some interest in the Ethiopian issue, raising funds and forming committees to oppose the Italian conquest. However, these were small-scale and uncoordinated efforts. Even if the Communists had succeeded in capturing all these organizations, they would have had little to show for their efforts.

Gradually the Party pushed the Ethiopian question into the background, at the same time placing greater emphasis on strictly domestic issues in approaching Negroes. The official press made fewer references to the matter, and refused to take cognizance of continuing criticism in the Socialist and Negro papers. Following the Ethiopian defeat the whole matter was for the most part abandoned—except for an occasional suggestion that if the Party's recommendations had been followed, the Italians could not have completed their conquest.[32] The Party, however, never quite overcame this setback in its initial efforts to build the united front among Negroes. Even today, fifteen years later, the double-dealing of the U.S.S.R. is vividly remembered by many American Negroes. It is a constant source of the deep mistrust with which they view the Soviet Union and the American Communist Party.[33]

Returning now to the means employed by the Communists to implement the new line on the Negro question, let us examine first the trade union program. So far as concerned colored workers, the Party's activities in the labor movement fell into three fairly distinct categories. First, it attempted to force the American Federation of Labor affiliates to abolish the numerous barriers against the admission of Negroes. Second, it supported the organizing drives of the CIO, abandoning the Trade Union Unity League and steering its affiliates into the new industrial unions which the Communists were helping to organize. Third, working through the National Negro Congress and through strictly Party organizations, it attempted to promote among the various segments of the Negro population an acceptance of the idea of unionism, and to enlist their support for organizational drives.

It was the latter two activities which the Party emphasized. The fact that John L. Lewis was willing to use Communist organizers in the big drives to unionize meat packing, automobile, rubber, agriculture and other industries provided an excellent opportunity for the Party to carry forward its program among Negro industrial workers. The Communists, of course, emphasized non-discrimination in the new unions in line with the program of the Party. However, the policies followed by the CIO in this connection were only in part the result of this influence. As Northrup has pointed out:

It is not difficult to comprehend why the CIO has pursued its liberal racial policy. Unlike craft unions, which are organized on an exclusive and narrow basis, and which depend upon their control of a few highly skilled and strategically situated jobs to obtain their bargaining power, industrial unions acquire their strength by opening their ranks to all the workers in an industry. The United Mine Workers, the Amalgamated Clothing Workers, and the Ladies' Garment Workers had been organized on an industrial basis for many years prior to 1935 when their leaders founded the CIO. Few, if any labor unions had better records for fair treatment of Negroes than did these three. Besides, their officers saw the projected campaigns to organize the workers of the iron and steel, the automobile, and the other mass production industries doomed to failure unless the unions in these fields opened their doors to workers of all creeds and colors. Finally, the CIO contains within its ranks most of the left-wing elements in the American labor movement. These groups have always most vociferously opposed racial discrimination in all forms. For these reasons then, the CIO has attempted to enroll workers regardless of race, creed, color, or nationality.[34]

The Communists gained their principal footholds in the automobile, meat packing, metal mining, waterfront, transportation, communication, electrical products and farm equipment unions, not to mention a number of the smaller organizations such as the American Newspaper Guild and the United Office and Professional Workers. A number of these industries, for example meat packing and longshore, employed thousands of Negro workers who had to be brought into the unions if organization was to succeed. The bitter intra-union struggles around the question of Party control which characterized the later history of such organizations as the United Automobile Workers, the United Packinghouse Workers, the United Farm Equipment Workers, the National Maritime Union, the Transport Workers Union, and the United Electrical Workers Union is indicative of the extent to which the Communists were successful in establishing their hold on the industrial union movement during the formative period between 1935 and 1940. More recently the fact that the CIO national organization has had to take extreme measures in ridding itself of Party-controlled affiliates is further evidence, not only of the extent but of the tenacity of the Communist grip.

From the very outset the Party was anxious to give full support to the CIO movement. Several factors explain this. The dual unionism program of the TUUL had produced few results. The limited effort to rejuvenate the AFL which was renewed in late 1933 and in 1934 had failed. The Party was anxious, as it had been for years, to develop a program of industrial unionism, not as a limited trade union strategy but for its larger purposes. Now that it was committed to building a united front, of which the trade unions were to be the back-bone, with a farmer-labor party as the ultimate political instrument, it was more desirous than ever of getting in on the ground floor of a movement, already backed by powerful unions, which would bring organization to the mass of unskilled and semi-skilled workers, and at the same time afford one of the best opportunities yet for carrying out its Negro program. Browder declared in 1936, for example,

... the Committee for Industrial Organization is launching the second great crusade to carry trade unionism into the open shop citadel of monopoly capital, to the half million slaves of the Steel Trust. Nothing so heartening has been seen in the labor movement since 1919.[35]

And further, that:

The Committee for Industrial Organization has taken up the task of organizing all the mass production industries of America in industrial unions. The success of this effort is a basic necessity upon which depends the future of the labor movement in all other respects. The Communist Party unconditionally pledges its full resources, moral and material, to the complete execution of this great project.[36]

The Party was aware that in the CIO it had a very effective instrument for organizing Negro workers and realizing the much desired Negro-white labor unity. Negroes, instead of being barred from the unions, as had been true in many of the AFL affiliates, were admitted into the CIO on an equal basis and actively sought as a necessary resource. Negro workers also stood to gain by their identification with the CIO, and thus the need was mutual. During the 1936 election campaign Ford indicated the Communists' keen appreciation of the possibilities inherent in this development, declaring:

... the great progressive unions united in the Committee for Industrial Organization—which is organizing the mass production industries —are breaking down these bars [against Negro workers in unions]. The colored people must support the organizing drive now going on in steel, automobile and rubber, for the fate of the black worker is linked up with the organization of the unorganized. A powerful labor movement in which all black and white workers are united is a bulwark against reaction, and a guarantee for higher wages and better working conditions.[37]

The Party had a number of advantages in approaching Negroes through the CIO. In the first place, it was seeking their support on a trade union basis, with an immediate program easily understood by the average Negro worker. Emphasis was put on increasing wages, shortening hours, improving working conditions, and on equality of opportunity at the job level and within the union. Second, it was working in cooperation with an organization that had tremendous economic and political resources. Third, it was participating in the unionization of workers who, after years of the open shop and company unionism, were reacting in a militant fashion and determined that racial prejudice would not again play into the hands of employers.

The CIO unions which the Party controlled later became a very valuable resource in the fight for other aspects of the Communists' Negro program. The funds of these unions were used to support other Negro movements, for propaganda, and for organization. Their political power was placed behind specific demands for an extension of Negro rights, such as anti-lynching, anti-poll tax, housing and other legislation. Responsible positions in the CIO gave Negro Communists a prestige in the black community which they would not have otherwise had; it provided them a platform from which they could speak, not only for the industrial union movement and in behalf of Negro workers, but for the united front program among all sectors of the race. For example, Negro Communists in the CIO were instrumental in the organization of the National Negro Congress, which climaxed the Party's hope for building a "people's organization" around the race question.[38]

Concurrently with its shift from revolutionary dualism in the trade union sphere, the Party executed a change in its policies toward the major organizations in the field of Negro protest and betterment. No longer condemning them in unmerciful fashion, it attempted to obtain their support, by agreement at the top or by infiltration from below. It rationalized this change by declaring that pressure from the colored masses, frequently articulated by Communists, had forced the NAACP, the NUL and other Negro organizations to adopt more militant, more pro-labor policies. The NAACP had indorsed the unionization of Negro workers, supporting a number of CIO drives in areas of large colored population. It had also become more active in the political and legislative spheres, expanding its cooperation with other groups in these important activities. As early as 1934 the National Urban League had established a series of Workers Councils with the aim of acquainting Negro workers with the trade union movement and promoting their more positive identification with it.

While these developments reflected no great awakening on the part of the NAACP and the NUL, Ford, for example, read into them great conversions, and declared:

> ... we Communists welcome this progress and desire to do everything possible to extend the work of building and broadening the movement of the Negro people in co-operation with the N.A.A.C.P., the National Negro Congress, and the Urban League and other organizations.[39]

For Ford, and for other Communists, it was always the opposition that had changed its policies—never the Party. It merely changed its tactics "in the light of the new situation," even if it did a complete about-face from the day before.

There was a limited amount of cooperation between these organizations and the Party during the united front period. However, it usually took place at the local level and on specific issues. The NAACP remained essentially aloof, not easily forgetting its relations with the Party during the past decade and a half. Communists were successful in capturing a few local branches but failed to obtain any large influence in the headquarters organization or in the official organs. The NAACP welcomed the Party's exposure of discrimination and injustice against the Negro. This did not imply, however, that it approved the Party's program or was willing to go along on the action it proposed. Both the NAACP and the NUL continued to criticize the Communist dictatorship in Russia, at the same time warning their members against infiltration tactics of the Party and suggesting caution in any joint action with Stalinists on local issues.

That the Party was willing, even during this united front period in which it "welcomed" the cooperation of moderate Negro organizations, to infiltrate and even destroy their programs was evidenced in the Workers Councils of the NUL. Lester Granger later described what happened:

The Urban League realized the country was on a wave of greater movement of organized labor, and realized if Negroes did not join they would miss the train ten years hence. We spent $30,000 or $40,000 indoctrinating Negroes on the importance of trade union membership and the ways members of a minority group can protect their status.

That [Workers Council] was an ideal organization for the Communists to capture, and they did. They grabbed one in New York City; we had to kill it off. They grabbed another, I think in Pennsylvania, and we had to kill that off. The Communists were never barred from entering, but as soon as we found that a council was being subverted from its true purposes and was becoming a mere mechanism for the propagation of Communist strategy, we would close it down and open another. That kept us going all over the country.[40]

The experiences of other Negro organizations were similar. Most of them were inclined to retaliate rather than stand idly by and watch their agencies become instruments of the Party.

While the Party obviously resented the fact that these organizations would not fold up and be had for the asking, its desire for cooperation was not dampened. Browder, whose mouthings Ford usually aped, insisted in his report on the Seventh World Congress that the moderate Negro organizations (within a period of months) had undergone fundamental changes and were displaying a much friendlier attitude toward the Communists. The NAACP, he said, had been forced to "reorientate itself towards the Left, to become more bold and more active in demanding equal right for Negroes. We must recognize," he continued "that it opens up new possibilities for joint work and struggle on a far broader basis than ever before." [41] To the NAACP a short time later he declared in the tone of a good friend wronged:

Would it not be better if, instead of attacking us, you would combine forces with us in fighting for Negro rights, for Angelo Herndon and the Scottsboro boys, and for defense of Ethiopia. We would welcome co-operation with you for these things instead of having to answer your attacks, which is indeed an unpleasant duty.[42]

The NAACP did not agree that "it would be better." By this time both the NAACP and the NUL were developing new strategies to deal with the larger problems which confronted

American Negroes. While these changes could be attributed in part to pressure from the leftists, they did not result from any drastic ideological conversions. Rather, they were shaped in the pragmatic day-to-day activities in which these organizations engaged.

While making an all-out effort to "cooperate" with the moderate Negro organizations, the Party did not neglect the nationalist movements. The ideological ghost of Garvey reappeared, faintly and briefly. The Party attempted to clothe it in a red shroud. The Communists who had vehemently fought the Negro nationalist organizations since 1928 now accorded them warm support. The Party held that the idea of a Negro national state in Africa or a 49th State in America except in the Black Belt was erroneous. However, it believed that the frustrations of the urban lower and middle class Negroes who formed the basis of the separate state movement could be directed toward support of its own program. Communists therefore employed a two-fold strategy. They attempted to infiltrate such organizations as the Peace Movement of Ethiopia and the National Movement for the Establishment of a 49th State at the local level; at the same time they carried on a campaign of criticism against both local and national leaders. The rank and file was treated with deference. It was assumed that by careful "educational" work, it could be brought around to the Party position—sold on a program of immediate action, sold on self-determination in the Black Belt as a substitute for the Negro state.

Even had the Party succeeded in taking over these and smaller Negro nationalist agencies, it would have captured only a few people in skeletal organizations. By 1935 most urban Negroes looked upon the Garvey ideology as "silly." Having resided in the cities for almost a generation, having become adept in the ways of survival and getting ahead in Harlem and Black Metropolis, the former immigrants, who had been the backbone of Garvey's Universal Negro Improvement Association in the 1920's, had no use for "Back to Africa" and "49th State" slogans. They were Americans; they were going to stay in America—all of it. In the South, while some Negroes might sign petitions for relocation of the race in Africa, this was primarily a means of protest against conditions at home; it did not reflect any concerted movement among blacks to seek their liberation abroad.

Although the Party met with only limited success in its efforts to penetrate or cooperate with the established Negro organizations during this period, it was instrumental in the building of several new ones in which it exerted a marked, and ultimately a preponderant, influence. One of these was the Negro People's Committee to Aid Spanish Democracy. With the outbreak of the Spanish Civil War in the summer of 1936, organizations of varying political orientations initiated programs to aid the Loyalist government. Numerous liberal, Socialist, radical and trade union groups, bound together to oppose fascism and support a foreign policy of collective security; these loose federations were quickly involved in raising funds, obtaining and shipping medical and other supplies, and in the recruitment of personnel for the Spanish Republic.

The Communist Party of the United States was among these organizations. It was especially active in the political field, and in the recruitment of nurses, doctors, technicians and soldiers. The Party not only solicited from its own ranks but also obtained a number of non-Communist volunteers. While an estimated 2,000 Americans served in the George Washington and Abraham Lincoln Brigades, many of these came from the ranks of liberal students, workers and intellectuals. Some of them were Negroes.

In carrying out its program the Party employed all the existing organizational apparatus at its command. In addition it established a number of special committees on a united front basis. In an effort to reach the maximum number of people, it set up organizations among American ethnic, national, and racial groups. The Negro People's Committee to Aid Spanish Democracy was the organization through which it worked in approaching American Negroes. The Committee was established a few months after the outbreak of the war; it functioned through 1937 and 1938, and was not disbanded until sometime after the end of hostilities.

In building this organization the Communists were able to enlist the support of a number of non-Party Negroes. However, upon James W. Ford fell the responsibility of carrying out much of the organizational work. Ford visited Spain in 1937. Upon his return he addressed numerous Negro groups, many of which, of course, met under Party auspices. Ford emphasized the contribution being made to the Loyalist cause by American blacks, while suggesting that their efforts be broadened and intensified. "The open intervention of fascism in Ethiopia, in Spain, in China, and the threat of reaction to labor and progress in our country," he declared, "requires a joint policy, on the part of the Negro people, with all of the forces of progress in our country and in the world." [43]

The principal branches of the Committee were organized in the larger urban-industrial centers, the largest one being in New York City. Others were organized in Chicago, Detroit, Los Angeles and San Francisco. Party control of the Committee apparatus was not always readily apparent, and the Party obtained the indorsement of some nationally and locally prominent Negroes. Though some of the non-Communist Negroes were aware of the Party's role, they were still willing to go along, believing that the seriousness of the fascist threat warranted their participation. Lester B. Granger of the National Urban League assumed the chairmanship of one of the local branches. His experience is most revealing; it not only sheds light on the operations of the Committee, but on the tactics of the Party in its Negro work. He described it as follows:

In 1936 or 1937 I wandered into the support, and ultimately became chairman, of a committee for the Loyalists in Spain. At that time most liberal Americans were concerned with the Spanish war and were actively supporting the Spanish Loyalist cause. I prided myself on being a person of liberal impulses. I made a contribution of an ambulance to demonstrate Negro support of the Spanish Loyalists.

My contribution must have been gratifyingly large, because almost immediately I had an invitation to become chairman of the committee. ... The Party members are very kind. They will take away from the chairman the responsibility of doing the work. I didn't keep up with what was happening. ...

Suddenly I found this committee was being used for the purposes of the Communist Party in denouncing aid to Great Britain. It was called to my attention by certain non-Communist members, and I immediately called a meeting.

As usual, the non-Communist members came or did not come, according to their convenience. The Communist members showed up. I found we were only a branch and did not have authority. When I expressed myself on keeping this organization out of Communist politics, there was a tremendous and well-organized resistance from a majority of those present, and they out-voted me. The vote was that the course would continue along the previous line. Whereupon, I, by letter, circulated a statement among the total membership of the committee, and we got a vote to close the committee down. That is the only thing we could do. It was captured then.[44]

Granger was not the only Negro to discover that the Committee had been captured by the Party.

Data are not available whereby we might measure the success achieved by the NPCASD. No figures on total membership were ever published, and there was no reliable accounting of the funds raised or the manner in which they were spent. It would seem safe to assume that contributions from individual Negroes and organizations were relatively meager, because, among other reasons, they were rarely able to do more than support their own protest agencies. Negroes did serve in the ranks of the American volunteers who fought in Spain, but the number is not certain.

The significance of the Committee, however, should not be overlooked. It did not develop mass support among Negroes for the Loyalist cause, but it did reflect a growing awareness on the part of American blacks of their interest in world affairs and the implications of fascism for racial minorities. The fact that the Committee was dominated and used by the Communists, and finally steered completely away from its first task, should not obscure the genuine concern of many American Negroes with the issues involved in the Spanish Civil War, or the fact that their sympathies were all on the side of the legitimate Republic. The Party, without doubt, would have made considerably more headway had its appeal for aid to Loyalist Spain not come almost immediately on the heels of its duplicity in the Ethiopian matter.

While the Negro People's Committee to Aid Spanish Democracy was established by the Party for very immediate and limited aims—at least originally—the National Negro Congress was developed as the instrument through which it was to pursue its larger united front program among all segments of black America.

The Communist Party realized that its change in line during and after 1935 would enable it to approach, possibly penetrate, "reformist" Negro organizations. However, it soon saw that it would be impossible to capture such organizations as the NAACP and the NUL, or to work out any program of joint action, satisfactory to itself. Even had this been possible, it is quite doubtful whether the Party would have attempted it. The Communists' aim was a broad Negro "people's movement," and these organizations were regarded as too narrow in scope to fulfill this goal. It was necessary for the Party to assist in building an over-all Negro organization whose primary purpose would be the unification of varied Negro groups around the immediate problems confronting the race, and around the general united front program.

The Party realized this aim at least in part through the National Negro Congress. In the early days of the New Deal a number of prominent Negroes had organized the Joint Committee on National Recovery, whose purpose was to look after the rights of Negroes in the administrative policies of newly created government agencies. The Committee's support came from some 22 Negro organizations—religious, fraternal, labor and political. However, the main financial responsibility was borne by the NAACP.[45]

In the spring of 1935 the Division of Social Sciences at Howard University, of which Ralph Bunche was Chairman, and the Joint Committee on National Recovery sponsored a conference which reviewed a wide range of Negro problems. The idea was advanced that a national Negro agency embracing all Negro unions, together with religious, fraternal, and civic groups, could give sharpness and unity to race organizations and arouse the Negro masses to effective political and economic action. A special committee for a National Negro Congress was set up with instructions to take the necessary steps to develop a permanent agency. John P. Davis, who had served as Chairman of the Joint Committee, was sent on a nation-wide tour to enlist the support of Negro leaders. In a pamphlet, *Let Us Build a National Negro*

*Congress,* Davis emphasized the special problems confronting Negro domestics, farmers, and laborers, and proposed united race action on all fronts.[46]

The Sponsoring Committee obtained the enthusiastic backing of A. Philip Randolph, President of the Brotherhood of Sleeping Car Porters, and later was indorsed by such prominent Negroes as Lester Granger and Elmer Carter, of the NUL; Ralph Bunche and Alain Locke, of Howard University; M. O. Bousfield, of the Julius Rosenwald Fund; and James A. Bray, R. A. Carter, and W. J. Walls, Negro churchmen. In addition, many Negro teachers, social workers, and lawyers, "gave their initial blessing." That the Communist Party approved the move was indicated in Ford's becoming a member of the Sponsoring Committee.

While Communists did not dominate the Sponsoring Committee or obtain full control of the Congress when it was organized in Chicago in 1936, they were prominent in the movement from the very outset. Davis was sympathetic toward the general united front program of the Party. In preparation for the first meeting of the Congress, Communists worked diligently in the Negro communities to build up general support and to see that organizations which they controlled or influenced sent delegates.[47] Ford had delivered a speech at the 1935 conference which established the Sponsoring Committee. In it he emphasized the importance of unified action among Negro workers and "intellectuals, teachers, doctors, and other professionals who are beginning to understand more clearly the need for a new policy in the struggles of the Negro people." [48] However, he did not propose the formation of a national agency. While Party representatives at the conference were apparently prepared to indorse a new congress-type national Negro agency, they felt that the public initiative should come from other sources.

There was a wide initial response to the proposals of the Sponsoring Committee. However, within a short time considerable skepticism developed among many Negro leaders, a skepticism based on the nebulous character and left-wing backing of the movement. Negro organizations were hesitant to put money into other organizations generally, and this particular program appeared too broad and indefinite. Conservative Negro groups were scared off by the prominence of Communists in the preparatory work and by "radical" points in the prospectus. But the time of the initial meeting the Congress had assumed a definite interracial character and a number of white and mixed groups were contributing funds and other assistance.

The organizing meeting of the Congress was held in Chicago February 14-16, 1936. The Committee on Credentials reported 817 delegates in attendance. These delegates came from twenty-eight states and represented 585 organizations with a "combined and unduplicated" membership of 1,200,000. The heterogeneous character of the Congress was indicated by the variety of organizations represented. The following table shows the major groups and the number of organizations:[49]

| | |
|---|---:|
| Churches and Religious Organizations | 81 |
| Fraternal Societies | 71 |
| Trade Unions | 83 |
| Farm Organizations | 2 |
| Youth Organizations | 26 |
| Civic Groups and Societies | 226 |
| Political Groups and Parties | 46 |
| Women's Organizations | 23 |
| Educational Organizations | 14 |
| Professional Groups | 6 |
| Business Organizations | 2 |
| Newspaper Groups | 5 |
| TOTAL ORGANIZATIONS REPRESENTED | 585 |

A great majority of the delegates came from the northern urban-industrial centers. From Chicago alone came forty-three per cent of the delegates. The states of Illinois, Indiana, New York, Michigan, Ohio, Wisconsin and Pennsylvania were represented by 743 of the 817 delegates. Only fifty-five came from the South.[50] As Cayton and Mitchell pointed out: "The Congress, then, represented the northern urban Negro population rather than the entire country and attempted to express the interests of the urban industrial Negro worker."[51] While the civic, educational, and religious groups held a majority of the delegates, they had no common and well-articulated views, as did the economic and political organizations. Consequently it was into the hands of the latter that control of the Congress quickly passed.

Out of the deliberations of the Congress came a series of proposals for unified Negro action on a wide range of problems. They can be summarized as follows:

1. To organize and struggle against war and fascism.
2. To build a powerful and more inclusive civil rights organization among Negroes.
3. To develop movements for improving the conditions of sharecroppers and tenant farmers.
4. To intensify attempts to draw Negro workers into the trade unions.
5. To build a mass consumers' organization among Negroes.
6. To develop an independent working-class political party.[52]

The specific resolutions adopted by the Congress were varied and in some instances contradictory. It is interesting to note that General Resolution 1 indorsed the suggestion of John P. Davis, the pro-Communist National Secretary, that "The National Negro Congress goes on record that it is not and will never be dominated by any political faction or organization." [53] Other resolutions committed the National Negro Congress to the support of movements ranging all the way from the organization of sharecroppers to the aid of Negro businessmen.* The resolutions on foreign policy adhered closely to the proposals advanced by the Communist Party in 1936.

James W. Ford delivered one of the principal speeches at the first meeting. He hailed the organization as the fulfillment of Frederick Douglass' dream of a unified Negro people, and declared that it was in the best tradition of the militant Negro past. Ford's principal remarks concerned the "Negro People and

---

* These resolutions are too numerous and lengthy to be listed in detail here. The reader is referred to *Official Proceedings of the National Negro Congress, 1936,* pp. 19-36. See also: Cayton and Mitchell, *op. cit.,* pp. 418-420; and James W. Ford, *The Negro and the Democratic Front,* pp. 73-76. Perhaps the most incisive evaluation of the first meeting of the Congress and the whole movement over a four-year period is contained in Ralph Bunche's, *Programs, Ideologies, Tactics and Achievements of Negro Betterment and Interracial Organizations.* Only a limited amount of Bunche's excellent material on radical Negro movements made its way into the published Myrdal study, *An American Dilemma.* One of the glaring shortcomings of Myrdal's work was the omission of any sustained examination of the Negro and radical movements.

a Farmer-Labor Party." He listed nine "fundamental and basic" points for the program of such a party. It should fight for the civil rights of Negroes, higher wages and shorter hours, the right of labor to organize and bargain collectively, government guarantee of the right to work, reduced taxes among lower income groups, relief to impoverished farmers, full support of youth as advocated by the American Youth Congress, and peace through collective security.[54] The Congress later adopted a resolution favoring the formation of a Farmer-Labor Party.

The resolutions were similar in a number of respects to those adopted by the League of Struggle for Negro Rights, which the Communist Party had organized as a successor to the American Negro Labor Congress back in 1930. The 1936 program, however, was more specific, being focused on more immediate problems and not permeated with revolutionary trimmings. No mention was made at the Congress of the right of self-determination for Negroes in the Black Belt. No effort was made to define American Negroes as an "oppressed colonial people." Party delegates and their sympathizers were well aware that advocacy of this now shelved "principle" would further stigmatize the Congress as "Red" and alienate many of the delegates who were already extremely skeptical of the Party's role in the Congress. These delegates had come to do something about unemployment, housing, education and civil rights, and to do it now.

Although the Party did not capture the Congress at its first meeting, the latter's acceptance of much of the current Party program and the naming of Davis as Executive Secretary (which assured Party influence in one of the key positions) was enough to evoke the widest acclaim by Communists. Ford declared:

The National Negro Congress recorded progress made by Communists and the many delegates who supported our program, in the increasing work we are carrying on in the various organizations of the Negro people. Our modest successes are, however, just beginnings. We must now undertake to profit from our experiences, mistakes, shortcomings and successes, by showing that changes are necessary in our methods of work to build the National Negro Congress.

The Congress has shown how, by overcoming sectarian methods of work we can help to develop still further the movement for Negro liberation already started by the American Negro Labor Congress, the League of Struggle for Negro Rights and the International Labor Defense.[55]

Browder sounded even more enthusiastic than Ford, declaring:

The National Negro Congress which met in Chicago in February and established a permanent organization, found the correct road to a broad unity of the varied progressive forces among the Negro people and their friends. It is a broad people's movement, which at the same time has a firm working class core of Negro trade unions and working class leaders. Communists and all progressives will continue to give it their energetic and steadfast support.[56]

Richard Wright, the Negro novelist, who later broke with the Party, employed his keen reportorial talents in describing the first meeting of the Congress and Ford's role in it.[57]

A number of Negro church leaders had indorsed the Congress and were present at the organizational meeting as delegates. Immediately afterward, however, they became markedly critical of the new agency and its "radical" program. These churchmen felt that the political and economic groups who controlled the Congress had assigned the religious bodies a completely secondary role. They were likewise quite critical of the prominent role played by the Communists in the Congress's proceedings, noting that Ford, Davis, Edward Strong (the Vice-President of the American Youth Congress) and others—openly Communist or closely associated with the Party—were among the more conspicuous participants. The Congress was likewise widely criticized in a number of Negro papers, particularly in the *Chicago Defender*.[58]

At the Chicago meeting the Presiding Committee drafted a detailed organizational plan for the permanent agency. This plan provided for three national officers—chairman, secretary, and treasurer. Fifteen permanent committees whose members were to be selected at large were established. The country was divided into fifteen regions, each of which was to be represented on the National Executive Committee by the president and vice-president of the regional subdivision. Local sponsoring committees were now to become permanent local councils. At the national level, Ford was elected Chairman of the Committee on International Relations. Edward Strong became Chairman of the Youth Committee. Ben Davis, Jr., B. D. Amis, A. W. Berry, Henry Johnson, Adam Clayton Powell, and Max Yergan—some of whom were Party members with the remainder being consistent fellow travelers—were elected to important committee or council posts.[59]

In spite of grandiose plans and hard work by the Communists, the National Negro Congress could point to only very modest accomplishments for its first year of operation. Its Chicago council had been helpful to the CIO in the organization of steel and meat packing. Local councils established in New York, Philadelphia and Pittsburgh were quite active on community as well as larger issues. Although a number of the councils, established immediately after the first meeting in February, 1936, were unable to function, they did keep the Congress idea alive and served as the hard core around which more effective agencies were later built. The headquarters organization in Washington conducted an intensive legislative campaign and tried to muster grass roots pressure on various bills. The Communists in the NNC were tireless workers and responsible for most of the limited success achieved during the first year. Much of the financial support came from the Party-controlled unions in the CIO.

The NNC, however, was laboring under the handicap of the Communist stigma, and it had a host of other problems as well. It lacked funds and had no way of building up the kind of reserves which community organization programs required. Although the delegates at the first meeting had indorsed the program, this did not spell support by the organizations which they represented. Unification of diverse Negro groups in the local councils was a particularly difficult task. The NNC program was still too broad and tended to overlook the basic differences— class, economic, political and religious—within the Negro community itself.

The second meeting of the Congress was held at Philadelphia in May, 1937. Its objectives had now been somewhat narrowed and included demands for decent jobs for Negroes, their right to join unions, adequate relief and security for the needy, abolition of lynching, and complete equality.[60] The 1937 meeting was attended by 1,218 delegates, 400 more than the previous year. While these persons came from all sections of the country, and represented varied types of organizations, the great majority consisted of Negroes from the North delegated by trade union and political agencies. Even more than at the first meeting, they dominated the proceedings.

While only a few individuals of national prominence participated in the first meeting, a host of very important persons appeared on the program at the 1937 sessions. Walter White, Executive Secretary of the NAACP; Norman Thomas, 1936 presidential candidate of the Socialist Party; Philip Murray, Chairman of the Steel Workers Organizing Committee; Thomas J. Kennedy, Secretary of the United Mine Workers; Frank Crosswaith, Secretary of the Harlem Labor Committee; and a number of other notables addressed the delegates. The presence of these persons gave the appearance that the NNC was moving toward its aim of uniting wide groups of Negroes with the labor movement behind a program of race and working-class goals. The Communists, one of the most influential but by no means the most conspicuous groups at the meeting, were delighted with the outcome and were more effusive in their praise than in 1936.

The Congress adopted some 174 resolutions covering a wide range of Negro and labor problems. The focus was sharper and the specific aims more precisely conceived. Emphasis was placed on the need for further organization, and a closer coordination of the work of the local councils.

The NNC was in a position to carry on its work more effectively after the 1937 meeting. It had the closer cooperation of some of the NAACP branches. It became more labor-oriented and received greater backing from the CIO, particularly from those affiliates in which the Party held a commanding position. A number of Negro intellectuals, impatient with the slow moving NAACP and aware of the need for concerted race action, were drawn into the NNC. Ralph Bunche, for example, refused to be frightened by the charge of "radicalism," and though aware of the dangers inherent in any "cooperative" undertaking with

Communists, insisted that moderate Negro groups should support the Congress and try to guide it.

The Congress held no national meetings during 1938 and 1939. The third meeting was held at Washington, D. C., in April of 1940. By this time the Party was in complete control; it dominated the meeting from the outset and alienated most of the non-Party delegates by forcing through a series of anti-Roosevelt and "anti-war" resolutions.* (The Russo-German pact had been signed in August, 1939.)

The Communist Party from 1936 to August, 1939, regarded the Congress as an ideal instrument for its "Unity" program among the Negro people. Largely through the help of the Party, the Congress had overcome many of its initial difficulties. The number of councils was greatly increased, and there emerged a more experienced and sophisticated leadership in the local and regional organizations. Myrdal noted that during 1938 and 1939, when he traveled throughout the United States, "the local councils of the National Negro Congress were the most important Negro organizations in some Western cities." [61] The moderate Negro protest and betterment agencies were not at the time capable of undertaking large-scale political organization among Negroes. The Congress was in a position partially to fill this gap, and the moderates in some instances were willing to support it for this reason.

The success of the Congress was also a result of its concentrating on a series of immediate issues, primarily economic, which made sense to many Negroes. These issues fitted into the Communist program during the period. The Party was particularly anxious that the Congress rally the Negro people behind the New Deal. Many of the affiliated organizations had supported these programs prior to the united front period and were therefore not required to do a *volte-face* in order to accept the position of the NNC. When the Congress, under Party control, opposed Roosevelt and his foreign policies after 1939, its membership shriveled to a handful of Party hacks and their entourage.

* The third meeting of the Congress and the role of the Communists in it is treated in more detail in the following chapter. See pp. 191-199.

At its 1936 meeting the National Negro Congress established a special Youth Continuation Committee and a National Youth Bureau with Headquarters in Washington, D. C. The specific purpose of the Bureau was to:

... develop concrete plans regarding finance, publicity, literature, office and executive arrangements, etc., to carry out the resolutions adopted by the Youth Section of the National Negro Congress and to extend youth divisions of the Congress, etc.[62]

Edward Strong, Vice-President of the American Youth Congress, was named Chairman of the Youth Continuation Committee, which was to exercise general supervision of the Bureau. Angelo Herndon, the Party organizer of the unemployed in Atlanta, Georgia, whose conviction under an outmoded "sedition" statute was on appeal, was named a member of the Bureau. The Party was thus well represented in the youth section, therefore, and in a position to influence its organizational policies.

One of the first activities of the Bureau was to assist in the formation of the Southern Negro Youth Congress, which was convened in Richmond, Virginia, in February of 1937. The Party probably would have preferred an extension of the American Youth Congress to develop its united front program among southern youth, Negro and white, but recognized that young Negroes confronted special problems in the region. It was aware of the limited work that could be done through interracial youth organizations. Consequently, it gave its full support to the Southern Negro Youth Congress.

John P. Davis, Ford, Strong, and James Jackson (who later became a paid Party functionary) were prominent participants at the first meeting. Angelo Herndon, Henry Winston (currently Director of Organization for the Party) and a number of other Party officials were there. The resolutions on civil rights, education, employment, relief, housing, trade unions, and foreign policy were similar to those adopted by the NNC a year previously and closely paralleled points in the American Youth Congress program.

Although Communists played important roles in the first meeting of the SNYC, the charge of "red" and "radical" was not generally raised. The meeting was indorsed by a number of educators and churchmen. Students and representatives of churches made up a majority of the delegates. A number of sharecroppers, industrial workers, and unemployed were present, but their participation in the conference was limited.

Edward Strong was elected Chairman, and a number of important committee posts went to Communists or those who had consistently adhered to the Party line. The Party, however, was not unopposed, and there was heated debate on a number of the resolutions, as well as on the report of the Nominating Committee. Student groups were the most articulate, and apparently more radically inclined than the church and other representatives. The former dominated the proceedings, and their ideas prevailed in the resolutions.

Following the pattern of the National Negro Congress, the SNYC undertook to organize a series of local youth councils. Their purpose was to conduct youth forums and work for crime reduction, health projects, vocational guidance, and other issues of immediate interest to young Negroes. A headquarters organization was established in Richmond, Virginia, and later moved to Birmingham, Alabama. Like the NNC, the SNYC faced an immediate financial problem; but it was able to employ a small paid staff and to distribute a considerable amount of literature among sympathetic white and Negro organizations.

The number of councils established by the SNYC was never large. The local programs which actually developed did not take any "radical" line. Some of the councils were instrumental in the organization of Negro workers by the new CIO unions. Others confined their activities to health, educational and employment problems. Although a wide variety of groups had been represented at the first meeting and though the SNYC program had been indorsed by their delegates, the proposed program never really took hold at the local level. While the SNYC was acutely aware of the difficulties facing young Negro workers and sharecroppers, it was never able to reach them in any large numbers on an organizational basis. It was primarily an agency of Negro student, church, and political groups centered in a few of the larger urban communities in the South.

The Communist Party, however, was enthusiastic about its possibilities. Ford, for example, said:

> The conference [first meeting of the SNYC] was an historic event in the life of the Negro people, and of the whole South. The young delegates came from all sections of the South, representing students, steel workers from Birmingham, sharecroppers—a cross-section of the Negro people. . . .
>
> The conference was one of hope and determination. The evils against which these young people came to fight did not deter them, but spurred them on to solve their problems and build a future of happiness for the Negro people.[63]

The *New Masses* in reporting on the third meeting of the SNYC declared: "The Southern Negro Youth Congress is symptomatic of the awakening of the Negro people. The Negro people are beginning to close ranks and learning to join hands with progressive whites of common democratic aims." [64]

The third meeting of the SNYC in 1939 occurred prior to the signing of the Hitler-Stalin agreement. Consequently, the new "line" followed by the Party after the pact was not reflected in the resolutions and program adopted. Subsequent meetings and programs, however, indicated clearly the extent to which the SNYC had been "captured" by the Communists. Ralph Bunche, observing the SNYC in 1942, declared:

> The Southern Negro Youth Congress is a flame that flickers only feebly in a few southern cities today. It started with promise but, lacking competent leadership, it failed to catch the imagination of the young Negroes of the South. Its program has been diffuse and recently, at least, seems to take its cue in the major essentials from the "line" laid down by the American Communist Party.[65]

Subsequent activities of the Congress which the writer observed at first hand bear out Bunche's earlier conclusions.

The National Negro Congress and the Southern Negro Youth Congress, then, were the two principal race organizations through which the Party attempted to carry out its Negro program during the united front period. The International Labor Defense, The American Youth Congress, and the League for Peace and Democracy, of course, worked with Negroes on the problems of civil rights, foreign policy, etc., but their primary concerns were not racially determined.

While the Party attempted to use the NNC and the SNYC councils in the South for the furtherance of its Negro program, it found in the Southern Conference for Human Welfare an organization offering wider possibilities not only for work among Negroes, but for the development of the united front line in all its major aspects.

The SCHW was organized in Birmingham, Alabama, in November, 1938. The Party, in line with its program of unifying "all the progressive forces in the South," participated in the preliminary efforts to establish the new agency. In addition, it sent a number of delegates to the Birmingham meeting and was further represented through some of the trade union and youth organizations which it controlled. The Party, however, did not play the key role in the organization or procedures of the first SCHW meeting. The initative came primarily from the Southern Policy Committee, which included white liberals and labor leaders, educators and churchmen, with a number of Negroes participating in a somewhat informal capacity.

The immediate inspiration of this group was the report of the National Emergency Council on the *Economic Conditions of the South*.[66] The *Report*, prepared by a group of widely recognized southern leaders,* was a classic summary of a host of regional problems—economic, educational, social, health and welfare. It concluded that the South as a region presented the nation's major economic problem; the phrase, "number one economic problem of the nation," was later popularized by President Roosevelt in his advocacy of special government aid to the region. The report was given wide publicity in the southern press. Some saw in it the basis for unifying the liberal and labor forces of the South around

* To mention only a few of the framers of the *Report*: B. F. Ashe, President of the University of Miami; Carl Bailey, Governor of Arkansas; Barry Bingham, publisher of the *Louisville Courier Journal*; Frank Graham, President of the University of North Carolina; The Hon. Blanton Fortson, Judge of the Superior Court, Athens, Georgia; Lucy Randolph Mason, Public Relations Director, CIO; General John C. Persons, President, First National Bank, Birmingham, Alabama; Paul Poynter, publisher *St. Petersburg Times*, and Alexander Speer, former president, Virginia Public Service Company.

a program of economic and political action that would result, in the words of one of the participants, "in a gradual, but significant transformation of the whole region."

The Communists, of course, gave the SCHW their official blessing and hailed its establishment as "brilliant confirmation of the line of the democratic front advanced by Comrade Browder at the Tenth Convention [May, 1938]." [67] There was a tendency at that time, one which has increased in recent years, to credit formation and initial control of the SCHW to the Party itself. To suggest that this was the case, however, is to misunderstand the nature and composition of the 1938 Conference, and greatly to overestimate Party influence in the South. The Party later captured the organization, but its initial influence was limited.*

The Party was represented by only five out of 1,250 persons officially attending. Its strength was augmented somewhat by delegations from trade unions and other organizations which the Party controlled. It would seem safe to assume that not more than ten per cent of the delegates were Party spokesmen. Nevertheless, a number of southern newspapers, conservative politicians and certain organized groups—some of whom had indorsed the *Report*, hurled the charge of "red" and "radical" as the delegates assembled for the first meeting. The Democratic Women's Clubs of Jefferson County and Alabama, whose program at the time was predicated largely on a "white supremacy" policy, charged that the Conference was of "questionable origin and purpose." Still other groups thought that it was a "racial equality" meeting, and pointed to plans for the unsegregated seating of Negroes as confirmation of their worst fears. Critics of the Roosevelt administration and the New Deal program in the South charged that the SCHW was an effort emanating from Washington to strengthen the President's political influence in the region.

* The upsurge of joint action among southern liberals and labor organizations during the 1930's could be said to have had its logical culmination in the SCHW. The program of the Communists in the South at that time was in line with these developments. This important—all-important point—was completely ignored in the *Report on the Southern Conference for Human Welfare* prepared by the Committee on Un-American Activities of the United States House of Representatives in 1947. Other critics of the SCHW who based their objections ostensibly on grounds of Communist domination likewise tended to misconstrue, probably intentionally, the nature and character of the organization during its formative years.

Even had there been no Communist participation in the meeting, the above charges would have been hurled by those who stood to lose much if southern liberals, trade unionists and Negroes could develop organizational unity around a minimal program of economic and political action. It was obvious that the SCHW, taking its cue from the *Report*, would oppose lynching, the poll tax, the farm tenancy system, and other underpinnings of the southern political edifice. It was also obvious that the Conference would favor a minimum wage, organization of labor, federal aid to small farmers and sharecroppers and a host of other items, many of which were included in the New Deal program. There was indeed cause for the southern conservatives to holler. They did.

Attendance at the Birmingham meeting far exceeded the expectations of the most optimistic planners. Though a maximum of four hundred delegates had been anticipated, official attendance, not to mention the large number of visitors, was three times this figure. Negro participants alone numbered between 250 and 300, coming from trade unions, churches, fraternal, professional and educational groups. Conservative groups in and around Birmingham, impressed by the huge turnout, sought to discredit the meeting as a "race equality" assembly and insisted that local ordinances against unsegregated seating of Negroes be enforced. It was thought that this would split the Conference, alienating the Negroes and dividing the whites into factions condoning or opposing enforcement of the Jim Crow laws. This maneuver failed. Segregated seating was followed after the first day, but Negroes stayed throughout the meeting and the whites were not split.[68]

An examination of the list of delegates and the composition of the various committees and panels at the 1938 meeting indicates further the limited role played by the Party. The resolutions committee, for example, was composed of such prominent non-Communists as: William Mitch, United Mine Workers; George Googe, Southern Director, American Federation of Labor; Lucy Randolph Mason, CIO Public Relations Director in the South; Donald Comer, President of one of the largest textile firms in the South; Barry Bingham, publisher of the *Louisville Courier-*

*Journal*; Arthur Raper, outstanding southern sociologist; Edwin A. Elliott, Regional Director of the National Labor Relations Board; and F. D. Patterson, President of famed Tuskeegee Institute.

The principal speakers at the meeting enhanced the SCHW's prestige. Eleanor Roosevelt, United States Supreme Court Justice Hugo Black, Frank Graham, President of the University of North Carolina, Aubrey Williams, Works Progress Administration, Congressman Luther Patrick, and a number of other liberal spokesmen of national stature appeared on the platform. Important churchmen, educators, publishers and government officials played prominent roles at the Birmingham meeting. (The Dies Committee was also represented, its investigators attending all the sessions, taking rapid notes and generally keeping tab on the proceedings).

While Communist delegates did not play a conspicuous role, the Party's views were expressed through a number of persons having no official identity with the organization. John P. Davis, Executive Secretary of the National Negro Congress, was a member of the panel on civil rights. He was later elected a vice-president of the permanent organization. Edward E. Strong, Chairman of the Southern Negro Youth Congress, was a member of the panel on youth problems. A number of delegates from trade unions in the Birmingham area also "carried the ball" for Rob F. Hall, Secretary of the Communist Party of Alabama, who directed them from a behind-the-scenes position.

However, the proceedings of the Conference and the resolutions adopted would have been pretty much the same had the Communist Party not been represented. The Communists at the time were identified with the prevailing liberal sentiment in the South; it joined in rather than loosened the landslide of reformism which culminated in the establishment of the SCHW. The resolutions adequately confirm this point.[69] Those on suffrage, civil rights, poll tax, lynching, youth, farm tenancy, education, trade unions, minimum wages, etc. did not vary substantially from what most liberal and trade union spokesmen in the region had long advocated. There was disagreement in some cases on methods, particularly where race relations were concerned. Generally, however, most of the delegates saw eye-to-eye on the minimal program. If the Communists, they argued, wanted to indorse such measures, then that was their privilege.*

The Party applauded the SCHW in glowing terms, declaring that "the Southern people, harassed by deep-seated problems, the solutions for which are long overdue, are determined to secure for themselves and their families more of the fruits of the New Deal, namely, broader democracy and a genuine improvement in their social and economic conditions." The Party's secretary in Alabama, however, noted that there were certain "shortcomings." He complained that the SCHW leadership "did not know on which forces to rely, even for the tasks such as the organization of a panel, the conduct of committees, the running of large sessions." He left no doubt about who constituted "reliable forces." He complained further that the American Federation of Labor was not widely enough represented and that the organizations of the southern middle class had not been sufficiently involved in the meeting. While he deplored the disruptive presence of "Trotskyites," he was deeply concerned that the American Farm Bureau Federation had failed to send official representatives! [70] The Party's appraisal of the SCHW participants—the southern liberals, churchmen, labor leaders, intellectuals, educators—was indeed a far cry from that of a few years before; 1934, for example. The question of who and what changed in the interim period is not difficult to answer.

The delegates at the initial meeting of the SCHW drew plans for the establishment of a permanent organization to "unite the Southern people, to promote the general welfare, to improve economic, social and cultural standards of the Southern people, and to advance Southern democratic institutions and ideals." An

* For a penetrating analysis of the role of the southern liberal during the period of the 1930's see: Myrdal, *op. cit.*, Ch. 21. Concerning the SCHW itself Myrdal noted: "The nearest thing to an organized political front was the Southern Conference for Human Welfare. . . . The author, who was present at the first occasion, had a feeling that the real importance of this meeting was that here for the first time in the history of the region, since the era of the American Revolution, the lonely Southern liberals met in great numbers—actually more than twelve hundred—coming from all states and joined by their colleagues in Washington; and that they, in this new and unique adventure, experienced a foretaste of the freedom and power which large-scale political organization and concerted action give." (p. 469)

advisory and executive body composed of seven representatives from each of the southern states, headed by Frank Graham, was set up. Later a headquarters organization and a permanent staff, made possible by contributions from the organizations represented at the first meeting and additional affiliates, were established.

To Negroes in the South the SCHW represented a hopeful development. While some colored leaders castigated the Conference for not taking a more forthright stand on Negro rights, they appreciated the fact that the organization held great promise for joint action among members of both races on a host of problems that had a special significance for southern blacks. Negro interest was indicated not only in the surprisingly large number of colored delegates, but by their very active participation in some of the panels and committees. Negroes were also given positions of some responsibility in the permanent organization. John P. Davis and Mary McLeod Bethune were among those named as members of the council.

Charles S. Johnson, Professor of Sociology at Fisk University, expressed the reaction—and hopes—of many southern Negroes when he declared:

If liberalism means anything at all it implies a willingness to subordinate personal prejudices and relax traditional sanctions where necessary in the interest of constructive social change. In this respect the Birmingham conference was as significant as it was historic. It drew together the largest group of liberals the South has witnessed. . . . It was the first bold emergence of the liberal South as a self-conscious group, inspired to action by the devastating government report on the region's economic and social plight. . . .

The strategy of the Conference was sound. It aimed at being neither a labor meeting, nor a social work body, nor a race relations assembly. It sought to present the total regional configuration, with special elements and problems in a functional setting. The labor relations section, for example, attacked the encrusted opposition of the region to State wage and hour legislation. While encouraging southern industrial development, it sought by proposals to reduce regional and racial wage differentials. Labor went on record as desiring greater unity in its programs in the area. It seemed unmistakably to be the feeling of the white labor delegates that the forward march of labor could not be maintained without according to the Negro worker full justice and fraternity. And it was not necessary in these discussions for a Negro to arise and ask for or demand such fraternity.[71]

Continuing, he suggested to Negroes the importance of changed attitudes and strategies in attempting to function within the framework of this broad, regionally-oriented coalition:

> If the Negroes are to be most effective in the new strategy, it will be necessary for more of them to be able to speak with knowledge and authority on issues other than the race problem. For they can never be presumed to speak wisely, other than as special wards seeking group protection, unless they are known to be acquainted with the total structure of southern life and the confusing interrelationship of all its problems.[72]

But these high hopes were not to be realized through the SCHW. Off to a good beginning, and with substantial organizational accomplishments to its credit during the first year, the Conference subsequently lost much of its earlier support; torn by internal rivalries, it ultimately split away from the liberal and trade union forces, an accomplishment for which the Communist Party can claim full credit. With the outbreak of World War II the Administration became increasingly occupied with foreign affairs to the neglect of its domestic program, especially in the South. The southern labor movement began focusing more and more on immediate wage and hour problems rather than on long-range regional goals. The southern liberals, momentarily encouraged by the great promise growing out of the Birmingham meeting, too often resumed their lonely wanderings. These were contributing causes to the decline of the SCHW.

The real splits in the organization, however, did not develop until after the Stalin-Hitler pact of 1939 and the *volte-face* of the American Communists. Between the first meeting of the SCHW and the outbreak of the war, the Party greatly strengthened its following in the Conference and attempted to use it to place the southern liberal movement, which had been united at the Birmingham meeting, behind the "anti-imperialist war" program. We shall consider this latter development in more detail in the following chapter.

While the Party was instrumental in building both Negro and interracial organizations in carrying out its united front program among black Americans, it did not neglect an important corollary activity, the reinterpretation of Negro history. Communists had always sought to depict the development of the American Negro in terms of a revolutionary tradition. Until the united front period, their efforts had been rather general and sporadic. However, beginning about 1935 a much more systematic and comprehensive approach was employed. In early 1936 James S. Allen published the *Negro Question in the United States,* attempting to use historical materials, current census data, and Stalin's definition of a nation to rationalize a Negro national liberation movement and self-determination in the Black Belt.[73] Although the book was widely read by the Communist faithful, the program of self-determination received little attention in the Party popular press. This resulted from the fact that, in line with the united front strategy, the Communists had dropped this goal as one of its immediate demands. Ford reviewed the book in the *New Masses* and explained that:

We hold no brief against a constant and persistent struggle against white chauvinism in the labor movement and elsewhere, but this in itself will not accomplish the desired end. Something more is needed: a clear and common understanding that the problems of the Negro extend beyond the limits of the "labor problem," that his most immediate needs are those of a people oppressed by another and more powerful nation.[74]

As an interesting digression at this point, it is worth noting that after the reconstitution of the Party in 1945, the basic idea of Allen's book became the core of a "new" self-determination doctrine.

Ford himself purported to be something of a historian, and in a series of pamphlets and articles emphasized the radical heritage of American Negroes.* International Publishers, which handled most of the Party publications, issued a series of biographies of Negroes and whites who had been prominent in the

* A number of his articles appear in condensed form in *The Negro and the Democratic Front* (New York: International Publishers, 1938).

anti-slavery movement. Included in the series were life stories of Abraham Lincoln, Frederick Douglass, Harriet Tubman, Thaddeus Stevens and Wendell Phillips.

But it was from the pen of Herbert Aptheker that the most voluminous and scholarly studies of the Negro came.[75] Aptheker is a tireless researcher, an excellent organizer of material, and an accomplished writer. However much one may differ with his appraisal of the Negro past in America, he cannot help being impressed with the technical quality of Aptheker's work.

While the reinterpretation of Negro history had been carried out by earlier historians under the influence of the scholarly Carter G. Woodson, who founded the *Journal of Negro History* and the Association for the Study of Negro Life, it remained for the Communists to produce and circulate widely the more popular versions and turn them to account in their propaganda work. A re-examination of the Negro past, outside the narrow bounds of traditional academic scholarship, was, and still is, needed. The Communist historians during the united front period, despite their limitations in other respects, made a significant contribution by further placing in question a number of the stereotyped accounts of the Negro's historical role. They challenged the premises on which such versions rested; they questioned the motives of previous writers; they made focal material previously relegated to the parenthetical; they gave to the Negro past a currency and relevance formerly lacking.

The Party historians sought to give to the Negro in America a radical past as a preface to a radical present. Thus Aptheker opened one of his books with the statement:

The desire for freedom is the central theme, the motivating force, in the history of the American Negro people. This has always determined their actions, policies and efforts, and has, indeed, permeated their religions, inspired their real and legendary heroes, and filled their incomparably beautiful hymns and spirituals.[76]

And he concluded a summary of the Negro in the Revolutionary War with:

The Negro people have always struggled and are now valiantly struggling for their liberation, and it behooves all Americans to come to their support, not only in order to have justice done for some fifteen million American citizens, but also in order to make secure and to advance their own economic and political well-being.[77]

Constantly emphasized by this group of writers were the instances of concerted action by Negroes and poorer whites against the dominant economic class. To quote Aptheker again as an example:

Negroes did not, of course, restrict themselves to independent work [in the abolition movement] but struggled side by side with white people in the common effort. Thus, for example, the production and sustenance of the chief organ of the Abolitionist movement, *The Liberator*, published in Boston from 1831 to 1865 by William Lloyd Garrison, were made possible by the encouragement and aid of Negroes.[78]

And he stated in still another book:

... The poor whites fled from its [the Confederacy's] armies and waged war upon it. The slaves conspired or rebelled, or broke its tools, or refused to do its work, or fled its fields and mines and factories. Many fought shoulder to shoulder with the Southern poor whites against a common enemy, and a multitude joined the army from the North and brought it information and guidance and labor and desperate courage.[79]

Woodson and DuBois were among the first to challenge the traditional interpretation of the role of Negroes in the Reconstruction period. The Communist historians drew heavily on these investigations and supplemented them with new data and concepts. They vigorously attacked the "bourgeois historians" for the falsification of the militant Negro political programs during the immediate post-Civil War period. Ford, for example, declared:

The reactionaries try to cover up the truth of this period and to conceal the revolutionary actions of the masses, particularly the Southern white masses. The book, *Birth of a Nation*, tries to depict the Reconstruction period as one of unrestrained violence, bloody terror, carnage and rapine, in which the naive but "semi-savage" Negro, freed from benevolent slavery, roamed the land robbing, stealing and venting lust upon unprotected white womanhood; while in the background, directing this horror, stalked the "carpet-bagger" adventurer.

A whole literature has been built up on such revolutionary distortions and misrepresentations of the Reconstruction period. The "carpet-bagger" bogeyman has been used to frighten little children and the whole population of Southern whites. The influence of the reactionary myth of "Carpet-Bagger Reconstruction" is not only confined to the South; this fallacy has been built up in the North also. It is one of the crimes of bourgeois historical scholarship that it has buried the profoundly significant revolutionary struggles of the Negro and white masses in the South during the Reconstruction period.[80]

Not only did the Party historians attack the southern apologists such as Thomas Dixon, Jr. but scholars like Charles A. Beard were denounced for conceding "the myth of the reconstruction."

Aptheker's works usually opened with a criticism of the standard history-book treatment of the slavery period and the reconstruction; indeed, his writing as a whole can be regarded as a sustained effort to "correct" the distortions perpetrated by the "bourgeois" historical school.

For the present discussion it is important to note that the Communist interpretation of Negro history, as indicated in the sources cited and in other works, had a rather clear-cut set of purposes. There is nothing unique in this, since presumably all historians are motivated by the desire to do something more than "write history as it actually happened." However, it is important that the reader know something of the motives which figure in the selection of data and its interpretation.

In the case of the Stalinist writers certain motives stand out clearly. In the first place, there was a recognized need to build up the Negro's belief in his own militant tradition. If he could see his forefathers as radicals and rebels, then he could visualize himself following in their footsteps. Second, there was a need to portray an identity of interests and joint action between Negroes and poor whites against a common oppressor in the past. Thus it would be shown that the desired solidarity of Negroes and whites in present working-class struggles had significant antecedents in the long and violent history of American workers. Third, it was important to depict northern industrialists and southern plantation aristocrats as the common enemies of Negro and white toilers, thus externalizing the evil against which the workers must struggle. Finally, there was a need to show that the Communist Party (and whatever program it happened to be following at the time) was in the main stream of the revolutionary tradition and therefore the logical instrument for securing the liberation of both Negro and white workers from their common oppressor.*

The Communists wrote American history, and especially Negro American history, with a purpose. The Party, like its mother organization in the U.S.S.R., demanded that the past explain and justify the present, and that it point to the future—a future in which great things were seen for the Party. If the role of great Negro figures was distorted; if small men were clothed in the garments of the mighty; if undifferentiated protest was imbued with heavy ideological overtones; if the accomplishments of moderate leaders were reduced to insignificance; if facts and scholarship suffered in the process, this could not evoke major concern. The Party historian was a Party man first and a historian second.†

Along with the reformulation of its theoretical line on the Negro question, its building of united front organizations among Negro groups, and its increased propaganda work around race issues, the Party continued to build up its own organization among Negroes and to develop a black leadership. The Party's membership increased substantially during the united front period, largely as a result of its discarding revolutionary goals and focusing on immediate domestic issues while aligning itself with

* For further interpretations of American history by Communist writers see the following books or pamphlets issued by International Publishers: Francis Franklin, *The Rise of the American Nation*; Herbert M. Morais, *The Struggle for American Freedom*; Jack Hardy, *The First American Revolution*; Charlotte Todes, *William Sylvis and the National Labor Union*; Herbert Aptheker, *Essays in the History of the American Negro*; and Harry Haywood, *Negro Liberation*.

† Aptheker is currently a good case in point. Silent for the most part on Myrdal's *An American Dilemma* from the time of its publication in 1944 until the shift in the Party program produced by the Duclos letter, Aptheker did not really take up the cudgels against the Swedish sociologist until 1946. Then he did a little book, *The Negro People in America*, which for its distortion reaches some kind of new low, even for a Party historian. Aptheker is now searching historical documents for the word "nationalism" which he is using to "prove" that the idea of a Black Belt black republic has deep roots in American Negro history.

a collective security foreign policy. By 1934 Party membership was estimated at 25,000, with an additional 5,000 youngsters in the Young Communist League. In 1936 the Party claimed a total membership of 40,000, with 10,000 in the YCL. According to official reports, membership in the Party almost doubled during the two-year period, from 1936 to 1938, reaching a total of 75,000. YCL membership also doubled to 20,000. If these figures are correct the basic Party organizations could show almost 100,000 members during the last full year of the united front program.[81]

The percentage of Negroes in these organizations was not revealed. However, it would appear on the basis of previous patterns as well as current estimates that probably not more than ten or fifteen per cent of Communist Party and Young Communist League membership was colored during any of the united front years. This would be a ratio approximating that of the Negro to the total U.S. population.* While the failure of the Party to build up a large Negro membership during the period was not viewed with alarm, there being other organizations through which it would carry on its program, the inability to develop Negro leadership was a disquieting factor.

Writing in 1938 Browder observed:

Recruitment of Negroes into our Party, and their training for leadership, have made some advances in the past two years, but we can by no means be satisfied with what we have accomplished. Constant attention to this question is necessary, constant critical self-examination of our work. Let the outstanding contribution to our Party of Comrade James Ford be a constant reminder to every one of us of the great resources waiting for our Party among the Negro masses. We have been called

---

* It is difficult to accept official Party membership reports at their face value. The Party has never hesitated to exaggerate its claims. Further doubts are suggested by the high turnover rate. One does not know just what the quoted figures imply—whether they refer to paid-up active members at the time of the report or include all persons listed as Party members during the year or during the period since the previous report. The claimed membership of the Party's basic organizations, or the votes received by its candidates, are very inadequate criteria for measuring its influence among Negroes or any other group. Such figures are particularly misleading when applied to the united front period. The Party's aim was not to build up its own organization *per se* or poll the highest number of votes for its candidates.

"the Negro Party" by enemies in the South; we repeat again that we claim this title as a badge of honor. But let us deserve it by serious recruitment of Negro members.[82]

And again in late 1938 he declared:

There are some disquieting signs of a relaxation of vigilance within our Party on the Negro question during the last period. We must call for a full reawakening of all our sensitiveness.

In this field a special review must be made of recruiting among Negroes and our promotion and training of Negro leading personnel. On the question of Negro leaders, local, state and national, we must give equal attention to two phases of the question: first, promotion of Negro leaders without mechanically weighing their qualifications for posts of leadership, technically and educationally, as compared with the qualifications of white candidates; and second, having promoted Negroes to leading posts, to give every possible assistance to raising their technical and educational qualifications to the highest level, never to be satisfied until our Negro cadres have gained, *not merely formal but actual equality in every respect.*

There is to be seen in some places among us, a shrinking away from the second phase of this work of promotion which threatens damage also to the first phase. There is too often a tacit exemption of the Negro comrades from the essential process of critical and self-critical evaluations of their work, which is the foundation of all Party advance in every field, and a relegation of this task to small closed circles of the Negro comrades themselves, separate from the rest of the Party. Comrades, let us speak boldly and frankly about such a tendency and call it by its right name—an inverted white chauvinism. . . . It is damaging to all of us to slip into cowardly abandonment of responsible accounting and criticism, according to carefully adjusted standards, of the work of even a few Negro comrades, and damaging most of all to the Negroes themselves.[83]

The Party's failure to build Negro leadership is only partially explained in the foregoing statements by the General Secretary. While more Negroes were brought into the organization during the united front period than at any previous time, they usually lacked any exceptional abilities. The institutionalized roles for Party functionaries required that a certain number of posts be filled by persons having a black skin. If they possessed few qualifications besides this primary requisite, this could not deter their assignment.

Race prejudice within the Party itself, veiled somewhat in the above admissions by Browder, was without question an important deterrent to sensitive and capable Negroes. Another factor of significance was the inability of Negro Communist leaders to pursue any kind of independent or imaginative course in their work. This was true from Ford on down to the lowest colored functionary. Bound by doctrinal and structural rigidities, like their white associates, they could act only within a very limited framework.

The Party attempted to recruit a Negro leadership among the younger intellectuals. These young Negroes came primarily from the colleges and universities, with a few drawn from the churches and trade unions. They were attracted to the Party because a wider exposure to liberal and radical ideas made them less inclined than their fellows to accept the status quo of second class citizenship. Like young people generally, they were dissatisfied with the ideas and organizations of their elders—the NUL was too limited, the NAACP too slow-moving.

In a sense they had no place to go. Discrimination blocked off every avenue of advancement. The outmoded admonitions of Booker T. Washington evoked little more than a sneer or a laugh among this group. They considered themselves talented, but they wanted to reach out and down among the mass of Negroes, not limiting themselves to the top tenth as DuBois had suggested. The resourcefulness of the Party had been demonstrated to them as they watched its functionaries operate in the NNC, the SNYC and the American Youth Congress. The Party welcomed them to its ranks; it flattered them; it gave them something to do, a feeling of belonging, a sense that they were going places. It was primarily from among this group that the Party augmented its Negro leadership during the united front period. Henry Winston, Edward Strong and James Jackson—subsequently to hold important Party posts—were among these new recruits.

However, it would be erroneous to suggest that any large number of Negro intellectuals sought an outright identification with the Party during the unity years. While an impressive number of black intellectuals looked with approval upon certain aspects of the Communist program and even supported a number of the organizations which the Party strongly influenced or controlled, they did not go over completely to the Communist ranks, aware of the stigma that would result from such a commitment, aware, too, that Party discipline and doctrine would involve numerous restrictions on their ideas and action.

The Party also drew its Negro leadership from the new CIO unions. The Communists at the time either controlled or strongly influenced the policies of a number of these organizations having large Negro memberships. Promising Negro leaders were singled out and developed by the more experienced Communist organizers, built up among the white as well as Negro members, and given positions of responsibility. In the process these Negroes accepted Party backing, and in turn became obligated to it. Revels Cayton in the International Longshoremen's and Warehousemen's Union, Ferdinand Smith in the National Maritime Union, Sheldon Tapps in the United Automobile Workers Union and Henry Johnson in the Packinghouse Workers Organizing Committee—each owed much of his success to the support of the strong Party factions in each of these organizations. And there were others whose leadership roles were a direct consequence of Party support. While these Negro leaders were not always directly identified with the Communist Party itself, they nevertheless constituted during this period a group on whom the Party could rely under most circumstances. Because of their trade union backing, they were probably the most effective Negro leadership resource the Party had. However, the outstanding Negro leader in the CIO, Willard S. Townsend, was never identified with the Party.*

James W. Ford, of course, continued as the outstanding Negro

---

* One of the big gaps in our information on Negro leadership during the past fifteen years is in the trade union area. We know who the colored labor leaders were; we know little of the political and sociological factors involved in their rise to positions of prominence. To rise to a position of leadership the black trade unionist must usually come from a local that has a large number of Negroes. To move further up the ladder he must be in an international that also has a substantial number of Negroes. What else is involved would have to be determined by a more extensive inquiry.

in the Party itself. He wrote copiously for the *Daily Worker,* the *New Masses,* the *Communist* and other publications. He authored, or had ghosted for him, a large number of booklets and pamphlets dealing with the Negro in the united front program. He served on numerous special committees and directed the over-all Negro program, taking his cues from Browder. Ford was neither independent nor original, only a high-placed Party hack, always anxious to do as he was told. He shifted so completely to the united front line and followed Browder's lead so faithfully that in non-Communist circles (and possibly within the Party itself) he was characterized as the "Red Uncle Tom." His hat-in-hand acceptance of the handouts of the Communist boss-man in New York outdid that of even the most impoverished colored sharecropper in Alabama.

The most outstanding new Negro Communist to emerge during this period was Benjamin J. Davis, Jr. who first became associated with the Party as the defender of Herndon in Atlanta. In New York he became chairman of the large Harlem Section and later a member of the National Board. Well educated, an effective speaker, and a skilled organizer, Davis attracted a large personal following which he was later to turn to account in winning a position on the New York City Council. But like all other Communist leaders—Negro and white—he could lead only as long as he was willing to follow without question the line laid down at any given time. The Davis who in July, 1939 insisted on American participation in a collective security program was the Davis who in August demanded that America get out and stay out of the "imperialist war." Davis became a Party hack with a law degree.

The old-time Negro Communists holding minor positions, now long schooled in the art of about-face, had no difficulty in shifting to the united front program or accepting its antithesis when the period ended. Harry Haywood, Abner W. Berry, and Richard B. Moore exemplified just how such twists and turns could be executed with the greatest of ease.*

* A Negro Party functionary during this period, Manning Johnson, who was also a business agent for Cafeteria Workers Local 302 in New York was active in such organizations as the National Negro Congress, the United May Day Provisional Com-

Browder at the close of the united front period might complain that the Party had been lax in the development of Negro leadership. This was true in terms of the goals the Communists set for themselves and in view of the Party's continued emphasis on the Negro question. However, there was a great deal more to show in this respect than during the preceding period when all-out, highly intensive work among Negroes had been a must on the Party program.

In its Negro program the Party could point to substantial gains during the united front period. Dropping much of its doctrinaire theory, foregoing dual revolutionary movements, and concentrating on a host of immediate issues important to Negroes, it was able to make a much more effective appeal. It reached a much wider Negro audience through its own and through the Negro and trade union press. It built up a number of special organizations for work among Negroes, including the Negro People's Committee to Aid Spanish Democracy, the National Negro Congress, and the Southern Negro Youth Congress. In addition it was able to identify with—and ultimately control —certain non-Communist agencies having a large and direct interest in the race question, the Southern Conference for Human Welfare being the most notable example. As a result of its strong position in a number of the new CIO unions, the Party succeeded in reaching a large mass of Negro industrial workers on the job and in the colored community.

While it failed to capture the NAACP, the NUL, Father Divine, or the Negro nationalist organizations, it did succeed in some instances in picking off some of their local branches; in others it obtained a certain amount of support on community issues. It developed a Negro Communist leadership by tapping the younger intelligentsia and trade union sources, a leadership that was quantitatively and qualitatively a considerable improvement over that of the preceding period. Among the organizations

---

mittee of 1939, the League Against War and Fascism and other Party-supported agencies. In addition he wrote extensively for Party publications. He later broke with the Communists and has since given numerous accounts of his association with them. However, his story is so confused and told in such an off-the-cuff fashion that one is disposed to place little stock in it.

which it controlled it developed spokesmen who, although not necessarily members of the Party were as committed to the Communists as the most devout card holder. Negro membership in the Party was more than doubled, although percentage-wise it remained about the same. All these gains, while small perhaps for an organization that wore the label, "the Negro party," as a "badge of honor," made the organization during this period a force in Negro protest. And had the trend continued, the Communists might have become an increasingly important factor in American race relations.

But the trend did not continue. The Party became more than ever an instrument of the Communist International. Adolph Hitler had not been stopped by the united front. The Stalin-Hitler pact was the alternative. To persuade the Nazis to accept the pact Stalin had to make many commitments. He agreed to pose his obedient servants in the United States against American aid to Hitler's scheduled victims, and against American intervention in behalf of those countries on the Nazis' calendar of conquest. That the latter were nations with whom the master of the Kremlin had only a short time before proposed defensive alliances evoked no concern. All this meant a complete change of line for the American Communists, a quick break-up of the united front edifice, a reversal of their entire program—including that on the Negro question.

# V

# "THIS IS NOT THE NEGRO'S WAR"
# 1939–1941

THE Stalin-Hitler Pact was concluded in August, 1939. This agreement between the respective dictators of the "socialist fatherland" and the super-race state set the stage for the Nazi blitzkrieg against Poland. It neutralized the eastern German frontier, giving Hitler freedom to act against the low countries, against Denmark and Norway, and later against France and England. The pact obligated the U.S.S.R. to refrain from military action against Germany. It went further; it obligated the former to take positive steps to support the Nazi régime in its aggressions. In dutifully carrying out this end of the bargain, the U.S.S.R., through the various sections of the Communist International in western Europe, sabotaged the defense efforts of Hitler's victims. While the Nazi war machine prepared to overrun the borders of Belgium, the Netherlands, Denmark, Norway, and France, the Communists helped to soften them up internally. They weakened the will to resist, they sowed the seeds of political confusion and even promoted treason in the armed forces. The most cynical Nazi could not have accused the U.S.S.R. of failing to deliver on its promises.

The Communist International directed the American Communist Party to do everything possible to prevent our government from aiding the allied powers. The Communists were ordered to sabotage the production of war materials through strikes and other measures, to prevent the shipment of these materials to France and England, to discourage American rearmament, even for its own defense, and to oppose the interventionist trend in American foreign policy. These aims became the sole determinant of Communist Party actions in the United States during the period from August, 1939, until late June, 1941. All other aspects of the Party program were so much window dressing.

This new directive required a drastic over-night shift in the American Communist Party program. The Communists dropped immediately their demand for a foreign policy of collective security which they had vigorously indorsed during the preceding four years. They joined with a queer collection of isolationist elements—America First and the German-American Bund, Gerald L. K. Smith and Fritz Kuhn—to demand a hands-off policy in Europe.* The agreement between the fascists and Communists in Europe was formalized in a pact at Moscow; in America the agreement was not solemnized in writing at Party headquarters in New York. But it was nonetheless real.

The Party did a complete reversal in its attitude toward President Roosevelt, to whom it had given increasing support as the united front developed. Now it joined his critics in branding him as a Wall Street spokesman, a warmonger, a desperate politician who was willing to involve the country in a war to cover his own mistakes and to clothe his fascist intentions in the garb of national defense. Turning on the New Deal Program, it characterized the gains of workers and Negroes as mere sops thrown out to cover basically sinister intentions. It joined with the extreme right-wing of the Republican Party, with a wide variety of reactionary groups, in calling for defeat of those who had developed and carried forward this grass-roots challenge to unrestricted economic privilege.

The Communist Party dropped its effort to build a united front program with liberal and reformist organizations whose

* I recall a conversation with a Communist Party organizer in Chicago in January, 1941, which may illustrate the point. We were discussing the Committee to Defend America by Aiding the Allies, an organization in which I was active. I referred him to an item in the *New York Times* in support of a statement I had made. His reply was: "Well, you *know* who runs the *Times*. If you want to find out what your so-called Committee is up to, then read the *Daily Worker* or the *Chicago Tribune*. They are the only ones with the courage to print the real truth."

hands it had attempted to grasp in "unity" since 1935. Now it denounced them as being fake liberals, weak-kneed "progressives," and, at best, "confused and timid" elements who did not appreciate the basic changes in the "new situation." Where it had formerly seen in these groups new sharpness and political courage, it could now see in them only empty slogans and fearful compromise.

The Party reversed its entire program in the trade union field, where since the formation of the CIO it had given wide support to the industrial unions while halting its attacks on the craft organizations in the AFL. Now it turned on those organizations and leaders whom it could not steer into the "anti-imperialist" war struggle, characterizing them as tools of monopoly capitalism and Wall Street warmongers. Now John L. Lewis' isolationism was seen as a manifestation of labor statesmanship while Sidney Hillman's interventionism was nothing short of a bureaucratic sell-out to the war party. The mass of workers, the Party now maintained, in direct contrast to its position of a few weeks previously, wanted no part of the Administration's "drive toward war."

A like reversal occurred in the Communist Party's position on the Negro question. During the united front period the Party made numerous overtures toward the moderate Negro organizations, especially the NAACP and the NUL, proposing joint action on a series of immediate issues. It had dropped its attacks on such leaders as Walter White, Lester B. Granger, and A. Philip Randolph, whom it had characterized as "friends" and as "responsible spokesmen" of a wide segment of black America. Now it turned upon them with a fury unparalleled in the two decades of Communist activity around the Negro question; now the NAACP and the NUL did not voice the aspirations of the Negro masses—rather, they were "betrayers of the Negro people," "traitors to the race," and "black handmaidens of Wall Street imperialism." The moderate Negro leaders had suddenly become paid agents of the Roosevelt administration, whose job was to line up Negro support for the "imperialist war."

Whereas the Party had attempted to build a number of "broad Negro people's organizations" during the united front period, it now sought to convert these same organizations—the National Negro Congress and the Southern Negro Youth Congress—into narrow but vocal instruments for building anti-war sentiment among American blacks. To accomplish this purpose the Communists were willing to destroy these agencies if necessary.

The self-determination doctrine, abandoned for all practical purposes during the united front period, was revived, and Negroes again became a nation under the heel of American imperialism. British and French exploitation of colored colonial peoples was paralleled by American exploitation of Negroes in the Black Belt, and the war was being fought to guarantee the continued slavery of them all. The American Negroes, said the Party, should not only oppose American aid to the Allied powers and American involvement in the war, they should struggle at the same time for the establishment of a black republic in the South.

In light of the "new situation," the Party's tasks were clear. After the jailing of Browder they were summarized by Foster as follows:

The Communist Party in the period ahead will do its full share to give the working class theoretical and practical leadership in the complicated struggles that are bound soon to develop. It will fight resolutely to have the United States get out and stay out of the imperialist war; for the American masses to demand a people's peace; for the defense and improvement of the economic standards of workers; for the preservation of civil liberties; for the release of Earl Browder and other class war prisoners; for friendly relations with the Soviet Union for the establishment of socialism.[1]

Translated, this meant that the Party would carry on intensive "anti-war" propaganda through its press, oppose lend-lease and all other forms of aid to the allies, organize strikes in major defense production plants, support free-speech fights for those denouncing the foreign policies of the Roosevelt administration, campaign for the release of Earl Browder, and in all other ways possible attempt to carry out the directives of the Communist International. It also meant that Communists would attempt to capitalize at every opportunity on the myriad grievances of the American Negroes in an effort to carry out its more basic aim.

In formulating a rationale for its Negro program in this period, the Party insisted that the rights of racial minorities were not involved in the European war. France and Britain, it argued, were just as vicious exploiters of darker races as were Germany and Italy, although the former might lack any official theory of racial superiority. The United States, as a potential ally of the Allied powers, was equally guilty in its treatment of minority groups. It exploited darker-skinned people not only in the colonies but within its own boundaries. Therefore, the Party insisted, the colonial peoples and Negroes in the United States should not support the Allied nations or the United States in a war whose outcome could only be continued slavery. The duty of American Negroes was to use their entire resources in opposition to America's aiding France and Britain, and to strive for a "people's peace."

Having executed a complete reversal of policy on the Negro question (and on all other issues), how did the Party propose to implement its new program among colored Americans? A number of items stood out on the agenda. First it attempted to discredit moderate organizations and their leaders, who though not giving a blanket indorsement to the defense program and American foreign policy were not taking unequivocal positions against it. Turning on such organizations as the NAACP, the NUL and others, the Party declared:

> The fight against discrimination by the "defense" set up is gathering friends and supporters throughout the country, primarily because the fight is being waged by the Negro people in unity with labor and progressive forces, through the National Negro Congress. But many of those who are raising their voices in denunciation of this evil are not friends at all. Some find it fashionable to do so—it gives the protective coloration of being for democracy. . . .
>
> Primarily their minds are centered upon how to win the Negroes for the imperialist war program for they practice discrimination in their own establishments. Still another group like A. Philip Randolph and Frank R. Crosswaith, red-baiting social democrats, Walter White and Eugene Kinckle Jones, reformists, use the fight against Negro discrimination to win their own people for a war which means continued misery and lynching under the capitalist system. *The Negro leaders are spokesmen for an anti-Negro program among their people. . . .*

The pamphlet* fails to take full advantage of the opportunity to explain *the treacherous role being played by leaders of the N.A.A.C.P. and Urban League, dismissing them as being "too timid" in the fight for Negro rights.* The policy of these social democrats is conscious and political. *They are persistently and openly trying to win the Negroes to the support of the British-American gang of imperialists as against the Hitler gang* as if both gangs were not contemptuous of the Negro people.[2]

Another technique employed by the Party involved efforts to place Negro trade unionists in opposition to the defense program. In those unions which the Party controlled special propaganda was distributed among black members. They were urged to act through their unions, but to go further and align themselves politically with other elements in opposition to the "imperialist war drive" of the Administration. In those unions having substantial Negro memberships but free of Communist domination, the Party attempted to use the colored workers for spearheading a minority movement in opposition to the Roosevelt administration. In the more vital defense production and transportation industries the Communists seized every opportunity to involve black and white workers in strikes, anticipating more success among the former because of the extent and character of discrimination.

The Party vigorously claimed that discrimination against Negroes in defense production industries was part and parcel of the drive to involve the country in the imperialist war on the Allied side. It was aware, however, that it could not halt the entire program and that at least some Negroes would obtain jobs, a fact which might make these lucky few less than completely opposed to the defense program. The Party's strategy here involved emphasis on the paucity of job opportunities for Negroes, coupled with the strong urging that colored folk use their economic and political power to halt defense preparations. Max Yergan, writing in the *Daily Worker* in late May, 1941, pointed out:

* *Democracy Means: Jobs for Negroes* (Philadelphia: Communist Party of Philadelphia, 1941).

The Negro people must insist on jobs while at the same time opposing this imperialist war and our intervention in it. It is a war which cannot possibly serve to strengthen democracy or to liberate the people for it is an instrument of oppression the world over.

It would be a mistake, and it would do serious harm to the Negro people, if they demanded jobs in exchange for support of the war-making plans and of war itself, so this war holds no good for the Negro but will usher in destruction of democratic rights and further denial of the meager civil liberties he enjoys already.[3]

Yergan and other Party spokesmen, however, were not clear about how Negroes were to demand and secure defense production jobs and at the same time bring a halt to the defense program. Although the Party complained at length about the denial of job opportunities to Negroes, it would have been extremely disappointed had obstacles to their employment been quickly removed. In that event Communists would have lost one of their most important weapons for building Negro protest.

Realizing that even limited employment gains among Negroes would greatly blunt this Party instrument, Benjamin J. Davis Jr. argued:

Even if all job discrimination were broken down, still Negro people are faced along with other Americans, with the prospect of dying in a useless war. . . . Thus not only are Negro people against job discrimination, but they are against the whole imperialist program of which this discrimination is an inherent part. And the real way to defeat discrimination is not by surrendering to the war program but fighting it. . . .

*There is a special duty upon the Communists to show that job discrimination is a phase of the war program, that Negro people are opposed to the imperialist war, and that the only effective way in which jobs can be won and the increasing lynch terror against Negroes combatted is through clear unity with labor and the general population to get out of this war and stay out.*[4]

It is hardly conceivable that Davis was unaware of discrimination in employment before the Stalin-Hitler agreement.

This two-fold strategy of the Party on Negro employment also explains its opposition to the NAACP and the NUL. The latter were ardently committed to opening up jobs for Negroes and were meeting with some success. However, they were not proposing all-out opposition to the defense production program at the same time. Their sins, according to the Communists, were not that they were failing to seek some jobs for Negroes, but that such efforts were made only for the purpose of garnering Negro support for the defense and foreign aid programs of the Administration. The same considerations governed the Party's attitude toward the National March on Washington Movement, which will be discussed later.

In a further effort to build opposition to the defense and foreign aid programs of the United States, the Party, beginning immediately after the Stalin-Hitler pact, attempted to convert the Negro organizations established during the united front period into outright opponents of the "imperialist war." The most notable example was found in the National Negro Congress. It will be recalled that between 1936 and 1939 the NNC emerged as a rather promising coordinating agency for Negro protest and betterment efforts in a number of larger urban centers. Up until August, 1939, the Communists had been willing to let the NNC function without too rigid restraint. This was due partially to the inability of the Party to take over the organization completely during its formative years. It also resulted from the fact that the NNC served the united front program well among Negroes from the Party point of view.

By mid-1940, however, the Communists were in key positions in the Congress and able through concerted efforts to take it over in support of the new line. While the Party was in control of the governing committees of the NNC, it was by no means satisfied with the response of the membership to the new program. Opposition to the "imperialist war" had been voiced by the Party spokesmen at the top; the rank and file was reluctant to go along. One Communist functionary complained that Negro Communists had not been sufficiently active in articulating the sentiment for peace among the mass of Negroes. This failure, he declared, was:

undoubtedly due to the weakness of the broad national Negro people's organizations which at the present time have not the ability to give national guidance to the anti-war sentiments. This is so especially with the National Negro Congress, which has a correct attitude to the war but has far too little organization below, in communities and cities, to act as an effective organizing and leading force in uniting and guiding the anti-war sentiment into correct channels. In those localities where local organizations do exist and function, their activities are not of a specific and concrete character. Consequently they fail to serve as organizers of the sentiments against war.[5]

The "correct" attitude, of course, was the attitude of the Communist Party. But this line could not be effectively forced on a majority in the NNC immediately. This was due in part to the structural weaknesses of the organization; but other factors must be taken into account. Negroes in the United States were frequently quite apathetic about the issues involved in the European conflict. While they obviously opposed the race superiority doctrines of the Nazi régime and feared their extension, they could not embrace France or Britain as exponents of racial equality. Remembering the experiences of Negroes during and after World War I, they displayed a justifiable skepticism toward another great crusade for the democratic ideal. This apathy was advantageous from the Party point of view, for it meant that the great bulk of American Negroes would not actively push for our intervention in the conflict. But this lethargy was not enough for the Communists; they wanted black Americans to line up solidly behind the new line.

Another reason why enthusiastic acceptance of the new line could not be immediately forced on the NNC was that large segments such as that led by A. Philip Randolph were not willing to place themselves in the forefront of any "anti-imperialist war" movement, particularly when this meant collaboration with the German-American Bund on the one hand and the Communist Party on the other. Many members of the Congress were reluctant to accept the pronouncement that the Germans and the English were cut from the same cloth insofar as concerned racial matters, particularly in view of the fact that the Communist Party had placed so much insistence on the latter's basic differences during the united front period.

But the Party was determined to convert the National Negro Congress into a completely controlled instrument for the realization of its own singular purpose. To do this it would be necessary to get rid of Randolph and the moderate elements who would not embrace the new line. It was necessary to shift the entire emphasis of the program from domestic issues to foreign policy and to stress such matters as civil rights, housing and job opportunities only insofar as it was necessary to secure Negro opposition to defense and foreign aid. "It is fundamentally necessary," declared a Party functionary,

to extend the greatest assistance to the building of the National Negro Congress as the broad expression of anti-war and anti-imperialist struggle on a local, state and national scale. That is why it is necessary to speak to the Negro people about the war on the basis of their tragic experiences in the last war; to prove that the war will not bring job and prosperity but tragedy and death and greater oppression; to destroy the legend of the "anti-fascist" and "democratic" and "freedom of small peoples" character of the war waged by British, French and German imperialism; to organize and unite the existing sentiment against war; to combat the demoralizing propaganda of enemy ideologists and the activity of the pro-war forces now working among the Negro people.[6]

And these aims were to be realized by:

. . . [the Party's] helping to strengthen and build progressive and anti-war organizations of the Negro people; by helping to assure the success of the coming Third National Negro Congress in Washington on April 26-28; by helping to draw into the Congress the trade unions, civic, church, fraternal and community white and Negro organizations; by helping to build locally the National Negro Congress through stimulating and encouraging the greatest united activity on a local scale around the specific issues affecting the Negro people and the multitude of common issues affecting all white and Negro people.[7]

Thus the National Negro Congress was to be converted into another instrument for realizing the primary goal of the Party at the time just as it was to be converted into an instrument for realizing a completely different Party goal a year later.

With strategy developed well ahead of time and their numerical superiority assured prior to the convening of the NNC in Washington, the Communists were all set to take over and eliminate any opposition elements. That they succeeded, perhaps even beyond their highest hopes, is evidenced by what happened at the 1940 meeting. A total of 1,264 delegates representing trade union, civic, fraternal, political, professional, educational, church and business organizations attended the Third National Negro Congress. Only 888 of the delegates were Negroes. From the North came nearly three-fourths of the delegates, the southern and border states sending only 315.

Following the earlier pattern, the largest state delegations came from New York, Pennsylvania, Illinois, Massachusetts and the District of Columbia. More than a third of the delegates represented trade unions, with the political organizations constituting a sizable bloc. There was a significant drop in the number from the religious, fraternal, and business agencies. The trade union and political groups, many of them under Party control, dominated the proceedings of the Congress, and it was upon them that the Communists relied in forcing Randolph from the presidency and imposing the "anti-war" program on the NNC.

Party strategists prepared the resolutions beforehand, forced them through the committees, and supported them on the floor with speeches that bordered on hysteria. Opposition speakers were hooted down. Randolph's efforts to provide non-Communists an opportunity to express their views were sabotaged by parliamentary maneuvers, or where necessary by boos, catcalls, and other disturbances. Frequently, delegates unacquainted with Party ways were unaware of what was going on or else were awe-struck by the turn of events and remained silent in disgust. The principal resolution adopted by the Congress at this 1940 meeting indicated quite clearly how effective the Communist move had been.

There is again a distinct danger of American envelopment in a war, a war already raging on the continent of Europe. The present war abroad is an imperialist war between fully imperialist rivals and is in no sense a war for the protection of the rights of small nations. . . .

The present drive of the administration to mobilize the American people to support either side in the war cannot receive the consideration of the Negro people because we have ourselves not yet secured full citizenship rights, Federal protection against lynching, the complete right to vote, the elimination of the lily-white primaries and the poll-tax or the abolition of the entire system of jim-crow discrimination, in other words we have not yet received freedom or democracy. . . .

The National Negro Congress declares that the Negro people have everything to lose and nothing to gain by American involvement in the imperialist war and sharply condemns the administration for the steps it has taken and the partiality already shown, and demands of the administration that it take no further action that might involve the country in war.

The National Negro Congress further declares that the battle for democracy lies at home in the war against hunger and misery and for jobs, security, opportunity and prosperity and for full democratic rights; and the National Negro Congress resolves to aid in the organization of the Negro people to act in concert with labor, youth and all other anti-war forces to keep our country at peace.[8]

A. Philip Randolph, who had served as President of the Congress since its inception, refused to stand for re-election as the third meeting drew to a close. He was aware that although the newly adopted permanent constitution and by-laws presumably prevented minority control of the organization, the NNC was now nothing more than an enlarged Party cell. He knew that to continue in office would mean acceptance of a program which he could not indorse in principle; he knew, too, that it would mean serving as a stooge for the Party bureaucrats and their errand boys, who now firmly held the reins of all the governing committees. Even so, he attempted to bow out gracefully; but such courtesy was not reciprocated by the Communists, who left the hall during his final speech, leaving only a handful of delegates. In his final address to the Congress Randolph made it quite clear that outright Party control would wreck the organization, committing it to a program that would alienate most Negroes and separate from the liberal and labor movement any who remained.

Randolph later charged that the NNC was largely under the domination of the left-wing CIO unions—that it had ceased to be representative of all Negro labor. He pointed out that the NNC was no longer self-financing, but was securing substantial funds from non-Negro sources; he warned that those who controlled the purse strings would likewise control policy. He complained with justification that the NNC was no longer a

Negro organization, pointing to the presence of some 400 white delegates at the Washington meeting. Finally, he charged that the Congress had passed under complete Party control as evidenced by the critical attitude toward American foreign policy coupled with nothing but praise for that of the U.S.S.R.[9]

The Party in turn bitterly attacked Randolph for daring to disagree with the new line and for breaking with the NNC as a result. "The enthusiastic Congress tensely awaited the message of Randolph," declared one Party delegate,

but his speech filled the audience with uneasiness, consternation and disgust. His words were not the words of Negro labor, of the Negro people. They were the words of the frightened Negro petty bourgeoisie, chattering with fear, pleading for mercy before the white master. They were the words of treacherous Social-Democracy. Of the progressive Randolph of 1936 only a hollow mockery remains.[10]

Again the answer to who and what had changed is not difficult to guess. Randolph was as much of a liberal and a pragmatic trade unionist before the Stalin-Hitler pact as he was afterward. But he was now a sadder and wiser man, having received another lesson in cooperation with Communists.

In spite of Randolph's withdrawal, the alienation of the moderate delegates, and the immediate reduction in the NNC's influence, the Party hailed the third meeting of the organization as a great success, declaring:

The convention marked an enormous step forward in the centuries-old struggle of the Negro people. It was not yet, in the full sense of the word, a people's congress. It represented, in fact, the advanced detachment of the Negro movement. A firmer basis has, however, been established for the unity of the Negro masses. A new note, of far reaching significance, was struck in the relationship of the Negro people to labor. The foundation for the historic alliance between the Negro people and the working class has been immensely strengthened.[11]

A different estimate, however, was made by Ralph Bunche, one of the founders of the Congress and a delegate at the 1940 meeting. His report represents an excellent case history of how the Party captured, and for all practical purposes, killed, an agency which at one time had displayed considerable promise for furthering Negro rights. Writing for the Myrdal project a short time after the third meeting of the NNC, he declared:

> In my estimation the Negro Congress dug its own grave at this meeting. It will now be reduced to a Communist cell. This certainly must have been the intention of the leaders, for John Davis [John P. Davis, Executive Secretary of the NNC] is an astute person. He knew therefore that when he openly pledged the Congress to a pro-Soviet policy, and when he stated American Negroes would not fight against the Soviet Union, the Congress would be publicly branded as a Communist front. Davis also knows that it is not possible to build up a mass movement among either Negroes or whites in this country under the banner of the Communist Party. Therefore, it can only be concluded that this was a deliberate retreat from any hope of the Congress as a mass movement, and that it was dictated by the change in the line of the Communist Party from pursuance of the popular front to a policy of closing ranks. . . .
>
> The Congress just ended was an amazing demonstration of controlled mass psychology, organizational and intellectual regimentation and skillful demagoguery.[12]

Max Yergan, a former official of the International YMCA and Director of the International Committee on African Affairs, and one of the early vice-presidents of the NNC, was elected by the Party's delegates to succeed Randolph. Yergan had adhered closely to the Party line during the united front period, and though he was not a card-carrying Communist, he was apparently considered "safe" by the Kremlin spokesmen. Just how safe was indicated by one Party delegate's statement: "The outlook for the Congress with Dr. Yergan at the helm is indeed bright. He is a man of sterling qualities, unselfish and indefatigable. He is staunch in his championship of Negro rights and unbounded in his devotion to human freedom." [13] Praise indeed for a man whose chief qualifications appeared to be a remarkable ability to say with firm conviction and a straight face just the opposite of what he had said the day before.*

---

* But even Yergan could not keep this up indefinitely. He broke with the Party during the post-war period after having executed with it a complete *volte-face* following the German invasion of the Soviet Union. The involved background of Yergan's break with the Communists need not be explored here. It hardly need be mentioned that the Party no longer regards him as a man of "sterling qualities."

That Yergan merited such confidence and that he was willing to carry out his orders without question was exemplified a short time later in his declaration before an Episcopal church group:

We [Negroes] do not believe we have any business allying ourselves with either of the belligerent sides now responsible for the war. We believe *that* to be the basic question for the masses of the American people both white and Negro. In this question are involved all other questions confronting the Negro people and, for that matter, all the people of America. On the eventuality of peace or war depends the possibility of carrying forward the struggle for fuller democracy, or turning to fascist dictatorship in America.[14]

Concluding, he declared:

America will most certainly not aid Nazi Germany. America must not become an ally of imperialist Britain. To help either of these powers is to use the tremendous manhood and material wealth of this country in the support of forces of human exploitation, of war and misery.[15]

But the efforts of Yergan and the Communists in the NNC were largely unavailing. While vague "anti-war" sentiments were widespread among American Negroes (and whites as well), the Party was unable to capitalize on them for its own purposes. The NNC never had a real mass base in the Negro communities, even when its program was focused largely on a series of immediate domestic issues. It could hardly hope to develop such a base on such far-removed questions as foreign policy and war. Party control of the Congress became widely known following the third meeting in 1940. Organizations which had formerly supported it were no longer willing to identify with what was now an obvious and single-purposed Communist instrument. By its rigid insistence on opposition to the defense and foreign aid programs, the NNC alienated groups that were immediately concerned with such problems as civil rights, housing and employment. The Congress presumably was interested in such matters, too, and it was very vocal about discrimination in employment and in the armed forces. However, many Negroes came to feel that such interest was not genuine, that it merely clothed a different set of aims.

Local branches of the NNC in New York, Philadelphia, Detroit, Chicago, and Los Angeles were active on the problem of Negro employment in defense industries. Attempts were made to form local fair employment practice committees and to secure support from other Negro organizations.[16] These efforts, too, were largely unavailing. The labor market pressures were not yet sufficient to force employers and trade unions to modify their discriminatory policies. The national administration was not convinced that it should take a more emphatic line concerning discrimination against Negroes in industry. More specifically, the NNC itself did not have a sustained interest in promoting Negro employment; its energies were frequently diverted to the promotion of "peace" movements and the larger propaganda efforts against the "imperialist war." In line with Bunche's prediction, the National Negro Congress became nothing more than a Communist cell and remained so until its demise in the postwar period.

By 1939 the Party was also in firm control of the Southern Negro Youth Congress. The third meeting of the SNYC took place in early 1939 prior to the signing of the Stalin-Hitler pact. While the organization had made some gains in certan urban centers in the South, it was still rather weak and ineffectual. Like the National Negro Congress, it was unable to establish any mass base or to formulate a program general enough to appeal to a wide segment of black youth while working for a series of specific and tangible goals. The resolutions at the 1939 meeting resembled closely those adopted in 1937 and 1938. The usual statements on civil rights, health, welfare, education, and employment were adopted. A program of collective security against aggression was indorsed.

Following the signing of the Stalin-Hitler pact the governing committees of the SNYC, now firmly under Party control, attempted to carry the organization along in opposition to the defense and foreign aid programs. However, there was not much to carry and no organizational strength to back the numerous demands. Such support as the SNYC now had come largely from the Communist-led trade unions in the South, and the latter were numerically weak with the exception perhaps of the Mine,

Mill and Smelter Workers in Birmingham. Church and student groups did not accord the SNYC the support that loomed so promisingly during the formative years of the organization. Party control was also becoming increasingly obvious, alienating some of the initial organizations and scaring off potential affiliates. Subsequent meetings of the SNYC were more and more to resemble small collections of the Party faithful.

The SNYC did make something of a comeback after America's entry into the war. However, it was never to recover from the severe losses it suffered during the period from 1939 to 1941, when it faithfully went down the "anti-imperialist war" line imposed upon it by the Communists. While the SNYC functioned through 1948, its real value to the Party was lost with the end of the united front period. As in the case of the National Negro Congress, the Communists were willing to kill any organization that could not be steered along the new and rigidly defined line which separated the saved and the damned into two hard and fast camps.

In addition to swinging the SNYC behind its new line, the Communists in the South also sought to capture the Southern Conference for Human Welfare. The second meeting of the SCHW was held in Chattanooga, Tennessee, in April, 1940. During the eighteen months since the initial meeting, the Party had succeeded in strengthening its earlier position by involving more of its members in the work of the permanent committees and affiliating additional organizations which it controlled. Communist gains derived also from defections within the SCHW ranks as some of the more conservative church, civic and trade union organizations withdrew their support. On the whole, however, the Conference showed a steady if not dramatic growth during the period between the first and second meetings.

Communist spokesmen and delegates at the 1940 meeting of the SCHW, under the direction of Rob F. Hall, Party Secretary for Alabama, attempted to force through the Conference an eight-point "uncompromising" peace policy. The Communists, however, were forcefully opposed by many of the labor and liberal groups under the leadership of President Frank Graham. Debate on the Party's proposals became very bitter and at one point fist fights threatened. The SCHW went on record as opposing war appropriations at the expense of the underprivileged people of the South, but at the same time it condemned aggression by Communists as well as Nazis.

The 1940 meeting led to further schisms within the SCHW, from which it was never completely to recover. Some groups thought that the Communists controlled the Chattanooga meeting and viewed the resolution on war and foreign policy as an indirect indorsement of the Party position. While few groups officially withdrew from the Conference, their support was lost for all practical purposes. The resolutions adopted on such issues as civil rights, labor, welfare, farm tenancy and others were similar to those of the first meeting of 1938. They represented a continuation of the program worked out at Birmingham, on which there had been an impressive amount of agreement. While the Party applauded these decisions and commended the work of the Conference in the economic and political fields, it was far from satisfied with the foreign policy program. Hall, for example, declared:

There were weaknesses in the Chattanooga conference, due partly to the failure of honest progressives to orient themselves to the new situation caused by the outbreak of the imperialist war and the abandonment of the New Deal by Roosevelt, and partly due to the failure of labor to come forward boldly to give leadership to the movement.[17]

The partial defeat of the Communists at the 1940 SCHW meeting, however, only strengthened their determination to capture and place the organization in opposition to the defense program and foreign policies of the Administration. And the Party thought it saw in the Negro organizations affiliated with the SCHW one instrument through which it might work. However, in June of the following year the Party completely reversed its position, and its task then became one of placing southern liberals and labor behind the "win-the-war" program.

The Negro delegates at the 1940 SCHW meeting were not appreciably influenced by the concerted efforts of the Communist spokesmen. The latter attempted to make a special appeal around Negro grievances in an effort to line up the black delegates for the eight-point "peace" program. Negro support of these proposals came only from those delegates representing Party-controlled organizations. It is significant that it was from among the white pacifist-inclined non-Communist churchmen that the Party found its most articulate supporters.

Negroes were obviously unwilling to accept a Party leadership which would place them in opposition to the main drift of American liberalism. However, they were willing to protest their lot and to organize betterment programs—as they had been long before August, 1939. As a matter of fact, the war was a stimulus to racial unrest. The rejection of Party leadership suggested political awareness and maturity rather than misguidance by "traitorous" leaders. The NAACP, the NUL, and various other moderate Negro organizations from the outset fought vigorously for the rights of Negroes to defense jobs and to unsegregated military service. To realize how early and how completely they were committed to such programs, it is necessary to review only briefly their histories during this period.[18] Their only sin in the eyes of the Party was that they did not stand squarely with Communists in unqualified opposition to the foreign policies of the Administration and the defense program.[19] That was enough to damn them to eternal hell (at least until June 21, 1941).

While the NAACP and the NUL had sought in various ways to eliminate discrimination against Negroes in the various areas of the defense program, they met with only limited success. The need for more dramatic protest on a mass scale was clearly evident. The March on Washington Movement was designed as an answer to this need. Randolph, after leaving the National Negro Congress, had become increasingly aware of the need for a Negro mass organization free of Communist Party influence. In late 1940, impressed by the continued discrimination against Negroes in the defense program, and with the aid of a number of other non-Communist Negro leaders, he mapped plans for a protest march on Washington by thousands of Negro workers. A series of local committees was established throughout the country, particularly in the larger urban-industrial centers which had substantial Negro populations.

These committees were responsible for enlisting the support of local groups around a series of immediate grievances. They used various devices in pressuring for jobs in the respective communities. In addition, they planned to have their members participate in the actual "March on Washington," which was scheduled for the latter part of June, 1941. Randolph's strategy was very astute. The demands of the MOWM were brief and to the point; they contained no visionary slogans or revolutionary jargon. The country was preparing to defend democracy the world over. It needed armaments—and manpower for the job. Negroes could provide the latter, but undemocratic practices barred them. The United States was appealing to colored peoples all over the world to support its policies. How could it make this appeal when it treated its own colored citizens as outcasts? Let the Administration clearly demonstrate that it meant what it said—to American Negroes and to all colored races. Let it open jobs to Negroes, end discrimination in the armed forces, guarantee minimum civil and political rights. Was that too much to ask of democratic America, asked the MOWM.

The Administration was well aware of the implications, domestic and foreign, of the March on Washington. Efforts were made to persuade or force Randolph to call it off. He refused in the absence of assurance that the Administration would take some positive action on the question of discrimination in the defense program. President Roosevelt offered to issue a mild Executive Order without any enforcement provisions. It was rejected. The President then issued Executive Order 8802, which prohibited discrimination in defense production industries and established the President's Committee on Fair Employment Practice to enforce this policy.*

The Communist Party and the National Negro Congress opposed the MOWM for four reasons. First, the MOWM was achieving phenomenal success in an area on which the Party and the Congress felt they had a prior claim. The MOWM met with

* Executive Order 8802 was issued on June 25, 1941. A Second Executive Order strengthening the original and making more specific the functions of the FEPC was issued May 27, 1943, following renewed pressure from the MOWM and other organizations. See: *Final Report, President's Committee on Fair Employment Practice*, (Washington, D. C. Government Printing Office, 1947), pp. 98-100.

a wide response in the Negro communities; Negroes attended its meetings, served on its committees and supplied it with funds. Second, the Party and its NNC had practically no influence in the MOWM and little possibility of obtaining control over it. Third, the leadership of the MOWM was in the hands of Randolph, who was ably supported by the NAACP, the NUL, and in many cases the Negro churches. Fourth, the MOWM was not committed to all-out opposition to the foreign policy of the Administration. It did not accept the idea that all the belligerents were cut from the same cloth. It proposed to use its bargaining strength to obtain immediately some of the goals the Administration had proclaimed, as in "the four freedoms."

The Party could not afford, however, to launch a frontal attack on the MOWM. It had to confine its opposition to sniping at Randolph and the other "reformist" Negro leaders associated with him.[20] Had the Party openly attacked the MOWM, it would have further alienated Negroes and lost even more of its own black membership (and that of the National Negro Congress). The MOWM was primarily responsible for Executive Order 8802 and the President's Committee on Fair Employment Practice. It was this influence, also, which evoked a subsequent Executive Order strengthening the first. These measures, which were widely hailed by Negroes as a "Second Emancipation Proclamation," were the achievements of an organization which the Party had not only refused to support but had attacked in a most irresponsible way. The Party's claim to being the "recognized spokesman of the Negro masses" had a peculiar ring, to say the least.

Later the Party was to pretend that it had supported the March on Washington Movement, asserting that through the National Negro Congress, the Southern Negro Youth Congress and the "progressive" labor organizations, Communists had been responsible for a substantial amount of the MOWM's success.[21] Just what is meant by "support" in this instance could involve us in a semantic difficulty. In some cases branches of the NNC and the SNYC did participate in organization of the local MOWM committees, but the results of such participation were possibly more of a hindrance than a help. Communists did attempt to take over at the local level but without much success. Officially the Party was extremely critical of Randolph and the entire movement, charging before June 21, 1941 that it was an instrument of Wall Street imperialism and after that date that it was impeding the war effort. Some of the most vitriolic attacks ever leveled by the Party at a Negro organization were visited upon the MOWM during this period. The Party's claim to have supported the agency must be viewed as a hindsight effort to get on the bandwagon after the MOWM had demonstrated its effectiveness in spite of the Communist's efforts to wreck it.

The Party was sharply aware that Negroes had little enthusiasm for the war, an attitude that persisted to some extent well after the German attack on Russia and the Japanese strike at Pearl Harbor. Communists sought to capitalize on this feeling. Negroes for a considerable time did display a marked lack of concern for the defense program, and with good reason. The policy of discrimination in the armed services relegated Negro recruits to the most menial assignments. Negroes were obtaining few jobs in war production industries; many major contractors were guilty of wholesale discrimination in training and hiring (a practice that continued throughout the war). Negroes remembered all too well the role played by black soldiers in World War I and the violent attacks leveled against them after their return from Europe. They found it difficult to become enthusiastic about the defense of democracy in Europe when they had so little of it in the United States.*

The Party in its various propaganda instruments, particularly in the *Daily Worker,* played up discrimination against Negroes in the armed forces and defense industries. The National Negro Congress, through its remaining local councils, conducted investigation of (and organized protest movements against) discrimination against Negroes in a number of defense produc-

* There is a large literature on the Negro and the war, some of which well portrays the attitudes suggested above. See: Walter White, *op. cit.,* pp. 102-119; Drake and Cayton, *op. cit.,* pp. 746-761; Horace Mann Bond, "Should the Negro Care Who Wins the War?," *Annals of the American Academy of Political and Social Science,* Vol. 223, September 1942, 81-84; Rayford W. Logan, ed., *What the Negro Wants,* (Chapel Hill: University of North Carolina Press, 1944). Note particularly chapters by Logan, Leslie Pinckney Hill, Charles H. Wesley, and Mary McLeod Bethune.

tion centers.[22] Its activities were reported in detail in the *Daily Worker* along with those of the Party itself.

The Party was placed in a ludicrous position when the line abruptly changed, with Hitler's attack on Russia on June 22, 1941. An article appearing in the June 21, 1941, issue of the *Daily Worker* gave much space to an account of a protest by Edward Strong of the SNYC against the OPM's handling of Negro employment in defense production industries. In the letter Strong accused the Administration of complete hypocricy in its job-equality pronouncements. The article was probably written on June 20. In any event few such accusations were to be lodged by the Communist Party, the NNC or the SNYC after that date.[23]

In an effort to obtain a rough measure of how the *Daily Worker* handled material on Negroes in war production industries and in the armed services during the period before and after the German attack on Russia, a survey was made of all such stories appearing in May, 1941, and May, 1944. The number of stories were roughly the same, and the amount of space did not vary greatly. However, there were some significant differences in the content of the articles. The May, 1941, articles editorialized on the connection between discrimination and the "imperialist" war. They stressed the extent of discrimination in employment and played down any successful efforts to deal with it unless action by the Party or the NNC was involved. They also emphasized the desire of Negroes not to be involved in the war and the cooperation of Negro and white trade unionists in opposing foreign policy and the defense program.

The May, 1944, articles editorialized in quite a different direction. They emphasized the gains made by the Negro workers in war production jobs, the Administration's effort to obtain job-equality, the curtailment of discrimination in the armed forces, the contribution of Negro workers to production records, the heightened employment of Negro women, and the general gains made by Negroes in industry as a result of the war. There is good reason to believe that these months are representative, since they cover periods in which two different lines were fairly well set. However, a more careful propaganda analysis would be required to support fully the above observations.

The Communist Party's membership declined significantly during the period from August, 1939, until July, 1941. While even the staunch Communists had some difficulty in making the abrupt shift demanded by the Stalin-Hitler pact of 1939, they managed it with remarkable agility, but the less faithful often found it impossible to execute these intricate acrobatics. Probably half of the several thousand Negro Communists dropped out of the organization during this period, and the Party found it difficult to recruit new black members. Most Negroes were conversant with the sins of British and French imperialism but they did not equate the Allied powers with Nazi Germany or Mussolini's Italy in this respect.

During this period, the Party undertook intensive recruiting drives among Negroes in an effort to augment its dwindling membership. Attempts were made to bring more Negro trade unionists into the organization. Negro churchmen of a pacifist bent were courted. Emphasis was placed on the recruitment of Negro youth, who faced two-fold discrimination—in industry and in the armed forces.[24] Efforts to organize the Negro unemployed around demands for jobs in defense production industries were renewed, while at the same time the Party put forth new demands for relief measures. But these efforts were largely unavailing. Few new colored Americans joined the Communist ranks; the exodus from the Party continued.

The National Negro Congress and the Southern Negro Youth Congress after 1940 experienced a loss in membership comparable to that of the Party and for essentially the same reasons. While they attempted belatedly to latch onto the March on Washington Movement and to carry out programs for increasing Negro employment in defense industries, their identification with the Party was now direct and complete. This was a handicap, for the Negroes in the urban communities were for the most part convinced that neither the NNC or the SNYC would carry on any struggle in their behalf unless it happened to coincide with the Party line; and there was no way of telling when and in what direction this line would change.

The Party during this period became increasingly antagonistic toward such organizations as the NAACP and the NUL. The vicious attacks by the Communists on such Negro leaders as Walter White, Lester Granger and Philip Randolph, all of whom were campaigning effectively for equality of job opportunity and equality for Negroes in the armed forces, further alienated Negroes, particularly when the Party and its organizations had so little to show in either of these fields.

Thus, by June of 1941 the Party had gotten itself out on a limb, isolated from the main trunk of American liberalism. And there it might have stayed but for a fortuitous stroke. Oddly enough it was Adolph Hitler who came to its rescue, on that fateful June day when he turned his tanks toward the East. Quickly the Communists crawled down from their isolated perch —for now the Party needed the help of the social fascists to win the people's war.

# VI

# "ALL OUT FOR THE WAR OF
NATIONAL LIBERATION" 1941–1945

WHEN the Germans attacked Russia in June of 1941, in all the major countries, including the United States, the Communist Parties abruptly executed a one-hundred-eighty-degree turn. The American Party, whose program since August, 1939 had centered around "getting out and staying out of the imperialist war," quickly discovered that the entire world "situation" had altered, requiring a new "orientation" and a new program just the opposite of that followed in the immediately preceding period.*

With the invasion of the U.S.S.R. the conflict, according to the Party, ceased to be a "contest between rival imperialist groups" in which the working class had no stake; it was now a war for "national liberation," for "survival," and for the "preservation" of the democratic institutions (and potentials) of

---

* The July, 1941 issue of the *Communist* reflects the difficulty in which Party spokesmen and editors found themselves immediately following the German attack on the U.S.S.R. The initial pages of the issue contained a Party resolution, "Support the U.S.S.R. in Its Fight Against the Nazi War." This statement emphasized the barbaric character of the German offensive and the stake of *all* Americans in the outcome of the struggle. It demanded all-out American support of Russia in resisting the attack. A few pages later, however, appeared an article by Henry Winston, "Professor Logan Is Ready for a Third World War." Logan, in a newspaper article, had suggested that Negroes in America had a definite stake in the victory of the Allied powers over Germany and Italy. He had urged Negroes to acquaint themselves with the issues and to support American defense production and foreign aid programs. Winston charged, however, that Logan was joining with other traitors to the race in trying to win "the support of the Negro people for the present criminal imperialist war."

people all over the globe. England and France, now allied with the U.S.S.R., were the defenders of western civilization against the fascist forces of evil. The United States had ceased to be the partner of a group of self-seeking capitalist nations and became an ally in the global struggle to defeat tyranny and prepare the way for a new world based on the four freedoms. No longer was President Roosevelt a warmonger leading the country toward a blood bath to preserve the interests of Wall Street; he was now cast in the heroic role of leading the American forces against the Axis drive for world conquest.* The war was no longer one whose outcome would further enslave the darker races; it was a crusade for the rights of racial minorities everywhere.

From this new meaning of the war flowed numerous changes in the program and tactics of the Communist Party. The latter began to plug the formerly distasteful lend-lease; it insisted that even more materials be made available—and that the U.S.S.R. receive the highest priority. It stopped opposing the draft; it urged the government to strengthen its whole military establishment and increase the number of men under arms. It abandoned its program of disruptive strike activity; it insisted that labor disputes could be settled by arbitration and without loss of man-hours and production. It moderated its emphasis on the free speech rights of Administration critics; it heartily condoned the indictment of certain groups under hastily enacted "conspiracy" laws.**

The Party immediately parted company with the nondescript band of isolationists and "America Firsters" with whom it had been consorting. It dropped its criticism of the great majority of American labor leaders against whom it had directed a two-year barrage of invective; these leaders suddenly became patriotic

---

* Thus Earl Browder, writing after the Teheran meeting of Roosevelt, Stalin and Churchill, declared: "Our country needs above all a stable policy in its foreign relations, it needs the feeling and atmosphere of stability, it needs to have the policy of Teheran adopted by the whole country in its overwhelming majority regardless of partisan alignments—therefore it needs Roosevelt, not as a partisan but as a national leader in the broadest sense." (Earl Browder, "Partisanship—A Luxury America Cannot Afford," *Communist*, Vol. XXIII, No. 3, March, 1944, 199.)

** It is interesting to note in passing that the Communists during the war indorsed the conviction of a group of Trotskyites under the same law that jailed the eleven top leaders of the Party in 1949.

servants of the interests of the nation—and of their constituents. It no longer attacked the heads of moderate Negro organizations as "black handmaidens of imperialism" and traitors of the race; these men were now supporting the basic rights of colored people by cooperating in the war production effort and facilitating Negro participation in it.*

According to the Party, aiding the U.S.S.R. and winning the war transcended all other questions and issues. The realization of this goal, Browder claimed, meant a subordination of differences, a minimizing of domestic conflict through common effort against an aggressor, the "unity" of all groups—farmers, workers, middle class, intellectuals—even the capitalists. Browder could declare with great force: ". . . this war has become a People's war of national liberation. Our very existence is at stake. That is why the obligatory slogan is: 'Everything to win the war! Everything for victory over the Axis!' " [1] And again:

I am able to speak thus [on national unity] forthrightly, when so many other public figures who think along similar lines keep silent, because my party, the Communist Party, is the only national political organization which has renounced all thought of partisan advantage and completely subordinated all other considerations to the needs of the quickest and most complete victory in the war. [2]

That all other "considerations" included the rights of Negroes was later admitted by Communist Party spokesmen themselves.

Along with the rest of its program, the Communist Party's position on the Negro question assumed an entirely different character. The previous "line" was not in error; the "situation" had changed. The *Daily Worker* indorsed the statement:

If there is any group that would know whether there's a people's stake in the war it is the Negro people. For years they have struggled with increasing support from labor and white progressives, for their full citizenship, their main enemies being the forces of fascism and Hitlerism at home. The Negro people can be found among the first to recognize the changed character of the European conflict since the invasion of the Soviet Union, and will see the world-wide dangers in-

* A short time later, however, the attack on Randolph, White, Granger and others was renewed because in the opinion of the Party these Negro leaders were not sufficiently enthusiastic about the war!

herent in Hitler's attack upon the stronghold of racial equality and freedom.[3]

Whereas during the preceding period the rights of American Negroes could best be secured by "getting out and staying out of the imperialist war," these same rights could be guaranteed now only by all-out support of the military effort. The attack on the U.S.S.R. was an attack on all racial minorities. "In the present new international situation," said Ford,

the struggle for the rights of the Negro people is an inseparable part of the struggle against fascism and reaction, for democracy and equality; it is an inseparable part of the international people's front to defeat and destroy Hitler fascism.[4]

While Ford had been proclaiming a few weeks previously that "this is not the Negro's war," he was saying just the opposite in October, 1941. In an article in the *Communist* Ford emphasized "the Negroes' stake in the fight against Hitlerism," the "changed character of the war," and the "Negroes' role in the national anti-Hitler front." Dr. Gordon Hancock, a contributor to the Negro paper, the *Norfolk Journal and Guide*, was "absolutely right," said Ford when he [Hancock] declared, "Negroes, this is our war." [5]

Though momentarily thrown off balance by the sudden change in the "situation," the Party's Negro "experts," well trained in the art of *volte-face*, quickly regained their footing and produced an itemized program for attacking the Negro question. It was suggested that the Party should attempt to realign Negro movements with the "progressive" sections of the labor movement on a much wider basis. It should make a sustained effort to unite all "forces and organizations of the Negro people" in order to develop their "full political strength." It should direct the influence of Negroes on American foreign policy, with emphasis on full aid to the U.S.S.R. In its Negro work the Party should strive for cooperation with all "sincere and progressive" people, and in approaching them it should avoid the danger of "sectarianism." It was to fight against discrimination and become the champion of the rights of Negro people in defense production industries and in the armed forces. It was to build further its organization among Negroes, with such immediate aims as the release of Earl Browder. At the same time its "ideological" program was to be intensified and the changed character of the war and role of the Party made clear to Negroes. Finally, Communists were to give:

... great attention to the problems of the Negro middle class and intellectual elements who bear in great measure the great cultural aspirations of the Negro people, and who play an important role in the struggle of the Negro people for democracy and for defense of the democratic institutions of our country.[6]

A completely changed attitude was displayed toward the moderate Negro organizations such as the NAACP and the NUL, on whom the Party had heaped its most irresponsible denouncements during the preceding two years. The NAACP continued to follow the same policies after the German attack on Russia as it had after the Stalin-Hitler pact. But Ford, seeing the Communist Party as the organization pursuing the only straight course, declared: "Many other organizations and groups among the Negro people are giving a good account of themselves. We can endorse wholeheartedly the reports of the convention of the NAACP in Houston, Texas, showing the changed tendencies in that organization." [7]

This new program required focusing on immediate issues in the context of the new world "situation." It resulted in the neglect and final abandonment of the Negro "national liberation" movement and the doctrine of self-determination for Negroes in the Black Belt. The "new" program with its "unity" slogans had a familiar ring. Adolph Hitler had again placed the Communist Party in the main current of the American political stream.

Although the Party had been very vocal about discrimination in defense industries and in the armed forces during 1939-1941, it had done little about it. It now took up the cudgels with even greater ostentation, impressed by the response of Negroes to the MOWM. It was now in a position to work more effectively, for opposition to the defense program no longer barred its cooperation with other groups.

The Young Communist League declared:

> The building of an invincible armed force requires the full integration of the Negro youth in all branches of the armed services without discrimination.
>
> ... The Negro youth of our country must be admitted to all branches of the armed services on the basis of full equality without discrimination, without segregation, and with the most severe and drastic penalties attached to all instances of Jim Crow violation of fundamental rights of Negro youth.[8]

Similar declarations were issued by the Party and the National Negro Congress. Formally, at any rate, the Party's demands for equal treatment of Negroes in industry and in military service were similar to those of organizations like the NAACP, the MOWM and the NUL. However, if we can take the subsequent word of Party spokesmen (speaking after the Duclos letter, of course) the Communists in their day-to-day work made no real attempt to implement these demands.

After the United States entered the war, the Party's willingness to subordinate its larger program to the immediate needs of the hour grew apace, and culminated in the dissolution of the Party and the establishment of the Communist Political Association in April, 1944. The Party's analysis of the Negro question in the United States underwent another tactical change; the possibility of achieving equality within the context of democratic capitalism was suggested. Benjamin J. Davis, Jr., observed:

> Although the Jim Crow system is still in force in our country it is slowly—too slowly—giving ground to the vast new forces of labor and the people united in the cause of victory. New developments are to be seen in the cracking of the walls of discrimination existing in war industries, in breaking down a limited number of barriers in the armed forces and in other phases of our national life.[9]

Basking in the magic glow of the Teheran agreement, Ford was even more hopeful. He declared that Negroes in the United States had always fought for their freedom. The Civil War had basically changed the Negro-white relationships in this country, and Negroes had indicated a desire to become a part of America as a whole (preface to the repudiation of the self-determination doctrine). Since the Civil War the interests of the Negro people had converged more and more with those of labor and progressive forces. During the course of World War II (after June 21, 1941), a basic change in the position and prospects of American Negroes had begun. Negroes were finding jobs, serving in the armed forces, and participating in an ever-widening political arena. In giving all-out support to the war effort and at the same time struggling for their basic rights, said Ford, Negroes would continue the process of liberation in an unbroken line.[10] No revolution. No self-determination.

The Teheran agreement became the principal orienting factor in the Communist Party program after 1943. It was to be the basis on which all issues—social, economic, and political—might be resolved. Its implications for the Negro question were not to be minimized; the "perspectives" which it provided for Negro-white unity were almost unlimited. Benjamin J. Davis, Jr., who was coming to the fore as the principal Negro in the Party, could thus declare:

The possibility of ending the Jim Crow system, with its related abuses against other minorities, is today greater than ever due to the patriotic war we are fighting and the character of that war as one of national liberation. The alternative to ending Jim Crow is civil strife, Detroits, Harlems, Mobiles, Los Angeles' and violence of a type which will effectively prevent the national unity which is necessary to win the war more speedily and fulfill the perspective opened by the Teheran agreements.

... The movement for the full freedom of Negro Americans is today on the broad highway of victory and Teheran. The job of speeding the movement is one for all Americans, whatever their station in life, capitalist or worker, white or black. [11] *

* A personal experience may further illustrate the point. In early 1944 I was stationed at a small Army air field in south Georgia where I was working in the base personnel section. I was approached one day by a corporal, a truck driver, who wanted to know if it would be possible to secure a transfer to an infantry unit scheduled for overseas shipment. This was an unusual request, for if an Air Corpsman feared anything it was transfer to the infantry, especially a "hot outfit." Anyone voluntarily asking for such a change would have been regarded as a "section eight," a candidate for the "psycho ward." I asked the corporal his reason for requesting the transfer. At first he was reluctant to talk. However, it eventually developed that, "the agreement at Teheran makes it incumbent that I, as a Communist, do everything possible to hasten victory over the Axis." The transfer was made.

It is difficult to establish in detail the correlation between Teheran and the dissolution of the Communist Party of the United States. But the preceding sources suggest that the Party for some time had been aware of this implication of the agreement and the necessity of preparing its Negro members and the Negro public for the step it was to take. In April, 1944, a Party publication prepared by Doxey Wilkerson all but conceded that the organization could best perform its mission among Negroes by merging with other "progressive" forces. He declared further that:

> The pro-Teheran coalition sorely needs the active political collaboration of the Negro people. Unless the Negro people are brought quickly and fully into the democratic national front, the victory of the anti-Teheran forces in the 1944 elections looms as a real threat, indeed imperiling the whole new perspective before the world.[12]

Under these circumstances what specific goals should the Party advance in its Negro work? According to Wilkerson, it should seek to bring about the "unequivocal support by Negroes of the war of national survival and liberation." More pointedly, it should increase its demands for democratic rights for Negroes as an essential condition of a lasting peace. The Party should renew its efforts among Negroes to draw them further into support of the "win-the-war policies of the Administration," particularly during the 1944 elections. Finally, the Party was to build the "unity of the Negro people," who would be firmly aligned with the progressive national front for victory in carrying out the Teheran agreement.[13]

In view of such pronouncements as these, it is not surprising that the Communist Party was convened in May, 1944, for purposes of ostensibly committing suicide, burying itself, and by a process of reincarnation emerging in the form of the Communist Political Association.

The Communist Political Association renounced Communism, at least officially. It was a bewildering spectacle. Revolutionists believed in gradualism, Socialists believed in capitalism, and Marxists believed in Adam Smith. The Lord embraced the Devil, and Lenin toasted Otto Bauer. Browder sang the "Star-Spangled Banner."

Acutually the Communist Political Association program did not differ from the "line" followed by the Party since July, 1941. Communists by fiat declared that they were not Communists, but continued to act in the same way without the stigma of Party membership and the implications associated with it. Browder was elected president of the Association and Ford, Foster, Robert Minor, Benjamin Davis, Jr., Robert Thompson, and Gilbert Green were elected vice-presidents. The party press hailed the "dissolution" of the Party, albeit permitting a few voices of protest to be raised.

But the officials of the Association had some explaining to do. They accordingly took the position that capitalism in the United States was a progressive force. Class antagonisms, which were usually inherent in a profit system, had not developed in the United States. Workers enjoyed political rights and a standard of living that could not be equalled elsewhere in the world. Liberalism in the United States had a long and successful tradition that would serve to steer social change in the right direction. Capitalists had evidenced a willingness to compromise and share power. Consequently, there was no need for class struggle or revolution, but only the continual assertion of the inherent progressive bent of the masses.

In the past, the Association declared, the Communist Party had fought for the advancement of the working class and for the national liberation and equal rights of Negroes. Now these goals were a fact, or had the possibility of becoming a fact under a gradual, slow process of economic and political development. The Communist Party was able to dissolve itself because its earlier aims were now a reality—and therefore ample testimony to the correctness of its theory and the effectiveness of its practical work. And there were dozens of passages in Marx which conclusively proved that the Association was the instrument of the working class.[14]

What were the implications of this general program for the Negro question? How did the Communists now rationalize their agreement with the once despised idea that Negroes could be integrated in the general American society, thus making it unnecessary for them to take part in a revolutionary working-class movement or set up their own black republic? The Association had the answer.

The Party, it maintained, had always been in the forefront of the struggle for Negro rights, but prior to 1928 it had followed an "unsound theoretical line" on the Negro question. When the theory of an oppressed nation and self-determination was advanced, it gave the Party an invaluable tool for its Negro work. But circumstances had changed, and the older theory was no longer applicable, for:

... the abolition of national oppression is a bourgeois-democratic reform; and such reforms are achievable within the framework of capitalism—rarely, it is true, and only under exceptional conditions. But these rare and exceptional conditions are exactly produced by the character of this war of national liberation that embraces the whole of the world when the Negro people pursue the correct course—the "Fred Douglass" course of full support of the war—and when a powerful labor movement takes sides with the oppressed peoples.[15]

The Association proposed to continue its campaign for the full equality of Negroes, concentrating its efforts on breaking down segregation and aligning Negro workers with "progressive" elements of the labor movement. But the theory of self-determination was out.

Browder explained as follows: After the Civil War the Negro people chose the course of integrating themselves in the American social and economic system, but were betrayed by the Republican Party. The Communist Party raised the right of self-determination to counter certain Negro nationalist movements that were "backward looking." Now in the crisis of World War II the answer to the Negro question had become clear. Negro people had found it possible to make a decision once and for all. The decision had been in the making for several years, from the time that the Roosevelt administration began to interest itself in the plight of the Negro people. Developments during the intervening period had further established Negroes as an integral part of the American nation.

The decision of the Negro people is therefore already made. It is that the Negro people do see the opportunity, not as a pious aspiration for an indefinite future, but as an immediate political task under the present system of approximating the position of equal citizens in America. This in itself is an exercise of the right of self-determination by the Negro people. By their attitude the Negro people have exercised their historical right of self-determination.

It is this choice which gives the possibility in this period of integrating the Negro people in the general democracy of our country on the basis of complete and unconditional equality, of solving the question now and no longer postponing it. The immediate achievement in this period, under the present American system of complete equality for the Negroes, has been made possible by the war crisis, and by the character of this war as a people's war of national liberation.

. . . I think that we can say that an approximation of that achievement is within our reach today under Capitalism, under the existing American system, under the changing relationship of forces, in which labor and the people exert an ever increasing political role and influence.[16] *

Thus was the Lenin-sired self-determination brain child of the Sixth World Congress of the Communist International disinherited by the Communist Political Association in 1944. Of course, two years later, the Communists were suddenly to realize (after the postman brought a letter from Mr. Duclos one day) that this "analysis" was "incorrect" and that Browder and Minor had read into a diplomatic document a great deal that was not there.

After June 21, 1941, the Party became as patriotic as the Daughters of the American Revolution and was probably more vociferous than the latter in denouncing "subversive" elements. In particular, it found that certain Negro leaders and organizations were "sabotaging the war effort," "aiding the Axis enemy," and endangering the "unity of the American people." The most "subversive" organization, according to the Party, was the March on Washington Movement; and the most dangerous Negro leader was A. Philip Randolph. The MOWM had been attacked

* Although this was written prior to the formation of the Communist Political Association, it clearly anticipated the shift in program that was to come. That this "analysis" was the rationalization accepted by the CPA later is patent from Minor's acknowledgement of it in *The Heritage of the Communist Political Association*, p. 44.

during the "anti-imperialist war" period on the grounds that it was collaborating with the Administration in the betrayal of the Negro people. After June 21, 1941, it was attacked for *not* collaborating in the war effort, thereby betraying the Negro people. Betrayal in either case.

For example, Ford in 1943 condemned the MOWM for being "too belligerent" in its fight for Negro job rights and the ending of segregation in the armed forces. This organization, he explained, was under the influence of the Socialist Party, and:

... was creating confusion and dangerous moods in the ranks of the Negro people and utilizing their justified grievances as a weapon of opposition to the Administration's war program and was following tactics that would lead to the isolation of the Negro people from their most important allies, the progressive white population and the organized labor movement.[17] *

Ford failed to mention his peculiar objections to the MOWM prior to June, 1941. He also did not indicate that the MOWM was almost solely responsible for the Fair Employment Practices Committee, which the Party in 1943 heartily approved and cited as an indication of the growing strength of Negroes in the United States! Finally, Ford omitted reference to the fact that it was the MOWM which, by again threatening a march to Washington in 1943, saved the FEPC from the axe wielded by War Manpower Commissioner Paul McNutt and forced a new and more effective Executive Order on discrimination. Ford also might have taken cognizance of the fact that a number of the trade unions, especially affiliates of the CIO, supported the MOWM from the outset.

Party spokesmen, however, were not easily swayed from their course by the facts of the case, and during the entire "win-the-war" period the attacks on Randolph and the MOWM con-

---

* It is worth noting that the Party in subsequently reviewing its "revisionist" position of the 1941-1945 period, declared: "We criticised, but seldom led, vigorous struggles against racial discrimination in the armed forces; indeed we characterized as unduly 'nationalistic' certain Negro organizations [March on Washington Movement] that demanded immediate and substantial correction by the Roosevelt Administration." Doxey A. Wilkerson, "Speech on the Draft Resolution of the National Board at the Plenary Meeting of the National Committee, CPA, June 18-20, 1945," (*Communist*, Vol. XXIV, No. 7, July 1945, 621).

tinued.[18] Browder and other Party officials rarely discussed the Negro question without singling out the MOWM for criticism.[19] What was the cause of these attacks by the Party on an organization that sought the same goals that the Party professed to embrace? Although the MOWM proposed to "bargain" with the Administration for Negro support of the war effort, there is no conclusive evidence that its program curtailed the output of war material or marred the effectiveness of the military forces. On the contrary, although it cannot be proved here, it seems highly likely that the MOWM raised the output of guns and planes by forcing the wider use of available Negro manpower; certainly it must have boosted the morale of Negro troops by seeking an end to discrimination in the armed forces. In addition, the FEPC enhanced the moral prestige of the United States in the eyes of colonial peoples. (Indeed, American propagandists made wide use of it).

Nor is there any evidence that the MOWM isolated American Negroes from liberal and labor forces in the United States. For it was largely these groups that assisted the MOWM and later backed the FEPC. Ford's charge will simply not stand up under scrutiny. It is difficult to be convinced that he did not have eyes averted and tongue in cheek when the accusation was made. Perhaps the Party's real quarrel with the MOWM was that it succeeded as the Party never had in rallying Negroes around its program; that it was an organization which the Party could not penetrate or control. Ford, Browder and Wilkerson knew this.

The Party posed the National Negro Congress against the MOWM. Hitler's attack on Russia gave the NNC another lease on life; or perhaps more correctly, it momentarily disinterred its remains. The NNC could now advocate non-discrimination in employment and in the armed services outside the context of an "anti-imperialist war" orientation. It sought to work with other Negro groups at both community and national levels; that the latter were somewhat skeptical of these overtures is not difficult to understand. By a curious bit of logic (indeed, with no logic at all) the Party claimed that the NNC had been the foremost instrument of unity of the Negro people and the most militant organization for Negro job rights in the past.[20]

In a number of local communities the NNC did become closely associated with anti-discrimination committees. It cooperated with those government agencies which sought greater Negro employment and housing in war production centers. However, in conformity with the Party "line," it did not display a militant attitude in the face of continued discrimination in these areas, as the Party itself was later to concede. Its propaganda among Negroes, like that of the Party, tended to emphasize the gains already made rather than new goals to be achieved. The Party wanted Negro manpower reserves to be tapped, certainly, and it was willing for black Americans to kick up some fuss to get their share of the war jobs. However, Communists were not willing to jeopardize "national unity" in the least, and they therefore tried to keep the lid on major unrest. Whenever labor demands or Negro protest threatened to disrupt arms production, the Party functionaries shouted "all out to win the people's war!" This sometimes momentarily endeared them to the reactionary employer, if not to the Negro workers.

In New York City the Party opposed the MOWM by organizing the Labor Victory Committee. While the ostensible purpose of the Committee was to end discrimination against Negroes in war industries and in the armed forces, its main purposes appear to have been to counter the wide support which the MOWM enjoyed, to build enthusiasm for the war among Negro workers, and to create additional pressure on the Administration for the opening of a second front in Europe. Ford hailed the Committee as a great step forward in the unity of the Negro people of New York behind the war effort.[21]

The Southern Negro Youth Congress, which had followed the Party's cue in attempting to array young southern Negroes against aid to the Allies during 1939-1941, again revealed its Communist control by switching to the new line after the German attack on Russia. At its 1942 meeting in Tuskeegee, Alabama, the SNYC refused to indorse the "Double VV" campaign being waged on a wide front by the major Negro newspapers. This movement was designed to bring about "Victory over the Axis abroad" and "Victory over discrimination at home." Party spokesmen, who were in commanding positions, objected that such a campaign was "disruptive." We may presume that the Governor of Alabama was quite pleased.

Although in the past the Party had been criticized by certain reactionary elements as a "Negro party" and as a "race equality" organization, its compromising behavior on the Negro question (as distinguished from its formal program), now led to castigation from other sources, some of which were formerly sympathetic. The December, 1944, issue of the *Negro Digest*, a monthly magazine of the *Reader's Digest* type, contained the results of a public opinion survey on the question, "Have the Communists Quit Fighting for Negro Rights?" [22] * The same issue carried a series of articles representing a debate between several distinguished Negro intellectuals and three spokesmen for the Communist Party.

William L. Patterson, Benjamin J. Davis, Jr., and James Ford defended the Communist position while George Schuyler, the journalist, and Horace R. Cayton, sociologist (*Black Workers and the New Trade Unions, Black Metropolis*), took an opposing view. One can guess what the first three participants had to say. In opposing them, Schuyler said:

The record shows that where and when the Communists seemed to be fighting for Negro rights, their objective was simply to strengthen the hand of Russia. When this was accomplished, they abandoned the fight and turned to something else.

Whereas at one time they were all for stopping production because of Jim Crow employment policies, low pay or bad working conditions, they are now all-out for the Government's policy of no wartime strikes and have actually endorsed labor conscription; i.e., human slavery. Everything must be done to save Russia even if Negro rights have to go by the board. [23]

Cayton, a recognized student of race and radical movements and certainly no "red-baiter," conceded that during certain periods and on specific issues the Communists had fought

---

* It will be noted that this "public opinion poll" carried no information concerning the methodology employed. The size and composition of the sample and the number of persons interviewed was not indicated. Consequently the results which might be interpreted as either favoring or not favoring the Communists were rather meaningless.

courageously for Negro rights, citing their contribution to the Scottsboro, Herndon, and other cases and their organization of the Negro unemployed. But, he maintained:

An increasing number of Negroes are becoming aware of the fact that, although Communists are giving verbal approval to their struggle, they are not supporting it in any organizational fashion. Most damaging to Communist prestige is their failure to formulate any program against Jim Crowism in the armed forces and their tacit acceptance of the Jim Crow practices of the Red Cross. . . .

There is great sympathy for the Communists among large sections of the Negro masses. This, I believe, is partly because of their admiration for Russia—the only great power which has abolished racial prejudice. Also, due to its activity during the depression, the Communist Party in America has become identified in the minds of most Negroes with a militant struggle against discrimination. Only gradually are they beginning to realize the change in tactics which subordinates the Negro's problem to the larger world struggle for power.

In all fairness, however, one should state that those trade unions alleged to be communistically dominated have been fairest to the Negro. But here too one wonders how far Communists will extend their position of compromise to achieve a so-called national unity. Harry Bridges' statement that it might be necessary to retain the no-strike pledge after the war is an indication of how far some groups in the left-wing movement are willing to retreat in order to support the foreign policy of the Soviet Union.[24]

After leaving the National Negro Congress and organizing the MOWM, Philip Randolph continued to be attacked by the Communists. The Party was an annoyance rather than a serious deterrent to the MOWM, which Randolph hoped might become a mass Negro organization in peace time. In outlining the plans for such an organization in 1944 he specified that Communists must be excluded:

It would be eminently unsound and destructive strategy for Negroes to tie up with Communists since the primary and fundamental interest of the Negro and labor are common and the same, but labor has long since recognized the danger of the Communist movement, and thus the A. F. of L. and CIO have condemned and repudiated the Communist Party, its policies, program, tactics, and so forth, and have adopted the policy of throwing Communists out of the unions whenever they are discovered. Hence, Negroes cannot logically and with sound wisdom tie up with a movement such as the Communist which organized labor in America condemns and rejects. The history and record of this political cult shows that it conforms with rigid fidelity to the rapidly changing, unpredictable climate of Soviet Russia, without regard to the national interests of any other group. When the war broke, the Communists who had posed as the savior of the Negro promptly dropped him like a hot potato. This was not the first time the Communists deserted the Negro.[25]

Such criticism of the Party as that voiced by Schuyler, Cayton, and Randolph reflected the failure of the Communists to make headway with their new Negro program. It is, of course, highly questionable whether they were anxious to advance any portions of it other than the "win-the-war" angle. This skepticism and mistrust of the Party was not confined to the sophisticated Negro intellectuals; it reached down into the popular attitude. Another source of criticism for the Communists came from the far left. The "Trotskyites" over a period of years had developed a special concern with the Negro question. One of their weekly publications, *The Militant*, maintained a regular department in which attempts were made to analyze various aspects of the race problem in terms of the left-wing program. In reviewing the shift in the Communist Party "line" after June, 1941, *The Militant* declared:

Many people have not understood how completely the Communist Party has deserted the struggle for equality for the Negro people since it came out wholeheartedly for support of the war last June. One of the chief reasons why their betrayal has been obscured has been the fact that they continue to devote a good deal of their literature to the Negro question.

But an analysis of their literature shows although they still write about the Negroes and address their appeals to them, the nature of their propaganda has changed completely. Instead of calling on the Negroes to fight for their rights in war time as well as in peace, 98 per cent of their message is concerned with explaining to the Negroes why they must join the poll-tax democrats and lily-white Republicans in support of the war.[26]

Whatever may have been the political orientation of the writer, the charge had more than a grain of truth, as even a cursory examination of the *Daily Worker*, the *Communist* and the various books and pamphlets published by the Communist Party during this period will verify in detail.

As if to confirm the above and similar charges that the Communists dropped the struggle for Negro rights during the war period, a high Party official later asserted: "A critical examination of Communist practice during the recent period [July, 1941—June, 1945] can but reveal a striking gap between ideological profession and actual performance." [27]

In summary, it may be said that while the Party attempted to build its organization among Negroes under the more favorable conditions prevailing after the German attack on Russia, it made only small headway. New recruits came in slowly, and those who had jumped off the train in September, 1939, were reluctant to climb back on in June of 1941, though the locomotive was now headed in the old direction. Organization drives were conducted among Negroes, especially in 1943, and one Party spokesman declared that "almost 5,000" Negroes joined the Party in the spring of that year.[28] One must regard these figures with extreme skepticism. They do not distinguish between new members and former members renewing their affiliation. In addition, they in all probability were considerably exaggerated for purposes of creating a "band wagon" effect for the membership drive. If they are presumed to be accurate, it would mean that the Party almost doubled its active Negro membership within a three-months period, which seems highly unlikely.

In March of 1945 the Communist Political Association viewed the future hopefully. The war was drawing to a successful conclusion; the Soviet Union had been saved. The program of the Association could be carried out in a gradual, even leisurely, fashion. But in France a paunchy, bald-headed little man with chubby hands and horn-rimmed glasses was writing a letter. His name was Jacques Duclos, and the letter was titled, "On the Dissolution of the Communist Party of the United States."

# VII

# "AMERICAN NEGROES! STOP WALL STREET IMPERIALISM!" 1945–1950

THE Duclos letter appeared in the April, 1945, issue of the *Cahiers Du Communisme,* the theoretical organ of the Communist Party of France. However, it was more than a letter; it was an order to Communists in the United States to reconstitute the Party and adopt a "line" more in keeping with the "new world situation." It was not just another instance of "self-criticism" among Communists. Duclos was second only to Thorez in the hierarchy of the French Communist Party; he had been an important cog in the machinery of the Third International. In this instance he was functioning in behalf of the Politburo, voicing its demand that American Communists now change their line in response to another "new situation."

In his "letter" Duclos presented a lengthy review of events leading to the dissolution of the Party in 1944 and the subsequent organization of the Communist Political Association. He charged that under Browder's leadership the Party had relinquished its function as the only independent spokesman of the American working class. The American Party, he maintained, had completely abandoned the Marxist theory of class conflict, substituting the mild reformism of the social-democrats. In making the Teheran agreement an instrument of political analysis, the Party had transformed a "diplomatic document" into a basic theoretical principle. As a consequence the Party played into the hands of the bourgeoisie and the monopoly business interests.

Duclos offered no explanation for the delay in calling these "errors" to the attention of American Communists, although a year had elapsed since the dissolution of the Party. He quoted from a letter which Foster had presumably written in 1944, in which the latter protested the action of the Party in disbanding itself and establishing the Communist Political Association. The Foster letter, however, apparently was known only to its alleged author and Duclos. If Foster was in disagreement with the course pursued by American Communists in 1944, his actions belied this. He made no public criticism, and he was elected and served as vice-president of the CPA during the entire period.

It is of no great importance whether or not Foster wrote such a letter. Authentic or fabricated, it served a real purpose for Duclos, the Politburo—and Foster. First, it suggested that an important American Communist and, presumably, a number of his followers were in disagreement with the action taken in 1944; this implied that rank and file Communists had been misled by Browder's high-handed methods. Second, it served as a means of indicating the new "line" which the American Communists should follow: the course suggested by Foster at the time he reportedly disagreed. Third, it was a technique for indicating that Foster, because of his "superior understanding" and steadfast adherence to "Marxist" theory, was the logical person around whom opposition to "Browderism" and "tailism" ought to center.

Shortly after the Duclos letter appeared in the *Cahiers Du Communisme* it was translated and reprinted in full in the *Daily Worker*.[1] Immediately thereafter the National Board of the Communist Political Association was convened for an emergency session and on June 2 adopted a resolution admitting its mistakes and calling for a review of its program since mid-1941, in light of the "friendly criticism" by "Comrade Duclos." The confession ran as follows:

While concentrating on our main wartime objectives, namely, that of subordinating everything to win the war, to smash Nazi Germany and militarist Japan, these mistakes were abetted by an over-simplified and one-sided approach. These errors were facilitated by non-labor bourgeois influences which unconsciously affected some of our policies as we participated and functioned ever more actively in the broad camp of national unity. And these opportunist deviations were accentuated by our reluctance to constantly analyze and re-examine our policies and mass work in the spirit of Marxist self-criticism especially the failure to draw our membership into the discussion and determination of basic policy.[2]

The "debate" on the Duclos letter began on June 4 and continued in a special section of the *Daily Worker* for a period of some two months. It would be questionable to construe what took place as a debate. The articles and letters for the most part were confessions reminiscent of the testimony of defendants at the Moscow trials. Prominent Communists who during the preceding month had fully praised the CPA and its "gradualist" program now attempted to outdo each other in beating their chests and admitting their "errors." According to their own testimony, they had been opportunists, "misleaders," "anti-Marxists," and "reformists." Browder, who chose to defend his course (indeed, he had no other choice), became the tempting serpent who had seduced the Stalinist virgins, and the whipping boy for those who required some evil influence to explain their past conduct.

But let the Communists speak for themselves on that aspect of their program which is relevant here, the Negro question. Confessed James W. Ford:

I share fully in the responsibility for the opportunistic line which has led our organization into the swamp of revisionism. . . . Because of my long standing in the leadership of our organization, I cannot and do not want to shirk my responsibility.

What are the sources of my error? I had a fear of factionalism. For a long number of years we have been warned against factionalism in the Communist movement. And I know what disastrous consequences factionalism would cause in all or any phases of work of the Communist movement, especially Negro work.

*My error here is grave, especially in regard to what I did to create illusions in my individual capacities, among the Negro people of expectation of democratic rights gratis from Roosevelt and the Democratic Party.* Closely connected with this *was the illusion I had that the bourgeoisie would industrialize the South and itself open up the path of bourgeois-democratic development.*[3]

Ford was a vice-president of the CPA and organizer of the Negro Labor Victory Committee.

Admitted Edna Lewis of the East Harlem Club of the CPA:

Our Negro comrades in the National Committee (of the CPA) share in the responsibility for the errors. Negro Communists have a special responsibility to the Negro people. Our knowledge of their suffering should have kept us on guard against accepting a program of compromise to last for many generations as proposed by Earl Browder.[4]

Said CPA journalist George Lohr:

Our revisionist estimation of the changed relationship of class forces in our country has also inevitably led us into some gross misconceptions regarding the integration of the Negro people into American life. *As a result we committed many tactical errors, which in my opinion, hampered the struggle for the rights of Negro people. On this front too we had become smug and complacent.*[5]

Declared H. V. Saunders:

By our revisionism of Marxism as it pertains to the national question, we weakened the whole struggle for the emancipation of the Negro people. . . . We cannot overcome the mistakes we made if we fail to examine every facet of our past policies—including the national question.[6]

Lamented Alice Burke of Richmond, Virginia, who for a number of years was active in the Communist Party (and later in the CPA) in the South:

We liquidated that force which led such tremendous struggles for democratization of the South and *more specifically struggles for rights of the nine millon Negro Americans.*
*Confused, disarmed by the "new historical period" we entered into a dream world of higher wages, rising standards of living, equal rights for the Negro people, and the prospect of eventual socialism without a struggle.*[7]

Statements of the type quoted above were not limited to the Negro question. Every aspect of the CPA program was treated in much the same manner in the course of the "debate" during June and July, 1945.[8]

Following the "debate" the Communist Political Association

called an emergency convention in late July, 1945, and promptly reconstituted itself as the Communist Party of the United States.[9] The resolution on the Negro question adopted by the Party emphasized the collective guilt of Communists in their failure to struggle for Negro rights during the war period, referring specifically to their neglect of Negro interests in employment, the armed forces, and the Red Cross blood bank. The resolution declared further:

The opportunist errors of our former general policy limited the effectiveness of Communist work on the Negro question. This was especially expressed in our glossing over the national character of the Negro question, [prelude to a return to the self-determination doctrine] and in our unwarranted illusion that the big bourgeois themselves would carry forward after V-E Day the wartime gains of the Negro people. ... The struggle for the national liberation of the Negro people as fundamentally related to the working class against capitalist exploitation and oppression was lost sight of.[10]

It is interesting to note that nowhere in the "debate" or in the proceedings of the emergency convention, or in the resolutions adopted, was there a suggestion by anyone that the "line" followed by Communists in the United States during the war period and the altered "line" precipitated by the Duclos letter afterward were the result of the changing needs of Soviet foreign policy.

In the Party discussion of the Negro question during the reconversion period, Thelma Dale pointed out that Negroes were not holding the gains in employment made during the war. One reason, she maintained, was that the Party (and the CPA) had not displayed sufficient foresight in planning for the job security of Negro workers. "In the win-the-war camp," she explained,

a false illusion existed that Negroes would *automatically* win their rights through all-out support of the war effort. Even the Communists, as part of the revisionist policies, to an extent were affected by this illusion which resulted at times in soft-pedaling of the fight against the inferior status of Negroes in the armed forces. Our politically phlegmatic position on the fight for equality within the armed forces became so untenable that even before the Duclos article we had been forced to re-evaluate and adjust our position.[11]

A more detailed but similar interpretation had been offered earlier by Doxey Wilkerson. He admitted, "It was inevitable that our over-all revisionist policy would weaken all specialized aspects of work—and this has unquestionably been true of our recent strategy and tactics on the Negro question." After Pearl Harbor, he maintained, the Communists began to soft pedal the issue of Negro rights, but this "lapse" was only temporary and the Party later insisted on a no-compromise position. However, in subsequent paragraphs he declared that the Party had taken few steps to insure Negroes' keeping their war-time gains. The Party, he charged, had failed to throw its full weight behind the drive to eliminate segregated blood banks in the Red Cross. It had failed to support the demand for Negro-white fighting units. It failed to fight for equality in the armed forces. It liquidated its own organizations in the South and preached reliance on the southern bourgeoisie. Finally, it had failed to develop a strong "corps of Negro cadres" in the industrial centers of the North. The result had been a loss of confidence in the Party among the Negro people, a sharp decline in Negro membership.[12]

If the liberal needed confirmation of his growing suspicion that the Party's approach to the American Negro question was largely opportunistic and manipulative, he had it now from the horse's mouth. For the Communists by their own admission had been quick to drop the cause of the colored American when the overriding war-time needs of the Soviet Union beckoned.

One final item on this point should be included. The Communists who confessed their errors and attempted to exorcise the damned spot of revisionism placed much of the blame for their sins on Browder. However, if Browder's contention is correct, the Party had given up the fight on Negro rights while he was still imprisoned in Atlanta under the passport fraud conviction. In defending his war-time policy, Browder declared:

When I returned from Atlanta in May, 1942 I found our main approach to the war problems correct but with two serious distortions. One was the idea that the struggle for Negro rights must be postponed until after the war; this had seriously undermined our relations with the whole Negro community. The second distortion was a similar attitude toward the colonial liberation movement and specifically toward

Puerto Rico. I secured the agreement of our leadership to the public corrections of these distortions in my first public speech in Madison Square Garden on July 2, 1942. But it took more than two years to dissolve this wrong attitude. . . .[13]

If this were the case, then the Party had dropped its fight for Negro rights within a relatively short period after the German attack on Russia and apparently without any prodding from Browder. The shift in the "line" after June 21, 1941, as summarized in the preceding chapter, would lend real substance to Browder's charge. But it also should be emphasized that Browder in practice agreed that the struggle for Negro rights should be postponed until after the war. Further, it should be noted that the above-quoted charge was made at a time when Browder thought he was fighting for control of the Party and his political life. He was defending his policies by suggesting that his critics were the first and biggest "revisionists."

The attack on Browder following the Duclos letter was as unscrupulous and as vicious as any he had visited upon his opponents, within the Party and without, during the fifteen years he had served as General Secretary and chief engineer of the Kremlin apparatus in the United States. It should not have surprised him too much to find himself the victim of the same brand of slander, abuse and recrimination of which he had become a pastmaster. But he had become used to being shown the same kind of adulation and deference in the United States (on a miniature and comic-opera scale) as was bestowed upon Stalin by the Communists in the U.S.S.R. While he had not been credited with discovery of the fundamental laws of genetics or the invention of the telephone, he had been accorded the recognition due the great leader. His every birthday had been the occasion of a mass meeting in New York and celebrations in the countryside. His every speech was quoted and requoted to establish the "correctness" of Party actions. His every article was published and republished in the Party journals. No Party functionary felt that a speech, an article or a resolution was complete unless the supporting word of the General Secretary was invoked.

No Party bureaucrat and no sub-dictator relinquishes power willingly—or gracefully. Browder was no exception. Although his long experience in Party machinations should have prepared him, he was unable to grasp the full significance of the Duclos letter; even if he had seen immediately its implications, it is questionable whether he could have saved himself from the wrath of the Kremlin or quickly adopted the necessary protective coloration. The same men who had called Browder the "leader of the oppressed," and the "heroic leader of the people," now called him a "revisionist" (and there is no more deathly accusation in the dictionary of Party epithets), a "collaborator of Wall Street," and "a stooge for the American imperialists." The same men who had applauded his "magnificent leadership" now condemned him for leading them into the "swamp of revisionism." They even forgot his birthdays.

Browder did not know, or refused to believe, that he was ticketed for oblivion from the time the Duclos letter was published. For when the old era ended, its symbols had to be replaced. At some future date, if there is a need for a "reformist-oriented" Communist Party in the United States, then "Browder the Renegade" may be dusted off and restored to the ranks of the faithful as "Browder the Comrade."

The Communist Party of the United States was "reconstituted" in late July, 1945. Browder was expelled, and leadership passed into the hands of Foster, Dennis, Benjamin Davis, Henry Winston, Robert Thompson and John Williamson. Although Ford had duly recanted during the course of the "debate" his identity with Browder and the "revisionist" line had been too close; he was relegated to a back seat in the post-war model of the Party machine. All top leaders in the Party, however, had participated without protest in the war-time strategy; all had been identified with the Communist Political Association during its brief existence. Their outstanding qualification in this instance was their ability to shift politically and ideologically in acceptance of a "line" that was the antithesis of that followed during the preceding four-year period.

The "line" of the Party during the post-war period was determined by "changing forces in the world situation." The Allied coalition which had defeated Germany, Italy and Japan was breaking up. The United States, Britain and France were beginning to question out loud the foreign policies of the U.S.S.R. Consequently, they were no longer "peace-loving, democratic" powers fighting in a common cause against fascism. They were now, according to the Politburo, imperialist nations bent on the enslavement of the world under a profits system and the destruction of the U.S.S.R., the socialist Fatherland.[14] This development is the key to an understanding of the Duclos letter, the "debate," the "reconstitution" of the Party and the new "line" it adopted. Thus *Political Affairs,* the official theoretical organ of the Party, declared in early 1946:

But the end of the war revealed that, while common interests exist between the Soviet Union and the peoples of Britain and the United States, as well as the entire world, there were fundamental differences between the outlook and aims of Anglo-American imperialism and the Socialist Soviet Union. It revealed that the deep-seated designs of monopoly capitalism were a threat to peace and the freedom of nations and peoples. It was bound to reveal that the Soviet Union now, as before and during the war, is the only great power which is a consistent fighter for the utter destruction of fascism, for peace, and for the freedom of nations.

The end of the war has revealed that Anglo-American finance capitalism is attempting to return to the old, to wipe out the progress made during the war in the direction of democracy and national freedom, of the unfettering of the forces of the people. It is attempting to prevent the strengthening of the newly emergent peoples' democracies, to restore and reinforce imperialist domination over the lands which had temporarily come under the control of German-Japanese fascism; to perpetuate the super-exploitation of colonial and semi-colonial peoples; and to rebuild the old *place d'armes* against the Soviet Union. It is, in short, taking advantage of its military and economic might to assert its will to world domination.[15]

Had the possibility existed that the western nations would condone Soviet expansion in eastern Europe, the Middle East and China, the Communist Parties in the Allied countries would have reacted quite differently. The American Party's theory and program on the Negro question in the United States might have been different. Browder would have remained in the driver's seat, and Ford would have been sitting beside him.

What view of the Negro question in the United States did the new "line" require the Party to take in the post-war period? One Party spokesman declared:

The political attacks that are being directed against the Negro people by Big Business have once again placed serious questions before the American working class.

These attacks reminiscent of post-World War I, are all the more serious because today the main danger of fascism to the world comes from the most colossal imperialist forces which are concentrated within the United States. The perpetrators of these attacks are representatives of the most reactionary section of monopoly capital and of the semifeudal economy of the Black Belt. This hook-up, expressed in Congress by the reactionary Republicans and the poll-taxers who draw their power from the oppression of the Negro people and the working class, makes it obvious that the two main forces for democracy are the working class allied with the Negro people.[16]

Another asserted:

The menace of this attack [by American imperialism] is expressed quite clearly in the drive to strip the Negro worker of the skills and discipline of industry; to split the working class by robbing the white workers of a basic Negro working-class ally. It is an attack which if not stopped, can lead to the smashing of the unions and the alliance of Negro and white labor, and thus retard the development of a democratic people's coalition, a third party movement.[17]

Negroes found their job opportunities and civil rights to be in great danger, and they were fighting to hold on to their recent gains.

In every community the Negro people are on the move, beginning to fight and solidify their ranks. Especially in the South the Negro people are playing a vital role. It is our task to further this struggle, to help strengthen the inner unity of the Negro people, and on the basis of a fighting people's program to strengthen the Negro-labor alliance. Labor as a whole must support the struggle of the Negro people; for it is an integral part of the struggle of the entire working class against the offensive of monopoly.[18]

The role the Party assigned to American Negroes during the immediate post-war period, then, was clear. They must stand with the left-wing labor movement in opposition to American imperialism both at home and abroad. But what tactical problems did this pose for the Party, and what specific issues would be the basis for its Negro work? The Party was to concentrate its efforts in the trade union field and develop support for fair employment practice legislation, elimination of discriminatory practices in the trade unions, and equitable training and rehiring programs. More specifically, it was to:

1. Oppose the effort to lay off Negroes in disproportionate numbers in each plant and industry.

2. Modify the seniority provisions of labor-management contracts so that their application to Negroes would be more "flexible."

3. Oppose the downgrading of Negro workers in plants where reconversion required the transfer of large blocks of workers.

4. Demand that an equal proportion of Negroes be hired in the expansion of old, or the opening of new, plants.

5. Demand the equitable retraining of Negroes in those plants where reconversion demanded different skills.

6. Eliminate Jim Crow practices from such unions as the Boilermakers and Machinists.

7. Insist that government agencies such as the United States Employment Service cease the arbitrary refusal to list Negroes in their proper job ratings.

8. Emphasize the hiring of Negro veterans and their inclusion in in-plant training programs.

9. Exert pressure "throughout the labor movement for a permanent F.E.P.C." [19]

In the South the Party was to support a series of drastic agricultural reform measures around which the "immediate struggle" would center. They included:

1. Abolition of the sharecropping system and "its economic and legal supports."

2. Reduction of land rents; Federal aid to small farmers in purchasing land and in establishing cooperatives.

3. Removal of "semi-feudal prescriptions for a living wage" and the extension of the Wages and Hours Law and Federal Unemployment Insurance to cover agricultural workers.

4. A vast program of public works, including the construction of dams, highways, schools, hospitals and irrigation systems.

5. Abolition of the Jim Crow caste system and the establishment of full equality for Negroes in all spheres.[20]

But these specific programs were to be developed by the Party within the context of the revived Negro nation and self-determination doctrine. For example, though the Party would attempt to organize Negroes and whites in the same units around the new agenda:

... under no circumstances should this objective be made a condition for the actual organization of the people. Experience, as in the case of the sharecroppers union in the Alabama Black Belt, shows that as a result of terroristic national oppression the Negroes may desire their own separate organization. This, in some cases, may be necessary as a stage toward joint organization.[21] *

In the South the struggle of Negroes for "national liberation" was to be joined with the struggle of white workers in the industrial centers; both in turn were to be geared to the larger fight of the entire American working class against "Big Business" and Wall Street "imperialism."

The carrying out of this program, in terms of our immediate tasks, means the orientation of the Party, organized labor and the National Negro Congress to the South. *It means all-out support politically, as well as concrete and practical aid, to the development of the struggle of the Negro Black population for land and national freedom. It means a final and decisive break with the Browder revisionist negation of the revolutionary, anti-imperialist role of the Negro people.*

The vast potential of the Negro Americans for anti-fascist democratic struggle has not been really tapped. Their full resources can be brought to bear in the cause of labor and American democracy only to the extent that white American labor understands and uncompromisingly supports their full and just demands. It is the job of militant labor and

---

* To one familiar with the ideology of the southern white conservatives the Communist contention that "Negroes may desire their own separate organization," sounds much like the former's argument that "Colored people like to be by themselves." But the white conservative has a morbid fear that Negroes don't want to be by themselves" and supports legal (and frequently illegal) measures to "keep them in their place."

the Communists to break down all barriers to the full unleashing of the struggle for Negro liberation.

It is their job to destroy the tank traps, set by the imperialist rulers and their wily agents, which block the bringing up of these strategic reserves of democracy and socialism. It is incumbent upon organized labor and, above all, its Communist vanguard, to knock from the hands of the enemy its secret weapon—the unsolved Negro question—and thus lay bare the Achilles heel of American imperialism.[22]

Condensed, all this meant that the Negro worker was again to be posed against the major trends of American foreign policy, that he was to be used in furthering the current interest of the U.S.S.R.

The Communist Party also gave considerable attention to Negro veterans during the post-war period, demanding that they be accorded equal treatment in the administration of the various laws affecting former servicemen, and that equal opportunities be provided for education and employment. Communists were to be instrumental in the organization of the United Negro and Allied Veterans of America.

Concerning Negro veterans the Party declared:

The Negro serviceman played a part in the war against fascism comparable only to his contribution to the cause of democracy and social progress in the American Civil War. As was the case after the Civil War, the record of the Negro people and in particular the Negro soldier in this war constitute a solid basis for a new upsurge and new sweeping gains in the struggle for Negro rights. Highly aware of this, monopoly capital, especially its spokesmen and slaveowner-minded allies of the South, are attempting to belittle and slander the role of Negro servicemen. Organized labor, and in the first place our Party, as a foremost democratic task, must undertake the responsibility of refuting all slanders regarding the war role of the Negro soldier and must bring to all sections of the American people a true understanding of that role.[23]

The Party proposed to push the expansion of the G. I. laws so that Negroes, along with other veterans, would derive increased benefits.[24]

While the Party developed specialized organizations for Negro industrial workers, sharecroppers, and veterans, it sought also to enlist the support of all strata of the Negro community for its foreign policy program. The NAACP, and other groups were regarded as potential allies of the Party in its fight against the international activities of the Truman administration.[25] In an effort to secure the support of these varied groups the Party made frequent overtures, buttered with warm praise. After the conflict between Russia and the United States waxed more sharp, the Party tended to become more adamant in its criticism of American policies. This tended further to antagonize many Negro organizations, which, though they often found fault with things American, were unable to stomach the Party line. And in time the Party turned upon them again, as in the days of old.

The new line on the Negro question was also characterized by a revival of the self-determination doctrine. Following the re-organizing convention of July, 1945, the Party established a special Negro Commission, whose purpose was to conduct an exhaustive study of the Negro question and prepare a basic "theoretical" line, as well as a more specific program of action.[26] It was apparent that the disagreement among members of the Commission was appreciable on only one important question: self-determination for Negroes in the Black Belt. The matter was "debated" by members of the Commission in the *Daily Worker* and in *Political Affairs*. The result, which could have been anticipated from the outset, was that the Party adopted the self-determination doctrine as a part of its official program.[27]

During the course of the "debate" within the Commission, only Doxey Wilkerson and Francis Franklin took a firm stand against the self-determination doctrine. Wilkerson's arguments are worth summarizing, for in rejecting them the Party bureaucracy revealed again quite clearly its inability to scrutinize the facts of Negro life in the United States. Wilkerson maintained, in the first place, that in the absence of further data it was presumptuous to attempt to formulate a basic "theoretical" approach in the self-determination context. Then he argued:

1. The Negro people had taken on the characteristics of a nation only in a very elementary form.

2. Marxist theory recognized that the problem of each na-

tion might call for a unique solution, and this did not imply some form of independent statehood as a necessary means to the exercise of the right of self-determination.

3. The prospects were that American Negroes would not disintegrate as a people or progress toward statehood but would develop further as a national minority and as "a distinct and increasingly self-conscious community of Negro Americans."

4. The overwhelming majority of the Negro people abhorred and rejected all proposals that separated them from the American nation as a whole.

5. The trend of the Negro people was toward a more intense (and successful) struggle against the special forms of discrimination to which they are subject.

6. A "correct Marxist approach" to the Negro question should contribute toward the maximum unity of the Negro people, and this the self-determination doctrine failed to do.

7. A correct approach to the Negro question should contribute to the maximum unity of the white and Negro masses in both the North and the South; the self-determination program tended to split them along racial lines.[28]

Wilkerson was attacked by James S. Allen, who charged that the former's position:

... confuses the basic theoretical principles of Marxism in relation to the national question, and therefore, also fails to supply the necessary tactical positions and programs of action required in the present situation.[29]

It is not necessary here to review the numerous articles which appeared in support of the self-determination doctrine. All were similar in form and content. Each echoed the analysis initially promulgated at the Sixth World Congress of the Communist International in 1928, which was discussed in Chapter III. Each followed the thesis that Allen had developed in his book, *The Negro Question in the United States,* in 1936. Each made continued reference to Stalin's definition of a nation and declared that it was applicable to Negroes in the United States. Each was liberally sprinkled with quotations from Lenin on the national and colonial question. Each insisted that it was not the doctrine that was at fault but the failure of Party members to understand it and apply it in their "day-to-day tasks." [30] The decisive factor in the Party's adoption of the self-determination theory appears to have been the fact that it was supported by the top bureaucrats, who had taken their cues from the Duclos letter.

Those who supported the self-determination analysis of the Negro question were aware that in preceding periods it had brought the Party little more than confusion from within and criticism from without. They were therefore very careful to specify the conditions under which the "slogan" was to be advanced. Benjamin Davis, for example, cautioned the Party to "avoid presenting the slogan [self-determination] in any manner whatsoever that creates the impression that self-determination would necessarily lead to the creation of a separate Negro Republic." He also insisted, "Our advocacy of the slogan must correspond more closely to the general stage of national development which the young Negro nation has attained." Further, "The adoption of this slogan in no way interferes with, but strengthens, the effectiveness of the fight for the basic policy of our Party on the current issues. . . ." [31]

During the post-war period the Communist Party has said little about self-determination in its mass propaganda work among Negroes. Its concern with immediate issues—the Progressive Party, a "United Front" against the "Wall Street Drive for War," and, more recently, survival as a legal Party—has made for a lack of emphasis on this long-range goal. However, within the Party itself an effort is being made to promote an acceptance, if not an understanding, of this "basic theoretical tool." For example, a publication of the National Educational Department of the Communist Party, which is used as a standard guide in intra-Party education, declares:

... Negroes are exploited and oppressed *as a people*. Discrimination and denial of rights and opportunities affect the Negro people *as a whole, including all classes*. Thus, the Negro question is not merely a class question; neither is it a national group question in the ordinary sense.

The Negro question in the United States is fundamentally a national question. In the Second Course of this series, [which is not yet available] we will show that the Negro people in the Black Belt constitute an oppressed nation which is fighting for the right to determine its own destiny.[32]

It is hardly likely that the Party will place any great emphasis on the self-determination theory outside Party circles in the near future. It must not permit such a doctrine to hamper its approach to Negroes on more immediate issues. If the Party should drop its effort to infiltrate moderate Negro organizations and embark on a program of dual organization in the race minority field, then the self-determination theory might receive wider emphasis. The Communists, however, will follow the latter course only as a last resort for it could only mean further isolation from Negroes and the labor movement, and their effectiveness as an advocate of the U.S.S.R. would be lessened.

Another feature of the post-war Communist Party program has been a renewed emphasis on eliminating race prejudice from within the organization itself. While Communists have prided themselves on the equalitarian character of their Party since its inception, they have frequently acknowledged that "white chauvinism" rears its ugly head even in the proletarian vanguard. During the period from 1919 to 1935 the Party carried on a vigorous campaign against this capitalist-inspired evil. However, after that time it hesitated to invoke drastic disciplinary measures against members found guilty of discrimination.

When the Party set out to rebuild its membership in late 1945, it apparently did not carefully screen applicants on the basis of racial attitudes. As a consequence, many of the new white members did not really accept the Party position on race questions. So extensive was the practice of intra-Party discrimination that it involved even long-time Party members and a number of highly placed functionaries.

The Party in 1947 declared that white chauvinism "is a system of ideas based upon the theory of 'white superiority.' It is used as an instrument of national oppression. In this country it is directed primarily against the Negro people." [33] It was an instrument employed by American imperialism to prevent the unity of Negro and white workers and thus split the trade union movement and "progressive forces." And, warned the Party,

Communists are also subject to the pressure of chauvinist ideas which capitalism pumps into the very atmosphere. Consequently all Party members must be constantly on guard against all open or hidden forms or expressions of white chauvinism in order to stamp them out wherever or whenever they manifest themselves. Some of the most important forms of white chauvinism to be found in sections of the Party are: failure to mobilize Party organizations or members to fight on issues of direct concern to the Negro people; lack of sensitivity to, or enthusiasm for such struggle; failure to promote Negro members to responsible posts; failure to train and prepare them for such posts; failure to develop personal friendships and relationships with Negro workers and comrades.[34]

These were serious admissions indeed from an organization which welcomed the characterization, "the recognized spokesman of the Negro masses." That the discriminatory practices indicated were widely prevalent within Party ranks is evident from the fact that they were openly acknowledged and made the subject of detailed discussion in the Party's educational program. The campaign against intra-Party prejudice, which was launched in 1946, however, did not produce the desired results. And in 1949 it became necessary for the Communists to take steps more drastic than "ideological work."

Such instances as the following are indicative of the prejudice of Party members (and leaders) against Negroes:

1. In one New York county forty-six members of the Party, including the local Chairman, signed leases containing restrictive covenant clauses.

2. In another New York county a whole group of Negro members were removed from leadership on the basis of a general allegation that they were "petty bourgeois elements."

3. In one Party unit white members "holding leading positions in the clubs were not on speaking terms with most of the Negro comrades because the latter had criticized them for white chauvinism."

4. In another instance, in which newspapers reported a case of rape, "white women in the Party began to develop the idea that they should ask for police 'protection' in a manner that fed the usual anti-Negro libels of the white ruling class."

5. In one Party unit in New Jersey a Negro woman who refused to re-register in the Party was threatened with the loss of her job by the local chairman.

6. In one of the southern districts the Party's "outstanding Negro trade unionist" was "energetically" removed from leadership for a slight breach of Party discipline, while similar breaches by white members were ignored.

7. In another district, when the Party's State Educational Director, a Negro, arrived at headquarters to teach a class, "he discovered that there were two classes—one for whites and the other for Negroes." [35]

But the most widespread form of race prejudice was "resistance by Party forces in the trade unions to waging an adequate struggle on behalf of Negro workers."

The interesting fact in this connection is that the most decisive battles for Negro rights being waged by the progressive forces in the trade-union movement are to be found in local unions which belong to the Right-led Internationals.[36]

Many white Party members had refused to "correct" their discriminatory behavior even when it was called to their attention. They attempted to rationalize their positions with such statements as, "You are trying to undermine the leadership and prestige of these comrades"; "Negroes are too sensitive about prejudice"; and "I know that I am chauvinistic. But all white people are chauvinistic and we will have chauvinism as long as we have capitalism." [37]

What were the causes of this resurgence of race prejudice within the Party? Party spokesmen were in general agreement in their explanation, as follows:

1. The imperialist offensive of big business had poisoned "the very atmosphere of the country," and Party members had breathed it.

2. The Party had extricated itself from the "swamp of opportunism" into which Browder had led it, but ". . . all of the necessary ideological and organizational steps were not taken to implement this [new] correct theoretical position" and enable

Communists "to develop an energetic ideological and political struggle against white chauvinism."

3. The membership of the Party was "virtually new" and had not been educated by the Party's previous campaigns to stamp out race prejudice within its ranks.

4. The labor movement, largely dominated by pro-imperialist "mis-leaders," had aided and abetted discrimination within the trade union movement and "poisoned" the minds of the white workers.

5. The Party had failed to apply correctly the self-determination doctrine and the theory of the Negro nation. Members had been misled by the "petty bourgeois" concept of "equal treatment." [38]

In combating race prejudice within their Party the Communists proposed "to conduct the ideological and political struggle against white chauvinism as already indicated; and to develop, in a consistent fashion, as an ever-present and unrelaxing feature of our work, the day-to-day struggles for the rights of the Negro people." More specifically, they were to intensify their educational work within the Party itself, emphasizing the "theoretical line" on the Negro question and requiring that all Party members, especially the leaders, "devote themselves to basic reading and study of the question." In addition, local Party units were to "intensify" the training of Negro leaders, promote "large numbers" of Negroes to responsible posts, and make special efforts to recruit Negro women. Cases of discrimination were to be thoroughly aired at local unit meetings, and where necessary, disciplinary action was to be taken.[39]

It is significant that the Party did not propose the expulsion of prejudiced white members. A number of disciplinary measures have been employed but these have taken the form of reprimands, temporary suspensions and "probation" followed by a period of "control work." In only a few cases have the practitioners of "white chauvinism" been expelled from the organization. "Educational" and "ideological" methods have been the principal ones employed by the Party during the post-war period.

There are good reasons for this. The Party believes that expulsion will permanently alienate many prejudiced whites. It realizes that prejudice is so prevalent that drastic measures might decimate the already dwindling Party membership. It believes that through education and milder forms of discipline, it will be able to instill "correct" attitudes. On the other hand, it is increasingly difficult for the Party to pose as the "champion fighter for Negro rights" when internal race prejudice "is a very material body of practices carried out by real people, and of ideas held by real people." [40]

The Party is now engaged in one of the most intensive efforts to reach Negro Americans in its thirty-year career. To build successfully the "anti-imperialist front" it must "win the Negro people." This is not an easy task, particularly in view of the Communist role in the 1939-1941 and the 1941-1945 periods. It is further handicapped by the growth of race prejudice within its own ranks, news of which gets about. (Indeed, the Party publishes its self-flagellations on this score.) As one Communist spokesman put it,

Many of our Negro comrades are not recruiting Negro workers into the Party because they are ashamed of the chauvinistic practices that exist in their clubs or sections. And many Negro workers refuse to join our Party because they do not see it waging a sufficiently sharp and sustained struggle on behalf of the Negro people. [41]

But "reaching" Negroes does not necessarily mean recruiting them for Party membership; and the Party is not likely to concentrate its efforts in this sphere. Its present "boring from within" tactics place great emphasis on the strategic location of Communists within moderate Negro organizations, and this could be accomplished with a relatively small number of Party faithful. A vigorous program that would result in large-scale expulsions of prejudiced whites is not necessary to a realization of this latter aim. Consequently, we can anticipate that the Party will continue to employ moderate forms of discipline in its effort to stamp out internal "white chauvinism." The Party also knows that even complete practice of racial equality on its part would not remove from the minds of most Negroes the belief that it is an instrument of the Soviet Union.

In spite of its emphasis on the Negro question in the post-war period, the Communist Party has made few efforts to form separate permanent organizations for realizing its goals. It did attempt to rebuild the National Negro Congress immediately after the war and to make it the center of Negro opposition to the "imperialist" policies of the Truman administration. To this end it convened the remnants of the Congress in Detroit in late May, 1946. Some 700 "delegates and visitors" were present; practically all of them were Party members or faithful followers. The major accomplishment of the convention was the adoption of a petition to the Economic and Social Council of the United Nations requesting the intervention of the latter body in the elimination of "political, economic and social discrimination against Negroes in the United States of America."

This was a highly dramatic gesture and was widely publicized in both the Negro and white press. It was not enough, however, to revive the Congress or give it the backing and prestige it had enjoyed during the united front period. Even so, the Party, was optimistic about the convention action, which, it declared, represented a "rebirth" of the Congress.

Indeed, in stepping forth boldly to confront the modern Goliath of U.S. imperialism, the Negro people have essayed the role of a doughty David. The boldness of the National Negro Congress, in articulating the challenge of the Negro people, marks a new advance in Negro America's organization, unity and political thinking.[42]

The action of the Congress could

... mobilize the Negro people to full participation in their historic role as an ally of the working class, thereby bringing desperately needed reinforcements into labor's present struggle to beat back the offensive of the big monopolies. By thus strengthening labor in this life-and-death fight, Negro America would be serving not only its own highest interests, but would be striking directly at the war plants of Wall Street.[43]

The two-pronged drive of American imperialism could be effectively opposed, and the

National Negro Congress, moreover, can be expected to be the appropriate spark-plug in this struggle. The Congress's predominantly trade union base, and its programmatic orientation toward the deepest unity with the labor movement, ensure that the character of the struggle will not be diverted into reformist or anti-labor channels.[44]

The Party, however, was not to attempt to develop its Negro program through the NNC alone. Although the latter allegedly had assumed a central position of leadership, it could not be expected "to mobilize and organize sufficient strength by its own efforts alone." The NAACP, the Negro press and church had "important roles to play"; valuable services and support could be contributed by Negro fraternal, business and social organizations. Indeed the struggle to unite the Negro people would have to embrace every section and penetrate all strata of Negro America.[45] Thus did the Party evaluate the National Negro Congress in August, 1946.

These high hopes were quickly dissipated. Few local councils of the Congress were revived. The quick switch on foreign policy by the remaining units indicated still further (if one needed additional evidence) that the NNC was continuing its ten-year adherence to the Communist Party line. While the NNC had reiterated demands for fair employment practice laws, abolition of the poll tax, anti-lynching legislation, and the elimination of discrimination it succeeded in winning only a handful of new adherents. It made no headway with other Negro organizations to whom it extended a grasping left hand.

In time the Party became painfully aware that the NNC was no longer an asset; it was a definite liability. Having no further use for what was once an organization with considerable promise in the field of Negro protest and betterment, Communists withdrew their support and the NNC collapsed. Within a year after its "rebirth" convention in Detroit the NNC had died again— permanently.

The Southern Negro Youth Congress, which the Party had been instrumental in organizing in 1937, did not fare so badly as the NNC during the 1941-1945 period. While it never had an influence comparable to that of the NNC, it had been able to build a number of fairly stable councils in a few urban centers. During the war period these councils developed limited programs around the issue of Negro employment, and in some cases were instrumental in modifying the traditional policies of employers, trade unions and government agencies. It was not as vigorous in action as the NAACP branches in the South, but with the support of such left-wing unions as the Food, Tobacco, and Agricultural Workers (formerly UCAPAWA) and the Mine, Mill and Smelter Workers it was able more or less to hold its own.

During the immediate post-war period the SNYC naturally followed the Party's lead in criticism of the Administration's foreign policies and later officially opposed the Marshall Plan. However, it gave some attention to questions of more immediate concern to young Negroes in the South. It campaigned for repeal of the poll tax, anti-lynching legislation, fair employment practice laws and equal education measures. In a few cities it conducted drives to register potential Negro voters; it attempted to rally southern Negro support for the retention of OPA.

The SNYC displayed some concern for violations of the civil rights of Negroes, and conducted investigations of a number of "race riots" in Tennessee and Alabama. In connection with this activity it raised funds by public subscription for the defense of Negroes who had been indicted as an aftermath of the riots. Some serious questions were raised by responsible persons concerning the use of this money; the SNYC never gave a full accounting of the amount raised or the purposes for which it was spent; the charge that the money raised in connection with the Columbia, Tennessee, cases, for example, was used for organizational propaganda rather than direct legal work in behalf of the thirty-odd Negro defendants appears to have considerable merit.[46] * This would not necessarily imply dishonesty on the part of the SNYC, which accepted the idea that the "mass pressure" which it claimed to be exerting through propaganda work was the more effective technique in freeing "class war" prisoners.

The SNYC held two general conferences during the post-war period; in both cases it publicly declared its opposition to the foreign policies of the Administration. Attendance at these meet-

* For a detailed account of the Columbia "riot" see: *Terror in Tennessee* (New York: National Association for the Advancement of Colored People, 1946) and *What Happened at Columbia* (Atlanta: Southern Regional Council, 1946). In the Columbia case all the indicted Negroes were eventually freed, largely as a result of the efforts of the NAACP with the assistance of the Southern Regional Council.

ings was small as compared to that of the pre-war and war periods. The reputation of the organization as an instrument of the Communist Party had become widely known; its actions more than confirmed such impressions. More and more the membership came to be composed of Party members and Party liners. In 1948 the Attorney General added the SNYC to his list of "subversive organizations." This further alienated non-Communist supporters.

In early 1948 the SNYC indorsed the Progressive Party and worked actively in behalf of Wallace and Taylor in the South. It sponsored the meeting at which Taylor was arrested for violation of a Birmingham segregation ordinance. During this particular period it gave little attention to the more immediate problems of southern Negro youth, which had been its major concern at the time it was organized a decade previously. If such matters as equal education, fair employment opportunities, and civil rights were mentioned, it was usually in conjunction with the Progressive Party program. The solution of all these problems was bound up with support of the Progressive candidates.

After the general elections of 1948 it was apparent that the SNYC could no longer serve Party purposes in the South. It had only a few hundred members; its funds were seriously depleted; its identity with the Party was complete. Though it tried, it had failed to penetrate local branches of the NAACP. It had never been able to reach young Negroes in the rural South. It was unable to rally Negroes, young or old, around the "United Front against imperialism." It had working relationships with only two or three left-wing trade unions.

In December, 1948, SNYC was voluntarily dissolved. Its central office in Birmingham, Alabama, was closed; the executive secretary went to New York, where he joined the staff of the Progressive Party. The remaining members were advised to join the youth section of NAACP branches or to form units of the Young Progressives of America, the youth division of the Progressive Party.[47] Thus the Party discarded another Negro organization which at one time had some promise of becoming an effective protest and betterment agency for young Negroes in the South.

The United Negro and Allied Veterans of America was formed

at Chicago in April of 1946. Kenneth Kennedy who had been associated previously with the Southern Negro Youth Congress was named the national commander and George B. Murphy, Jr., was designated acting adjutant. A short time after its organization the UNAVA was indorsed by the Fraternal Council of Negro Churches, the latter representing organizations having an estimated membership of 6,000,000.

By March of 1947 the UNAVA claimed a membership of 5,000 in 22 states and the District of Columbia. The bulk of this membership was Negro and was concentrated in a few chapters in the major urban centers. The UNAVA held its first constitutional convention in New York City on May 30, 1947. An estimated 500 delegates including twenty women and about seventy-five whites attended this meeting. At the close of the convention the national commander claimed that the organization then had a membership of 10,000 in chapters organized in 31 states. These figures were probably exaggerated, representing signed cards or applications rather than active participants. This organization was unique in that it accepted for membership former merchant marines and veterans of the civil war in Spain.

The UNAVA's headway among Negro veterans was slow; the more liberal Negro elements preferred the AVC; some Negroes joined the segregated units of the American Legion; the vast majority of Negro veterans joined none of the organizations which mushroomed in the immediate post-war period. Insofar as Negroes were concerned, the Party dropped its earlier aim of "penetrating" local posts of the American Legion. It was to discover again that Negroes viewed with extreme skepticism any organization that tended to separate them from the rest of the community, which, in this case, was the veteran community. Thus an agency which already carried the stigma of Communist control assumed the further taint of segregation.

The failure of the UNAVA can also be attributed in part to the vigorous activity of the NAACP in looking after the rights of Negro veterans. Prior to the end of the war the latter established in its Washington Bureau an Office of Veterans' Affairs with Jesse O. Dedmon, Jr. as Secretary. The purpose of the Office was two-fold. First, it attempted to secure the passage and fair enforcement of laws covering veterans, to the end that discrimination against Negroes would be eliminated or minimized. Second, it prepared for local NAACP branches material considered useful in handling Negro veterans' problems. Local branches of the NAACP served frequently as the agency through which Negro ex-servicemen initiated complaints or sought advice.[48] It was largely to the NAACP rather than separate organizations that Negroes turned for help on veterans' matters. The NAACP terminated the Veterans' Affairs Office in 1949, transferring its activities to the Legal Branch. Within a relatively short period the UNAVA made the Attorney General's "subversive" list, which climaxed its many difficulties such as lack of leadership, meager funds, poor organization, and vagueness of program. Again it was questionable whether a separate Negro organization—in this case, of veterans—could any longer serve immediate Party purposes. It came as no surprise that the UNAVA was liquidated by the Party. Its members were directed to penetrate the AVC or join the segregated units of the American Legion. It is not likely, however, that the Party in the future will place any special emphasis on Negro veterans apart from its general program. Also it must realize that its chances of penetrating such organizations as the AVC, the American Legion, the VFW and the AMVETS are extremely limited. It is safe to predict that the Party will make no effort to build a separate veterans' organization in the immediate future.

Perhaps the most important single Party instrument active in the field of Negro work at the present time is the Civil Rights Congress. After the German attack on Russia in June, 1941, the Communists not only gave up the fight for Negro rights in war industries and in the armed forces but abandoned their efforts in behalf of civil rights for Negroes and other minority groups. It will be recalled that from 1925 until 1941 the Communists waged a dramatic struggle for the rights of Negroes in the courts, using not only standard legal devices but "mass pressure" and "mass protest" as well. Because of the International Labor Defense's working affiliation with Communist organizations in other countries, this campaign frequently functioned on an international scale.

The Communist International was dissolved in 1943, and during the following year the American section transformed itself into the Communist Political Association. While the ILD was not disbanded, it dropped much of its emphasis on Negro civil rights during this period. The Party no longer established defense committees or special funds to handle cases of Negroes and other victims of prejudice. It no longer organized large-scale demonstrations, the purposes of which were to influence the courts, juries, and administrative agencies handling important cases. The "capitalist-controlled courts" which the Party had challenged with some success in the Scottsboro and Herndon cases were now regarded as impartial instruments through which workers and Negroes might ultimately secure justice. The Party did protest some court decisions involving Negroes and criticized the laxity of law enforcement officials whose negligence often contributed to lynchings, race riots and other forms of violence against Negroes. However, such protest was relatively mild, and it was not backed by any demands for action which might have "interfered with the war effort."

After the Party was reconstituted in July, 1945, it became apparent that a separate organization to function in the field of civil rights would be required. The Communists convened the remnants of the ILD and a number of other organizations in Detroit in the latter part of April, 1946. Three hundred and seventy-three delegates from twenty-three states attended. The Civil Rights Congress grew out of these deliberations. An organizational campaign was initiated, resulting in the establishment of a number of CRC chapters in the larger urban centers. Later the country was divided into a number of regions, with branch offices being established to direct and service the local chapters.

The bulk of the support for the CRC, local and national, came from two sources—the Party organizations such as the National Negro Congress, the Southern Negro Youth Congress and the United Negro and Allied Veterans of America, and the trade unions under Party control. Initiative for the organization of local CRC units came from Party functionaries, who were joined by a relatively few non-Communist elements. Communists supplied much of the volunteer help without which the CRC would have been unable to function. In addition, they held responsible administrative and policy-making positions. Rank and file Communists were and still are active in fund-raising drives and in protest demonstrations.

The position of Executive Secretary, the most important job in the CRC, was awarded to William L. Patterson, the former Executive Director of the International Labor Defense, which had been an affiliate of the Red International of Class War Prisoner's Aid. Non-Communist individuals such as Harry F. Ward were placed in important elective positions, but basic policies were and still are developed by Patterson and George Marshall, the Chairman of the CRC National Board. Among the vice-presidents were George F. Addes, former Secretary-Treasurer of the United Automobile Workers (CIO) and leader of that union's left-wing faction until his defeat by Reuther in 1947; Hugh Bryson, President of the recently purged Marine Cooks and Stewards Union (CIO); Dashiell Hammet, the writer; Jerry O'Connell, a former congressman; Lee Pressman, former Department of Agriculture attorney and ex-General Counsel for the CIO (who recently broke with the Communist-led American Labor Party in New York); and Paul Robeson. (Mr. Pressman, without doubt, has been removed from his CRC position by this time.) Within the past few months some changes have been made in the top leadership of the CRC. However, Patterson continues as Executive Secretary and the organization's commitment to the Party line is as strong as ever.

The CRC claims that it is a "national, non-partisan mass organization." However, those familiar with its origins and program did not require a declaration by the Attorney General that it was "subversive" to know that the CRC was and remains an instrument of the Communist Party. The claim that it is a mass organization must be taken more as an expression of hope than of fact, for the CRC following remains relatively small and is composed largely of the Party retinue. The claim that it is an organization, "democratically controlled by its members, who set policy at annual conventions," must also be discounted. The bulk of the delegates come from local chapters where Party strength is greatest, and the conventions are in effect an assembly of Communists and their ever-narrowing group of followers; the policies adopted reflect this basic fact. There is no evidence that any dissenting or independent views in conflict with the Party line are advanced.

The CRC also claims that it is dedicated to "the great struggle ... for constitutional liberties, ... civil and human rights." Its practices, however, indicate clearly that it is concerned with such issues only when Communist interests can be served. The CRC is not dedicated to the liberties or rights of Trotskyites, social-democrats, or liberals. In line with its current attitude, it regards such groups as "collaborators of Wall Street," and "traitors to the working class," for whom capitalist injustice is an appropriate punishment.

The activities of the CRC fall under some half-dozen major headings. It organizes protest and political campaigns on local and national civil rights issues. It provides attorneys to handle selected cases in the courts. It carries on bail- and fund-raising campaigns for those persons and organizations it elects to defend, the selection being based on political considerations. (It lost plenty of money on Gerhardt Eisler, who it now appears may shortly become a victim of "Soviet justice" in Eastern Germany). In this connection it usually establishes special defense committees without direct Communist identification. It develops publicity and protest campaigns around specific cases, attempting to create "mass pressure" on law enforcement agencies and the courts. At the same time it seeks to have outlawed certain organizations to which it is opposed on ideological and other grounds. An official publication declares: "CRC does not believe freedom of speech means license for Klan, anti-Semites and fascists to spread hate, incite violence and terror and destroy democracy and the constitution." *

However, it is not clear just where the CRC would draw the line, or just what groups it would characterize as "fascist." If some of Paul Robeson's statements are indications, the CRC

---

* *Whoever You Are* (New York: Civil Rights Congress, 1949), p. 17. The above summary of the composition and program of the CRC is based on this publication and supplemented with other documents which will be subsequently cited.

would be definitely opposed to defending the civil rights of individuals and organizations composing the non-Communist left. If the CRC and the Party did not now stand in need of help from impartial organizations like the American Civil Liberties Union, having a basic rather than a tactical interest in civil rights, it would probably place them in the Klan and fascist categories.

A number of considerations govern the CRC's selection of cases and issues. If the individuals involved are members of the Communist Party, or if they are closely identified with programs and organizations which the Party supports, their chances of receiving assistance are good. If they are members of a large racial or national minority, the CRC is likely to come to their aid, for it believes that it can advance its own program and that of the Party among such groups by a dramatic identification; besides, such cases make good anti-American propaganda in the cold war. If the individuals are members of one of the Party-controlled trade unions, and especially if they occupy positions of leadership, the CRC is apt to be among the first groups coming to their aid. The operation of this selective process is demonstrated in the cases of the "Top Twelve," the "Trenton Six," and the Ingram family.[49]

Following much the same pattern as did the ILD, the CRC attempts to make wide use of the technique of "mass pressure." The way it currently works was described by the Educational Director of the Communist Party of New Jersey in the case of the "Trenton Six."

The New Jersey *Worker* took up the story [of the conviction of six Trenton Negroes for murder] and started a campaign of mass action. The New Jersey *Worker* lifted the campaign from a humanitarian and legalistic level to one of class struggle by showing that such persecution was not accidental, that it was part of the scheme of big business and the government to maintain its political and economic stranglehold on all the toiling people, Negro and white. The people were urged to demonstrate their opposition to this most brutal mass-lynching decision. They were admonished not to place confidence in the courts. They were shown the ruling class character of the courts. They were shown that they, the people, are the great directors of history. They would be the final judge. In short the New Jersey *Worker* made it clear that the lives of the Trenton Six depended upon the people . . . and that the civil rights of the people depended upon what they did about the Trenton Six.[50] *

The similarity of these techniques to those used by the International Labor Defense in the Herndon and Scottsboro cases of the 1930's is quite apparent. Under the present circumstances, however, they are not apt to be so successful. The effective use of the technique of "mass pressure," whether employed by the IWW or the Communists or some other radical political minority, depends on the sympathetic cooperation of a wide non-radical element. And this the CRC does not have and cannot obtain.

Because the Communist Party of the United States and the CRC have close connections with organizations serving the Communist cause throughout the world, they are able to mobilize the latter groups behind cases which the CRC elects to defend. For example, the Cyprus Progressive Women's Union in Africa in a letter addressed to the President of the United States declared:

> Your excellency and the various Secretaries of the U.S.A. Government often speak and write about the adherence of your country and your people to the principles of freedom and equality. The Ingram case is a good opportunity to prove it. . . . We respectfully request you to intervene and order the release of Mrs. Ingram and her sons [convicted in Georgia on a murder charge and originally given a death sentence] from prison. This will be an act of justice.[51] **

A similar declaration from the Democratic Women's Union of Rumania stated:

> Women are indignant seeing the persecution to which Negro citizens of U.S.A. are submitted. On the behalf of 1,6000,000 members of the Democratic Women's Union in the Rumanian People's Republic, our

* The merits of the cases of the Trenton Six are not involved in this discussion. The matter is introduced here for purposes of demonstrating how the Party and the CRC are currently operating in the civil rights and legal fields. It is the opinion of the author, based on a limited examination of the cases, that certain denials of the rights of the defendants were involved in the actions of the prosecution and the court. If this is true, it is also the opinion of the author that ultimate justice is more likely to obtain if the courts are approached as instruments of impartial justice rather than as tools of "big business."

** As in the case of the Trenton Six, the merits of the Ingram case are not involved in this discussion.

Central Committee requires that the human rights inscribed in the United Nations Charter should be respected and that Mme. Rosa Lee Ingram and her sons should immediately be set free.[52]

Another declaration, this one from the Hungarian Women's Democratic Union, with headquarters in Budapest, followed the line of the above communications, insisting:

Mrs. Ingram's arrest and confinement are grave violations of the human rights and of the law of racial equality . . . the Hungarian women demand energetically the release of Mrs. Ingram and her sons.[53]

Similar communications were dispatched from Communist organizations in Syria, Argentina, England, Norway and other countries.[54]

Whether or not world-wide propaganda campaigns such as the Communists have conducted around court cases involving Negro Americans have any appreciable influence on the trials themselves is difficult to determine. Actually, legal justice is a secondary consideration for the Party. One thing is certain, the treatment accorded American Negroes in the courts, particularly in the South, is one of the most important bases for the anti-United States propaganda campaign waged by the U.S.S.R. among colored peoples all over the world. What more welcome event could occur for such propagandists than a lynching in Georgia, legal or otherwise?

The CRC's use of the technique of mass pressure follows from the assumption that American courts are not agencies through which impartial justice can be dispensed. Indeed, the CRC in terms of its basic ideological orientation can have no concept of impartial justice. The courts in its view are inevitably instruments of the state, and the state is the embodiment of the ruling class. The ruling class in America is capitalist. In Russia the ruling class is the proletariat, and the courts are inevitably instruments of the proletariat. In the Soviet view, a crime is always a crime against the people and therefore an act of treason to be punished accordingly.

The CRC's program must also be understood as an integral part of the Communist world movement. The cases which it identifies itself with must serve not only its immediate propaganda aims but also must fit this larger strategy. If any of the Trenton Six or members of the Ingram family were publicly to repudiate left-wing support, that agency would suddenly find that they were not victims of "capitalist injustice."

The CRC is not the organization that the ILD was. Times have changed. There is not the widespread public interest in the cases which it has handled; and what interest there is is likely to be unsympathetic. It needs to produce favorable court decisions, in at least a few cases, in order that those who do not partake of its ideological aims may nevertheless be impressed by concrete results. Although it may be able to carry on extensive propaganda programs around the Ingram case, for example, in which the shortcomings of American justice for Negroes are widely exposed, Negroes are likely to judge the organization by whether or not the Ingram family is released from prison. Such ends are more likely to be accomplished through the use of standard legal devices; it is significant that the CRC has retained exceptionally able lawyers in addition to skilled propagandists to handle its outstanding court cases.

The CRC is also in dire need of allies. Although it has been extremely critical of the NAACP and other moderate organizations, it has made frequent overtures for "unity" and cooperation with such groups. The latter, now familiar with the tactics of the Party and of the CRC have displayed a marked reluctance to accept such offers. This attitude was well exemplified in the decision of the NAACP to exclude the CRC from the National Civil Rights Emergency Mobilization, which met in Washington, D. C. on January 15-17, 1950. Prior to the convening of the Civil Rights Mobilization William L. Patterson, the Executive Secretary of the CRC, requested that his organization be allowed to participate. Roy Wilkins, acting Secretary of the NAACP, flatly rejected this bid, stating:

We remember the Scottsboro case and our experience there with the International Labor Defense, one of the predecessors of the Civil Rights Congress. We remember that the present Civil Rights Congress is composed of remnants of the ILD. We remember that in the Scottsboro case the NAACP was subjected to the most unprincipled villification. We remember the campaign of slander in the *Daily Worker*. We remember the leaflets and the speakers and the whole unspeakable machinery that was turned loose on all those who did not embrace the "unity" policy as announced by the Communists.

We want none of that "unity" today.

We of the NAACP remember that during the war when Negro Americans were fighting for jobs on the home front and fighting for decent treatment in the armed services we could get no help from organizations of the extreme left. They abandoned the fight for Negro rights on the ground that such a campaign would "interfere with the war effort." As soon as Russia was attacked by Germany they dropped the Negro question. During the war years the disciples of the extreme left sounded very much like the worst of the Negro hating Southerners. American Negroes and especially the NAACP cannot forget this.[55]

But the Communists were not excluded completely from the January meeting. In spite of the careful work of a well-informed credentials committee, a number of Party spokesmen got under the wire. However, they were soon identified and isolated. The refusal of such organizations as the NAACP to cooperate in any way with the CRC has, of course, brought down upon them the usual Party abuse. Confirmation of Wilkins' suspicions was supplied shortly afterward by the Party itself when it declared:

Negro businessmen, educators, physicians, lawyers and social workers, through depending primarily upon a Negro market for their economic survival, are increasingly subjected to the ideological, political and economic offensive of Wall Street. It is from this strata of the Negro population that the leadership of the N.A.A.C.P. has been historically drawn; it is primarily the interest of this group that the Wilkins-Current forces endeavor to represent and speak for. This wavering, petty-bourgeois type of leadership has set as its objective the subordination of the Negro people's liberation struggle to the overall strategic and tactical aims of American imperialism. The Wilkins-Current leadership with their [sic] reformist and Social-Democratic allies in all parts of the country, seek to police the Negro people's movement, to water it down and to misdirect the mass anti-imperialist upsurge among the Negro people.[56]

It is perhaps worth remarking again that the Wilkins-Current leadership which Strong condemned for "subordination" of the "Negro people's struggle" to "imperialism" was the same leadership which Strong and other Communists condemned during the war period for being too radical. It was also the same leadership with which the CRC only a month before had hoped to consort in the Civil Rights Mobilization.

Not only has the CRC failed to obtain any support from among the moderate organizations; it has failed to fire the imagination of American Negroes as did the ILD at one time. Yet the CRC continues to make a certain headway among American Negroes. This is largely explained by the default of other organizations, which lack either the interest or the resources to tackle an ever-growing number of cases involving the rights of Negroes.

The future of the CRC is bound up with that of the Communist Party in the United States. Even if it received wide support from American Negroes, which it has no hope of obtaining at the present time, it would still labor under the basic handicap of being a Party instrument. When it no longer serves Communist purposes it will be liquidated, as were a host of other organizations—the ANLC, LSNR, ILD, NNC, SNYC and UNAVA.

During the past four years the Communist Party has placed increasing emphasis on "boring from within" moderate Negro organizations as a means of implementing its Negro program. Three considerations are involved here. First, the Party-controlled Negro organizations have fared ill, as the preceding section indicates. Second, a number of Negro protest and betterment organizations, and especially the NAACP, have grown rapidly in recent years in terms of members and influence; the Party now recognizes that the NAACP is the "decisive organization" of the "mass of Negro people." [57] Third, Party strategy calls for a united front program in opposition to "Anglo-American imperialism." If the Party is unable to carry out this program through instruments of its own, it must seek to penetrate others where the bulk of Negro protest and political action is centered.

The technique of penetration employed by the Party is too well known to require detailed explanation here. Party members or fellow travellers join local units of the NAACP, attend every meeting, work diligently in committees, obtain positions of leadership, especially in the executive and publicity functions, secure control of the local branch, and then employ it as an instrument for forcing "reactionary" leaders of the national organization from positions of authority and for forcing a new "line" on foreign policy.[58] In accordance with its usual tactics the Party has attempted to make a distinction between NAACP leaders such as Walter White, Clarence Mitchell, and Roy Wilkins, and the "rank and file." The former, it charges, are trying "to tie the Negro people to the bi-partisan war program of U.S. imperialism," while the latter are interested in the development of a "genuine Negro mass movement against the Wall Street drive for war" and a "militant struggle for Negro rights."

Recent developments in Berkeley, California, provide an example of the effort of a local Communist group to carry out this "line." In the spring of 1949 the NAACP organized a branch among University of California students. Immediately afterward the Berkeley Campus Section of the Communist Party sought to penetrate the new branch and secure control over it. The technique closely paralleled that employed by the Party on a national scale.

The Berkeley Campus Section conceded that the NAACP had been responsible for many of the gains of Negro people over a period of the past four decades. It contended, however, that the NAACP, since its origin, had been "restricted by white paternalism; it has fought results not causes." It claimed that because DuBois had "protested the growing trend of the [NAACP] leadership to sell out to the war drive," he had been discharged from his position as research director, though he was one of the NAACP's founders. The Party students also attacked the Regional Director of the NAACP, who, it charged, "has been diverting the campus group in the same manner of the National Organization." Under these circumstances "local groups can and must be the centers of resistance to a sellout from the top." The campus section concluded by calling upon "all students, particularly Negro, who want to fight discrimination on campus, to join the NAACP and work for a program that will produce deeds rather than dreams." In effect, this was a call upon all student Communists and fellow travelers to get in the NAACP and carry out the program of the Party.[59]

The 40th annual conference of the National NAACP held in Los Angeles, California, July 12-17, 1949, provides an excellent case history of Party tactics in action. Prior to each conference local branches of the NAACP submit to the national office resolutions proposing changes in policies and programs. These proposals are usually printed in *The Crisis*, official publication of the NAACP. At the conference these resolutions, along with others which may be introduced at the time, are discussed and voted upon. The action of the conference then governs the policy of the NAACP until the next general meeting.

In June, 1949, the Jamaica, Long Island, branch of the NAACP, over which the Party had secured control, proposed a series of resolutions which, among other things, called for the following steps by the conference:

1. Disapproval of the action of the Board of Directors in its previous indorsement of the "Marshall Plan."

2. Disapproval of aid under the ECA or other forms of assistance "to nations which hold colonial areas in subjugation and exploit the people of colonial areas only for benefit of the imperial power." (This would have included Britain, France, Italy, Belgium, the Netherlands, and other recipients of Marshall Plan aid; presumably it would have placed Poland, Hungary, Rumania, Czechoslovakia, and Albania [but not Yugoslavia] on the eligible list).

3. Disapproval of the Atlantic Pact between the United States and the Western countries.

4. Reinstatement of Dr. W.E.B. DuBois to his "former position or one of like stature without prejudice." *

---

* DuBois left Atlanta University in 1944. Later he rejoined the national staff of the NAACP as Research Director. He was dismissed from this post on September 12, 1948 at a time when he was active in behalf of Henry Wallace and the Progressive Party. Just how much his political activity had to do with his discharge is difficult to determine. The full facts in the case have not yet been made public. During the late summer of 1948 DuBois charged, without consulting the NAACP Board of Directors, that the designation of Walter White as a consultant to the United Nations General Assembly was committing the organization to an indorsement of the foreign policies of the United States. He had raised no such objections, however, when the NAACP had designated him [DuBois] as a consultant for the organizational meeting of the

5. Establishment of an elected fifteen-man committee to review the failure of the NAACP to project "its vast potential in the mobilization of the vast body of both Negro and liberal white citizens" in the struggle to attain Negro rights.

6. Authorization of local branches of the NAACP to join with other organizations in the fight for Negro rights "if the National Office shall fail to effectuate such changes as shall bring about greater efficiency and branch participation. . . ." [60]

Delegates from the same branch also proposed that the editors of *The Crisis* be castigated for printing an editorial criticizing Paul Robeson for his statement that American Negroes would not fight against Russia.

Only two of the Party-sponsored resolutions reached the floor of the conference—those dealing with the Economic Recovery Program and the Atlantic Pact. Both were defeated by overwhelming majorities. Although Party spokesmen had an opportunity to carry the other resolutions to the floor for decision by the full body, they refused to do so in the face of such a strong non-Communist opposition, centering around Acting Secretary Roy Wilkins. The resounding defeat suffered by the Communists at the Los Angeles conference was further indication of their inability to penetrate the NAACP. The Party spokesmen fared even worse at the 1950 conference. This does not mean, however, that the Communists will drop the fight for control of the NAACP; on the contrary, their efforts will probably be intensified.*

The NAACP has long been aware of the designs of the Party and has taken steps to combat the infiltration threat. It has

United Nations in San Francisco in 1945. (See: "DuBois to Leave NAACP," *Crisis*, Vol. LV, No. 10, October, 1948, 302-303.) It has been suggested that other factors were also involved, but the author is not sufficiently acquainted with the details to make any final assessment. The Party was concerned with DuBois' reinstatement because it felt that he would be a valuable and safe man in the national office of the NAACP, which it had theretofore been unable to penetrate. Whether or not he would have lent himself completely to its purposes while inside the NAACP is a matter for conjecture. No one could contend that he has failed to do so outside of it.

* It is interesting to note that the *Daily People's World*, the West Coast counterpart of the *Daily Worker*, in its summary story on resolutions adopted by the conference made no reference whatever to the defeat of the Party-sponsored measures. See: *Daily People's World*, July 18, 1949, p. 1.

learned from bitter experience in the past that Communists are concerned with Negro rights only insofar as such issues serve the Party's immediate purposes. "The American Communists," *The Crisis* editorialized,

are busy stirring up disaffection, dissension, and unrest in every segment of American life they can penetrate, such as labor unions, church bodies, youth groups, college campuses, community organizations, and Negro groups, including the NAACP.

The purpose in all this is *not* to build a better NAACP to fight more effectively for civil rights for Negroes under the American Constitution, using legitimate American methods, but to operate one more front group to confuse and embarrass Americans and the American government in the present contest of ideologies.

There is no mystery, except to the unthinking and uninitiated, about the Communist program on the Negro. Their characterization of the NAACP as "reformist" reveals the line: they do not believe American democracy can be improved or reformed, hence anyone who does, who keeps alive a faith in the American way of life, is a criminal and a "betrayer of the people." As long as the NAACP and similar groups exist and push programs of reform, the Communist doctrine takes root slowly, if at all, in the nation's largest minority group. Hence the NAACP must either be captured or destroyed.[61]

Having set forth this estimate of the Communist Party attitude, the NAACP then warned its members:

Our NAACP membership . . . should be on guard against this campaign. It should remember that the Communists do not hesitate to lie when lies will serve their purpose, that they are masters of misrepresentation through misinterpretation, that they prattle about democracy in other organizations, while maintaining an iron-handed non-democratic procedure in their own party, and that their aim is to use the Negro and his problems mainly in support of Communist Party policy and only incidentally in support of Negro rights.

This does not mean the Communists should be fought, as such. They constitute a political party and have rights under the Constitution as do other parties. These rights must be maintained. Free speech and free assembly must be maintained for all. Let them enjoy their rights in this democracy and push their program as well as they can in their own groups. But this campaign of infiltration, disruption, and destruction of other organizations such as the NAACP can be prevented if members will not be deceived by their words, and will elect the proper officers and committees, choose the right delegates to conventions, attend meetings faithfully and out-vote the party followers, and see that the resolutions and public statements adopted by the NAACP groups are NAACP statements in truth, and not those of a group using our name for its own political purposes.[62]

The Party has had more success in penetrating NAACP locals on the West Coast than elsewhere, but even here it is unable to claim more than a few branches. Its hold over these was established immediately after the war. As early as 1947 the national and regional offices of the NAACP acted to break the Party grip on branches in Richmond, Los Angeles and San Francisco; they have been partially successful.* More recently the NAACP national office has been empowered to seize the charters of local branches falling under Party control and to issue new charters to newly constituted, non-Communist groups.

One explanation of the Party's failure to penetrate the NAACP is found in the over-critical attitude of Communists themselves toward this "reformist" organization. And Party propagandists are largely responsible for this turn of events. The all-out attack on such men as White and Wilkins has created certain confusions in the minds of Party members themselves, resulting in efforts on the part of the latter to crush rather than

* Report of the Resolutions Committee, West Coast Regional Conference NAACP, San Francisco, California, March, 7-8, 1947. (mimeographed) The resolution reads as follows:

Reaffirming our faith in democracy we maintain our unalterable support of the basic NAACP program which for 38 years has striven to integrate the Negro completely within the framework of the United States Constitution. Our Association has grown in size, prestige and power, now having more than 500,000 members. An inevitable consequence of this growth has been the attempts of various groups, particularly Communists, to either secure control of our branches outright, or use the branches as sounding boards for political and other ideas, and for the support and furtherance of programs other than that of the NAACP itself. We condemn and actively oppose these tactics. There should be no discrimination in offering NAACP membership to any person on account of race, color, religion or politics. All who honorably subscribe to the objectives and procedures of the NAACP are welcome. However, we urge our branches in the West Coast Region to be diligent in carrying forward the basic program of the NAACP and to be alert to check the injection of any doctrine or course of action not consistent with our program. We urge officers and members to scrutinize candidates for any office in the Association in order to prevent them from gaining control of our branches.

capture the NAACP's local branches. One Party spokesman recently warned:

> Some of the Left and progressive forces have occasionally fallen into sectarian tendencies, maintaining that it is "impossible" for them to bring about any changes in the Association [NAACP] due to the domination of the reformist and Social-Democratic leadership. They insist that the organization is purely reformist in character and that nothing important can be achieved by remaining in it; and they claim that the decline in membership [of the NAACP] during the past two years is proof that the Association [NAACP] has never basically won the allegiance of the Negro people. This attitude has at times been expressed in a withdrawal from active participation in the life and work of the organization and in a search for other channels through which to develop militant action.
>
> It is clear that underlying this sectarian tendency is a serious underestimation of the central role played by the Association [NAACP] in Negro life. Such an approach misses the whole point that by withdrawing from active participation in the work of the organization and by leaving its struggle for national civil rights legislation to the present reformist and Social-Democratic leadership, the Left forces would merely strengthen the control and domination of this leadership and serve to isolate the Left-progressives from broad sections of Negro life.[63]

The aim of the Party remains that of "capturing" the NAACP in spite of the numerous setbacks Communists have recently suffered in the organization and are likely to suffer in the future. The Party's main chance might come if a prolonged depression intensified current race problems beyond the capacity of the NAACP to deal with them in any meaningful fashion.* The fact that no such economic crisis is now in prospect and that the NAACP has shown a remarkable degree of flexibility argues against this possibility.

---

* Rejection of Party criticism of the NAACP does not imply blanket approval of the structure and policies of the latter. However, criticism has come frequently from those lacking any acquaintance with the day-to-day problems which the NAACP must confront. Myrdal has correctly pointed out that, "different as these critical judgments are in motivation, they all express the fundamental defeatism in regard to the upholding of law and order which has become so widespread among American intellectuals of all colors and political creeds. . . . This pessimism is exaggerated and consequently, criticism against the NAACP is largely unjustified." Myrdal, *An American Dilemma,* p. 831.

The Party has been extremely critical of the National Urban League during the post-war period, and its efforts to penetrate that organization have resulted in complete failure. Like the NAACP, the NUL is wise to the Party tactics, having had long experience with infiltration efforts.[64] The NUL is not an organization that readily lends itself to penetration by a determined and closely organized political group. It is primarily an employment and social service agency that does not depend on local, volunteer personnel for carrying out its program or upon clients for funds. The NUL works within a relatively narrow sphere of job training and employment and has no program or base for mass political action as does the NAACP. Policies are determined by a national board of directors with local boards mapping community programs; they are carried out locally by paid executives under the general supervision of the governing bodies.

At the present time the NUL has a paid professional staff of some 400 persons working in local offices in 29 states. An estimated 4,000 persons serve as members of the executive boards. These boards are usually made up of businessmen, educators, lawyers, union representatives and civic leaders. Only in rare cases is there an identity of such members with left-wing groups. It would be only as a result of obtaining control over such boards or of the national board itself that the Party would be able to advance its program within the NUL; this does not appear to be even a remote possibility. However this does not stop the Communists from trying. The Party's penetration tactics might conceivably work if the Workers Council program should be revived. However, such a program at the local level would be under the close scrutiny of the executive secretary and executive board, and infiltration would be extremely difficult.

Under these circumstances, the Party seeks to discredit the NUL in the eyes of the latter's potential Negro clients. It does this by denouncing the national as well as local executives with the usual charges of "sellout," etc. Another technique has been to invite the local NUL to participate in "joint action" with other organizations under Party influence. When the NUL refuses, it is charged with "obstructing united action of the Negro people." Neither technique has paid off for the Party.[65]

No Negro nationalist movements of any consequence have developed during the post-World War II period—in sharp contrast to what occurred after World War I. Such political and economic gains as have been made by Negroes—in large part as a result of the actions of organizations like the NAACP and the NUL—have been sufficient to convince a great majority that their interests lie in seeking full citizenship *within* the United States. The fact that many Negro workers now have unions for protection of their job interests and more effective protest organizations in the political and social spheres has provided positive outlets for frustrations that formerly found expression in movements like Universal Negro Improvement Association. Were such organizations as the latter to develop in the immediate future (a highly unlikely possibility) then the Party would seek to turn them to account for its own purposes. They would not be attacked as in some previous periods, even if composed of "bourgeois" elements.

At present the chief stimulus to Negro nationalism is the Communist Party itself, which through its "Negro nation" and self-determination theories seeks to bring to the fore any latent Negro aspirations for a separate culture and state.[66] The Party in language reminiscent of the Sixth World Congress of the Communist International can now declare:

The Negro arts defy adequate and fundamental understanding unless they are viewed as the expression of a *distinct people* within the general population of the United States, reflecting their *special relations* to the society as a whole, giving expression to their special memories, traditions and aspirations. Only in relation to the development of Negro Americans as an increasingly organized, self-conscious political entity within the American scene does the concept of Negro culture take on full meaning.[67]

And further:

Negro culture is illustrative of what Stalin's famous definition of a nation characterized as "a historically evolved, stable community of ... psychological make up manifested in a community of culture." It is a national culture whose origin and forms and content are to be understood as reflecting the emergence and development of an oppressed people, struggling for national liberation.[68]

And with respect to Negro artists the Party can declare, again in language reminiscent of *New Masses* editorials in the early 1930's but with new phrases popularized in *Pravda:*

> Not unrelated to this pervading insistence upon Jim Crowism in cultural content is the tendency of many Negro artists to escape into cosmopolitanism and formalism. On the one hand they deliberately avoid Negro themes, rationalizing on the irrelevant premise that they want to produce art "as good as any other." On the other hand, they seek refuge in "art-for-art's sake" avoidance of any realistic themes whatever, travelling down the fruitless and meaningless road toward non-objective "beauty" and "delight." [69]

However, the Party's intensified effort to cultivate a consciousness of Negro nationalism or to persuade Negro artists to incorporate its advance in their themes has not come off well during the post-war period. The increasing industrialization of the South and the changing character of the plantation system has redefined the agrarian status of black Americans in the South. The large-scale migrations occurring during the war and continuing afterward have made for a significant redistribution of the Negro population in the United States. Even in the South, there is an increasing tendency for Negroes to migrate to the cities, where they constitute not a majority but a relatively small minority of the total population. The Negro nation concept of the Party in its inception was predicated on the questionable premise that (1) Negroes were spatially situated in a contiguous territory that constituted the physical foundations of a distinct nation; and (2) that they possessed the other requirements for a nation as defined by Stalin. Such a thesis is even more fallacious at the present time.

Negro artists are no more inclined than they have been in the past to serve as propagandists for the Communist Party (Paul Robeson is now the only notable exception). On the contrary, if there is any theme which might be said to be predominant in their work, it is the idea of *integration*—not *alienation*. This, in the party's view, of course, is "bastard cosmopolitanism" and "formalism." While Communists have construed the protest expressed by Negro artists as a "striving for national manhood and self-determination," the great bulk of it, if one may attribute sociological and political implications, represents a striving for equality.

Probably at no previous time has the Communist Party been more bent on separating the Negro from the main stream of American life. This approach to the Negro question conforms to the Party's general post-war strategy of fomenting factionalism in American society. The party's failure to rejuvenate its separate Negro organizations, to build new ones, or to penetrate the moderate "reformist" agencies, has not exhausted its resources for "Negro work." It has also concentrated on Negroes in the trade union movement, meeting with a bit more success than in the other areas of Negro protest and betterment. Three major considerations have governed the Party's approach to the black worker and the labor movement during the post-war period. First, the Communists, as they themselves have admitted, dropped the fight for Negro equality in industry and in the trade unions during the period from July, 1941, until July, 1945. The result was that Party influence among Negroes in industry rapidly declined. The frenzied activity around "guaranteeing that Negroes would hold their war-time gains" was an effort to compensate for this neglect and recover the party's Negro following. Second, the Communists were aware that in the Party-led trade unions they would have their most valuable resource for dutifully carrying out the line of opposition to American "imperialism," and that Negro unionists would be a significant part of such resource. Third, the Party anticipated that in time it would face a show-down fight for control within the Communist-led unions and within the CIO itself. It believed that it would be possible to build Negro blocks within a number of the affiliates which it could turn to account in this power struggle. It is in conjunction with these three motives that the Party's work among Negro unionists in the post-war period must be examined.

In an effort to re-establish itself in the good graces of Negroes in industry, the Party advanced a program which merits examination in some detail. It supported, of course, a series of legislative proposals designed to facilitate the post-war economic adjustment of Negro workers, demanding increased unemployment compensation, public works programs, and substantial relief measures where necessary. At the same time it supported proposals for fair employment practice legislation at the state and national levels which would have penalized employers, trade unions and government agencies for discrimination in hiring or admission practices. These were measures which the Party had soft-pedaled during the war period, measures which in some instances it had condemned other organizations for advancing. The Party was now among the most vocal proponents.

Within the trade unions themselves, the Communists advanced a series of unique proposals which they thought would win adherents among Negro workers. These demands centered around modification of hiring and seniority provisions in standard labor contracts. The Party took the position that where such agreements affected adversely the hiring, promotion or lay-off of black workers, they should guarantee "the Negro workers *equal* job opportunities with the white workers in the shops and in industry." [70] On the surface this was a laudable proposal, but it carried two dangerous implications. First, it tended to split the workers in the industry and in the unions along racial lines. Second, it tended to weaken the principle of seniority by injecting the racial factor as one of the major determinants.

Negro unionists viewed these proposals with an unexpected skepticism. As trade unionists they were extremely doubtful about the implications for the seniority structure from which many of them benefited, along with white workers. While a few of them, as Negro workers, looked with favor on such proposals, these never constituted a large or influential group. Negro unionists were also skeptical of the proposals on the basis of the source from which they came. They were inclined to look this latest gift-horse in the mouth. Even a superficial inspection indicated that he was the same old dobbin who had once whinnied "everything to win the war." Even in the Communist-led unions themselves, only limited efforts were made to apply these proposals, the more significant examples being found in the relatively small United Office and Professional Workers and in the Food, Tobacco and Agricultural Workers unions.

This super-seniority program advanced by the Party was rejected by the great bulk of Negro unionists because they did not wish to be played against their fellow white unionists, and because they appreciated the general seniority principle which would have been threatened if the Party demands had been carried out. In addition, colored workers saw little to be gained in the long-run fight for equality by currently insisting on being placed in a special category. They did not ask that new contracts afford them exceptional treatment but that they be equitably applied.

However, Negro workers would have been more responsive to this special Communist appeal if there had not been positive evidence that the non-Communist elements in the CIO were working in other ways to equalize job opportunities and union participation. For a number of years the CIO has maintained its National Committee to Abolish Discrimination. This agency has worked on a wide front, seeking not only to eliminate discrimination within industries in which CIO affiliates have contracts and within the individual unions themselves, but in the government service, armed forces, and in various communities and public services. The Committee currently consists of twelve members including James B. Carey, Chairman; Willard S. Townsend, Secretary; and George L-P Weaver, Director. In the operations of this Committee and in other activities of the CIO and its affiliates, Negro workers have seen convincing evidence that the industrial union movement's declared principle of organizing without regard to race or color is more than an empty slogan.[71] While racial discrimination continues to be a problem in the CIO affiliates (as well as in the Communist-led unions formerly affiliated with the CIO) there has been substantial progress in its elimination. Had there not been, a great many more Negroes might have supported the "super-seniority" proposals of the Party and followed its unions out of the CIO.

One of the outstanding anti-discrimination programs among CIO affiliates is that of the United Automobile Workers, a union in which the Communists until some three years ago had a substantial though not widely distributed Negro following. For a number of years now the UAW has maintained a Fair Practices and Anti-Discrimination Department, of which Walter Reuther and William H. Oliver are currently the Co-Directors. The program of this agency is closely coordinated with that of the Department of Education. It assists in the establishment and servicing of local anti-discrimination committees. It conducts training and informational programs for local officers and shop stewards, advising on ways and means of integrating minority workers in the industry and in the union. In addition the Department is active in the political and legislative fields at the local and national levels.[72]

It is such programs as these that have largely offset the special appeals by the Communists to the Negro trade unionists in the post-war period. While anti-discrimination programs in a number of the CIO affiliates have not been as widely supported as that of the UAW, they have offered some possibility of obtaining Negro job rights within the program of the moderate elements. However, a great deal remains to be done; the CIO can effectively counter the Communist appeal to Negroes only by a sustained effort to realize its declared goal of racial equality in industry and in the trade union movement. The American Federation of Labor, and a number of its affiliates, is now taking a much more positive position in combating intra-union discrimination. It is to be hoped that such efforts will be expanded and intensified.

The American Communist Party has waged a constant attack on the right-wing elements of the CIO during the post-war period, characterizing the latter as "race-baiters" in an effort to draw off their colored support. But during the same time the Party has not been blind to the fact that these same "race baiters" have been more concerned with the integration of Negroes in terms of equal union benefits than the Communists themselves. In its periodic sackcloth-and-ashes sessions, the Party has admitted that the right-wing groups have in fact accomplished more in this respect than have the Party-led factions.[73] Such admissions are further indication that the Communists have engaged in a lot of fuss about race equality in the post-war period, but have done little about it, even when they controlled the instruments for doing so. In those unions where Party influence was dominant, the Negro question was subordinated to the political problem of opposing American foreign policy. In those unions where the Party did not have control, but was supported by a sizable bloc, the Negro question was subordinated to the internal power fight, with the effort to use colored workers against the right-wing elements. In the Party's post-war policy of factionalism and disruption, the ruckus itself is the important thing.

Unable to recoup their Negro losses in the CIO through advancement of the "super seniority" principle, or to win colored followers by characterizing the opposition as "anti-Negro," the Communists were weakened in their subsequent fight to retain control over a number of CIO affiliates and to remain within the general body itself. In an effort to hold their positions in such organizations as the Transport Workers Union, the National Maritime Union, the United Packinghouse Workers Union, the United Electrical Workers Union, the Farm Equipment Workers Union, and the United Automobile Workers Union, the Communists attempted to make special appeals to Negro workers. Some of the most irresponsible "smearing" ever practiced by Party functionaries was visited upon the right-wing leaders of these unions. The charge, in practically every case without any foundation, that non-Communist leaders were "Jim-Crowers" and "race baiters" was levelled broadside, mounting in intensity as the Communist position became more precarious.* These efforts, however, did not result in winning decisive Negro support. Had the Party been able to swing the Negro members of these unions

* For a catalogue of this invective and a summary of the attitude of the Party with reference to specific unions see the following: Henry Winston, "Party Tasks Among the Negro People," *Political Affairs*, Vol. XXV, No. 4, April, 1946, 353-357; Carl Winter, "The Face of a Social-Democrat—Walter Reuther," *Political Affairs*, Vol. XXV, No. 5, May, 1946, 407-422; George Morris, "The Menace of Social Democracy and Our Fight Against Opportunism," *Political Affairs* Vol. XXVII, No. 8, August, 1948, 757-762. See also Henry Winston, "For a Fighting Party Rooted Among the Industrial Workers!" *Political Affairs*, Vol. XXVII, No. 8, August, 1948, 834-856. For indications of the shift in the Party's attitude toward the right-wing elements during the period from 1946 to 1948 see: Eugene Dennis' Report to the Plenary Meeting of the National Committee of the Communist Party, July 16, 1946 in *Political Affairs*, Vol. XXV, No. 9, September, 1946, 795; and Eugene Dennis, "The Fascist Danger and How to Combat It," *Political Affairs*, Special Convention Issue, September, 1948, pp, 787-788.

behind its bid to retain power, the outcome in a number of instances might have been different but this is questionable.* In such organizations as the Food, Tobacco and Agricultural Workers Union, the Fur and Leather Workers Union, the United Office and Professional Workers Union, the Mine, Mill and Smelter Workers Union, the International Longshoremens and Warehousemens Union, the Marine Cooks and Stewards Union, and in the remnants of the United Electrical Workers Union, the Communists have succeeded in retaining their hold, at least at the present writing. Only in one or two instances could it be suggested that their grip depends on the support of Negro Communist factions.

Thus the Party appears to have been unable to capitalize on any discontent among Negroes in the CIO in its post-war struggle for power with the right-wing elements. The primary aim of the Party among the trade unions in the post-war period has been to use their political and economic power in opposition to the Economic Recovery Program and other aspects of the Administration's foreign policy which do not meet with the approval of the Kremlin. One of the prerequisites for so manipulating a trade union is, of course, control of its apparatus. This control the Party has lost, step by step and day by day until at the present time its influence in the labor movement is only a fraction of its former strength. The more the Party emphasized its primary purpose, defeat of the Truman administration's defense and foreign aid programs, the more it alienated the industrial workers, white and Negro. CIO members were not convinced that their failure to secure wage increases was a consequence of a plot between Truman and Churchill to destroy the Soviet Union. The Negro unionists in particular were unable to see any relation between the CIO's support of the Marshall

* The party at one time had a substantial following among Negroes in the automobile industry in Detroit. In an effort to secure support for the left-wing faction in the show-down fight with Reuther, the followers of George F. Addes promised to propose a Negro for one of the UAW vice-presidencies. While some support was obtained on this basis, it was not a significant issue for many of the Negro members. An outstanding authority on Negro labor recently remarked in an interview that while Negroes in the automobile industry sometimes followed the Party program, they did so "only insofar as it led to specific and concrete gains, which the opposition couldn't deliver."

Plan and the existence of discrimination in industry, a connection which the Party insisted was clearly evident. The Party was to learn again that it could hold few American trade unionists when its commitment to an agency outside the labor movement, indeed even outside America itself, was so patent.[74]

The Party attempted to offset its losses in the trade union area by intensified political activity, particularly among racial and national minority groups. In the Progressive Party the Communists saw an almost ideal instrument through which opposition to American foreign policy might be carried on. That the Party would welcome such a movement was evident from the time of its break with the Truman Administration following the Duclos letter in 1945. Communists at that time, however, apparently did not anticipate that within a short period the former vice-president of the United States would present himself as a willing helper in such an undertaking. The part played by the Communists in launching the Progressive Party and the mechanics of its central need not be examined in detail here. Suffice it to say that the Communists played a decisive role, with the result that the Progressive platform embodied both the major and secondary aims of the Communist Party at the time.

The Communists in the Progressive Party were largely responsible for the great emphasis placed on Negro rights in the platform and during the political campaign itself. This was a part of the Communists' strategy of making special appeals to racial and ethnic minorities. A good example is supplied in the following statement:

The new Progressive Party and the Negro people are partners. Like the partnership the Negro people had with Abe Lincoln in 1863. Like the partnership that won the Civil War and saved the nation.[75]

And further:

Inside that moving, fast-growing partnership that is the Progressive Party are Negroes and whites from every social, economic and intellectual level. There are giants like the world's greatest sociologist and historian, Dr. W. E. B. DuBois. There are millions of Negro workers, union members, farmers, professional men, sharecroppers, businessmen, students joined in the only mass-scale political party fighting discrimination and jim crow on a seven-day-a-week basis.[76]

Concerning Henry Wallace himself, it was asserted:

And from the activities of this man who stands alongside the Thomas Jeffersons, the John Browns, the Frederick Douglasses, the Wendell Phillipses of yesteryears, thousands of Negro and white Southerners have gotten inspiration to reach across the color-line and grasp hands and join together in this New Party of the common man.[77]

And finally:

Win, lose or draw, the Negro people are in closer partnership with the Progressive Party than with any other mass political party in America.[78]

Just how tenuous was this partnership was illustrated at the ballot box on November 2, 1948. Appeals of the above type were common in the Progressive Party's campaign. As the formal campaign got underway, and as the Progressive Party's identification with the Communists and their cause became more apparent, there was considerably less enthusiasm among Negroes in volunteering for Gideon's Army.

It was thought by a number of observers during early 1948 that the Progressive Party might be able to swing a large number of Negro votes in decisive states such as New York, Illinois, California and Ohio. This anticipation without doubt influenced the Democratic Party subsequently to incorporate the now well-known civil rights proposals in its 1948 platform. In this respect it can be said that the Progressive Party made an important indirect contribution to the advancement of Negro rights in the political arena. This was one of the unanticipated consequences of its actions; and it was an unwelcome consequence because the ADA elements in the Democratic Party thereby stole some of the Progressive Party's thunder. Negroes had established a growing identification with the Democratic Party since 1932, and they had no wish to sever it in favor of a minor third party movement; the liberal and labor elements in the Democratic Party gave them convincing reasons for continuing their alliance.

The Progressive platform was much more detailed in proposals affecting Negroes than were those of the major parties, reflecting the Progressive's effort to capitalize on Negro discontent. Among its proposals were: (1) outlawing all segregation in the government service by Presidential proclamation; (2) enactment of a permanent fair employment practice law; (3) halting federal aid to any and all state and local agencies practicing discrimination; (4) outlawing the dissemination of anti-semitic and anti-Negro or racist propaganda; (5) federal inspection of all primary and general election polling places to prevent blocking of the right to vote; (6) special programs for Negro health, housing and education; (7) withholding of federal funds from states denying equality of opportunity to persons on account of race or nationality; (8) a federal program to combat racial and religious prejudice; (9) a civil rights act for the District of Columbia; (10) the abolition of segregation and discrimination in all public housing; and (11) anti-lynching legislation and the prohibition of segregation in interstate travel.[79] Such a platform, incorporating all items in the Communist Party program except self-determination in the Black Belt, was widely publicized among Negroes.[80]

Initially Negroes rallied to the new Progressive Party, not only because of its stand on civil rights and segregation, but because a number of prominent Negroes were given positions of leadership. Prominent among them were W. E. B. Dubois, Charles P. Howard, Earl B. Dickerson, T. P. Lochard, and Larkin Marshall. Howard, a Des Moines attorney and former Republican, delivered the keynote address at the Progressive Party founding convention in July, 1948. Marshall, editor of the Negro newspaper, the *Macon Herald*, placed Senator Glen Taylor's name before the convention.

The convention was attended by approximately one hundred and fifty Negro delegates and alternates. Negroes were prominent in the convention committees and on the floor, twelve of them making seconding speeches following the nomination of Henry Wallace for the presidency. The convention went far in electing Negroes to permanent offices. Paul Robeson was designated co-chairman of the new Party and Alvin Jones, a student at Southern University was named to a vice-chairmanship. Jones was also elected co-chairman of the Young Progressives, the youth arm of the new party.

The Communist Party, beginning in early 1947, channeled the bulk of its "Negro work" behind the third party movement. While aware that the Progressive Party was not a completely ideal instrument for achieving "Negro liberation," it could declare that:

The Progressive Party has added something both qualitatively and quantitatively new to the Negro liberation movement. As the anti-monopoly electoral coalition of labor and the people against war and fascism, it flies the colors of Negro rights against the twin parties of reaction.[81]

And further:

The Progressive Party is by its very nature a great coalition of labor, farmers, the Negro people, youth, and professional and small business people.[82]

Such resources as the Party had among Negroes in the trade unions and in separate Negro organizations like the Southern Negro Youth Congress, or in mixed organizations like the Southern Conference for Human Welfare and the Civil Rights Congress, were used full blast in an effort to get out the Negro vote for the Progressive Party candidates. All other activities were subordinated to the election campaign, one consequence being that the headquarters of the various Party organizations and their local branches came to resemble campaign offices of the Progressive Party.

Following another technique of the Communist Party, the Progressives nominated Negro candidates in a number of states in an effort to garner the colored vote as well as to demonstrate the interracial character of the new movement. Mrs. Paul Robeson was nominated for Secretary of State in Connecticut; Mrs. Margaret Wilson was nominated for a congressional post in Missouri; in Georgia, Larkin Marshall was their candidate for the United States Senate; Stacey Adams carried the Progressive Party banner for the governorship in Texas, and William Brown was its candidate for the United States Senate in North Carolina.[83] A number of strictly local branches of the Progressive Party nominated Negroes for county and municipal offices. These measures proved no more effective for the Progressives than they had for the Communists. None of the New Party Negro candidates for state or federal offices was elected, most of them receiving only extremely small personal and protest votes.

Wallace and Taylor campaigned dramatically for the Negro vote, carrying their appeals into the South, where it was thought they might be able to secure the votes of some of the newly enfranchised blacks and at the same time curry favor with the more important Negro voters in the key northern states. These campaign tactics drew wide attention; Wallace and Taylor were subjected to vicious treatment in the South, frequently being denied the right to present their program in public speeches and over the radio. Henry Wallace was rotten-egged on a number of occasions, and in Birmingham, Taylor was arrested for violation of a local segregation ordinance. This was probably the best publicity the Progressive Party received for its civil rights program throughout the campaign. But in spite of the assistance of the southern bigots, the Progressive Party failed to obtain many Negro votes below or above the Mason-Dixon line. In this connection *The Crisis* aptly commented in an editorial:

> With little or nothing to lose by campaigning against inequality and segregation, Wallace's zeal and sincerity were discounted (unfairly perhaps) by a vast section of the public. But the silliness, if not the viciousness, of segregation was exposed by ropes being solidly erected between two groups of citizens of a town standing at an outdoor meeting—citizens whose white and black parents and grand-parents had grown up in the town and had helped build it. Fanaticism and hatred were laid bare, but often it was difficult to determine whether Negro equality or Communist support of Wallace was responsible.[84]

But regardless of the intense efforts of the Communists to shift the Negro's allegiance to the Progressive Party, or to divert it even temporarily, the movement was a distinct failure. This failure was all the more glaring in view of the special effort to capitalize on Negro discontent. Wallace and Taylor received less than two million votes, and a somewhat casual examination of their distribution suggests that considerably less than ten per cent were cast by Negroes. In Harlem, Wallace ran a poor third to Truman and Dewey. In five election districts Truman received

108,643 votes; Dewey, 34,076; and Wallace only 28,903—fourteen per cent of the total. A similar ratio prevailed in Brooklyn, where Negro voters made up a substantial portion of the total.

In Harlem the Progressive Party's Negro candidate for the State Senate (running under the banner of the American Labor Party, an affiliate of the Progressive Party) received only 12,719 votes, while the white Democratic Party candidate obtained 55,784. In Chicago, to take another example, three congressional candidates in "Black Metropolis" divided the total vote as follows: Democrat, 98,204; Republican, 43,620; Progressive, 5,188. A similar distribution was found elsewhere. Even in the South the Negro vote went to the Democratic Party and only in few instances did the Progressives poll more than a mere handful of votes, white or Negro. Doris Fleeson, writing a few days after the elections, observed:

> All parts of the country . . . report that the Negroes were overwhelmingly for President Truman, a vital factor in his Illinois and Ohio victories. In New York the Wallaceites cultivated Harlem intensively. Harlem gave the President 65% of its vote, Thomas E. Dewey 20 per cent, and the remaining 15 per cent was Wallace's high among Negroes in the cities of the nation, according to their own studies of the returns.
>
> Philadelphia says that nine out of 10 among its Negroes voted for the President and emphatically rejected all Wallace Party candidates. In Chicago, the ward of the only Negro congressman, gave the President more votes than any other ward in the city, 93 per cent of the total.[85]

The election results were a blow to the Communist Party, which had placed its entire apparatus behind the Progressives. They were likewise a blow to its Negro program, indicating again that when the showdown came Negroes would not permit themselves to be used as the instrument of a single party, particularly one which set itself so squarely against the dominant trends in American politics and tended to separate them from the main forces in the labor and liberal movements. The Progressive Party, contrary to its claims, was not the party of the farmer, the worker, or the Negro. As *The Crisis* observed editorially

> Many Negroes became emotionally involved in the Wallace campaign, but the tabulation shows that few voted for him. Best proof that the Wallace campaign was collapsing under the strict control of the hard

Communist core of workers and advisors was furnished in late September when the party [Progressive] announced withdrawal of its candidates in certain Congressional districts. The opponents in these districts were liberal congressmen whose only "crime" was their failure to follow the straight Communist line. Up to September the "Commies" had insisted that these people must be opposed, but the waning away of support forced a change in policy. After the elections Mother Russia spoke through the voice of Molotov to tell bewildered American liberal, non-Communist supporters of Wallace that after all Truman was not so bad, and that it was really Dewey who was a "war monger!"

It must have come as a shock to non-Communist Negro Wallace supporters that they had been merely used by a disciplined pro-Communist group.[86]

While the liberal and labor elements in the Democratic Party have thus far been unable to carry out any of the basic provisions of the 1948 civil rights platform, the President through executive action has made certain changes in the status of Negroes in the government service, particularly in the armed forces. In addition, the Supreme Court in a series of recent decisions, has extended Negro rights in the fields of higher education, private housing, and in interstate travel. While these have represented only piecemeal gains, they are none the less real and of direct benefit to Negroes. The liberal elements of the Democratic Party have projected the civil rights question squarely into American politics, and it is not likely that either of the major parties can afford to ignore it in the future. The Progressive Party has disintegrated since the 1948 elections, and with the recent departure of Henry Wallace it becomes an empty shell. (In the Party's estimation Henry Wallace has now become a "Wall Street collaborator" because he refused to sanction Communist aggression in Korea.)

As long as the labor movement is committed to the Democratic Party and so long as the working alliance between the trade unions and the moderate Negro protest and betterment organizations is expanded, there is no possibility that any third party movement can draw much Negro support. Negroes during the past two decades have found that they have important political resources if they are properly deployed. They are not going to dissipate this newly found bargaining strength by diverting it to any splinter movement which would jeopardize their balance-of-power position in relation to the two major parties. This is the basic fact of American Negro political life which the Communists in the Progressive Party ignored when they tried to swing the black vote to Wallace in 1948. Negroes will be reluctant to abandon the Democratic Party until they despair of its ultimate ability to deliver; Negroes will turn to a third party when it is launched by a genuine liberal-labor movement, lodged in the context of the native radical tradition which Negro slaves and citizens have helped to shape.

The failure of the Progressive Party to capture the Negro vote climaxed the Communist Party's loss of influence among black Americans in the post-war period. During the five years since the Duclos letter the Party's separate Negro organizations which were carried over from the united front and war periods have disintegrated. The one or two rather feeble attempts to build additional organizations, for example among black veterans, have met with quick failure. The Party has not been able to stimulate a consciousness of nationalism among Negroes or to develop any instruments for its organizational expression. It has failed, even after sustained efforts, to make any significant penetrations in the moderate Negro agencies. In the South its influence among Negroes was largely eliminated as a consequence of the collapse of the Southern Negro Youth Congress and the Southern Conference for Human Welfare following the fiasco of the Progressive Party. Its all-important trade union base has been whittled and chopped away as non-Communist elements took over Party-led unions in the CIO and as the latter body itself expelled those organizations which continued to hew to the Communist line. One consequence of this has been a marked decline in Party strength among black workers in the mass production industries. Negro membership in the Party has declined sharply and the total number of black Communists in the United States at the present time is probably less than 4,000. The Party is fighting for its very existence as a legal organization, and the prospects are that it will shortly be eliminated and forced underground. It can be anticipated that few Negroes would participate in any illegal, conspiratorial instrument of the Politburo.

The decline of the Party's organizational influence among Negroes has been paralleled in the ideological sphere. The anti-liberal implications of the Russian totalitarian state, although supposedly coupled with racial and ethnic democracy, have become increasingly apparent to Negroes as well as to other elements in American life who in times past were vaguely sympathetic with the "socialist experiment." This has tended to destroy any prestige which American Communists might have enjoyed as spokesmen of a country in which "race prejudice is outlawed." The Party's revival of the self-determination doctrine has occurred at a time when American Negroes have good reason to believe that their centuries-old fight for full participation as American citizens is producing results. Increasingly, Negroes have become aware that a separate republic in the Black Belt would mean nothing more than a new form of segregation.

All this is not to say that Negroes are unaware of the gains which they have made as a result of the Communist Party's activities. These gains, to be sure, always have been incidental to major Party purposes, never having been sought by Communists as ends in themselves. This is not to say, either, that the organizational and ideological decline of Communism among American Negroes means an end to Party influence or efforts. The American Communists at the present time are desperate, but they are also determined. Their set-backs in the trade union and in the political spheres may lead to a renewed emphasis on agitation and organization among racial and ethnic minorities, particularly Negroes, whose burdens, in spite of recent gains, remain many and heavy. Only if the extension of Negro rights begun in the context of the New Deal reforms and carried forward by the liberal, labor, and Negro movements themselves are continued, can there be any assurance that the Communist Party, as long as it remains a legal organization, will fail to capitalize on Negro discontent. America has a great weapon against Communism among racial and ethnic minorities in America. It is the Constitution. We would do well to apply its equalitarian potentials.

# VIII

# "RED AND BLACK: UNBLENDING COLORS"

THE Communist Party of the United States, cast in the image of the mother organization, is a monolithic structure. Its program is shaped by the Party bureaucracy, whose general—and frequently detailed—orientation is supplied by the Politburo. Its analysis of the Negro question, or of any other question, is never an independent one; and it is not an eclectic one, because it does not recognize the possible validity of any opposing point of view. This has been the case especially since the Sixth World Congress met in 1928, at which time the hand of the Stalinist dictatorship was firmly fastened on the world Communist movement.

It is not possible to characterize any specific interpretation of the Negro question in the United States as *the* Communist analysis. For the Party, analysis is a *function* of immediate program rather than its *cause*. This is amply illustrated by the Party's approach to American Negroes over a period of time. The real Negro question has remained essentially the same for decades: it is the persistent issue of basic economic and political equality for our largest racially differentiated minority group. The Negro question in the United States did not change fundamentally between the fifth and sixth meetings of the Communist International. It was no different on June 22, 1941, than it was on June 21 of that year. Though the Duclos letter of April, 1945, altered the line of the American Communist Party and replaced some of the top bureaucracy, it did not introduce any novel element in the race problem. And yet, with each shift in the Party line, the analysis offered by the Party has suggested that the Negro question then became something fundamentally different.

It would be pointless to search for consistency in the Party program. The well-known vacillations of the Party line have led superficial analysts to the conclusion that the Communist approach is illogical. But there is an overriding logic to the Party's various positions: it is rationally grounded in the premise that whatever serves the interests of the "workers' fatherland" is *right*—for the Negro and for the human race. It is one of the characteristics of a monolithic organization that the usual rules of analysis are never permitted to intrude upon the development of rationalizations for programs of action. When there is placed in the hands of the organization's bureaucracy full control of the instruments of communication coupled with the power of censure and expulsion, changes of line, however abrupt or contradictory, can be justified and their acceptance forced. In this the Party bureaucracy is aided by the fact that the dedicated Party member comes in time to feel that the "leader" can do no wrong.

Such an organization as the Communist Party requires that the actions of its hierarchy be considered "right" without exception—and without question. If error is admitted, it is always error in the past; the possibility of fallacy in the present could not be countenanced. Lovestone and Browder were bounced from the top rungs of the ladder, but the principle of leadership was never placed in question.

The function of the Party leader is not now, and has never been, that of examining a series of varying points of view and then resolving them in some tentatively advanced synthesis. It is not the job of the leader to select principles and ideas and offer them in the political market for whatever they may be worth. The role of the Communist leader is primarily a priestly one; he takes from on high whatever commandments are given and interprets them in terms of the duties which they impose on followers. When some shift in the line causes him to be momentarily uncertain as to just what the commandments are, he must mark time or go into hiding until the new Mosaic tablets are found. A correlative function of the leader is to denounce relentlessly the false prophets and heathen doctrines of competing organizations; the latter are composed, he claims, of either stupid and misled people or vicious seekers of power. In any event, he can question Kremlin infallibility only at the risk of being defrocked. And at the same time he must see to it that there are no "deviations" within the ranks.

The latter task is a perplexing one; it has never been solved by the leaders of the American Communist Party. A Browder, a Foster, or a Dennis can be caught between the cross-pressures of carrying out Kremlin edicts on the one hand and building an effective organization on the other. It is only rarely—as in the united front period—that the two are really compatible. However, if a choice must be made, numerical strength and political influence will be sacrificed in favor of the first pressure every time. The Party's top bureaucrats are balanced on a shaky fence, and it is easy to fall off.

It does not matter that the point of view which the Party spokesman attacks on one day may be the same that he so stoutly defended the day before. It can be a "lying misconception" to suggest that the Negro question in the United States is a "national" question *prior* to the Sixth World Congress. To assert that it *is not* a "national" question *after* the meeting is to be guilty of "bourgeois cosmopolitanism." Consistency in this respect is not a virtue; efforts to achieve consistency carry the possibility of confusion and suggest a lack of faith in revealed truth. The penalties of such behavior can be drastic, ranging from reprimands, followed by confessions of guilt, to possible excommunication from the ranks of the saved, with a one-way ticket to purgatory. Where conflict between his own inclinations and orders from on high occur, the Party functionary must search for a higher integrating principle that will cast out doubt and shed light on the new road he is to travel.

While Communist spokesmen in the United States have frequently found this a demanding task, they have ultimately discovered the requisite rationalizations in a conviction that whatever serves the needs of the Communist Party of the Soviet Union also serves the greater glory of the American Party—and of humanity. If they have been caught off guard by sudden shifts in the line, or temporarily made mute by the turn of events, they have shown a remarkable resiliency, sustained as they are by a nearly automatic set of reflexes and a long-term faith in the ultimate righteousness of their cause. Woe be unto those who fail in the effort.

To one who demands intellectual consistency, the behavior of Communists is disturbing at best. The former cannot understand how the latter can declare on Wednesday that the Negro question must be resolved by the establishment of a separate black republic and then on Friday, with just as much conviction, assert that the answer lies in the integration of Negroes in all phases of American life. He is at a loss to comprehend how the Communist on one day can proclaim that the war is an imperialist blood bath and the next "prove" conclusively that it is a holy war of national and cultural liberation. He cannot understand why the Party in one instance regards Walter White as an outstanding Negro leader and his class as the "chief bearers of the aspirations of the Negro masses" and in another situation contend violently that White and his colleagues are "traitors to the race."

But if one can appreciate the peculiar structure of the Party and the psychological make-up of the individuals who join and remain with the organization, then a measure of understanding is possible. To assert that Communists are traitors, or agents of a foreign power, or conscious instruments of the Politburo, is much too simple a view. Harold Rosenburg in a penetrating article, "The Communist: His Mentality and His Morals," has observed:

The readiness of the Communist to clasp to his bosom the hated enemy of yesterday and to denounce as traitors and monsters his former allies and even adored leaders has often led him to be considered cynical or immoral. Quite the contrary—such reversals of judgment and feeling are the very key to the Communist morality and the fullest expression of his constructed character. Accompanied by the strongest passions, they have nothing in common with the switches in attitude resulting from a mere absence or relaxation of principles. Morally weak or indifferent people may, for the sake of expediency, collaborate with individuals whom they have denounced and drop former friends as a liability; but this is merely a shift in relations. With the Communist a change in the policy of the Party transforms *the nature itself* of the former friend or ally. At one stroke the imperialist Roosevelt disappears and is replaced by Roosevelt the democratic champion of the peoples— while the isolationist peace-lover of this morning emerges this afternoon as a masked Nazi. It is as if Roosevelt or Hitler had never lived before the day of the change—as if their entire existence were conferred upon them by the party line. Thus the Communist's judgments stem from a metaphysics of being, and are the moral extension of that metaphysics. The question of what a Churchill or a Browder *is* having been decided, the Communist bestows upon him the complete measure of his contempt or adulation. When a new decision is made, a new Churchill or Hitler or Browder appears, and the present judgment is extinguished in its opposite.[1]

Whatever attitude one holds toward the Party—whether enthusiastic, tolerant, or antipathetical—should be grounded in a full appreciation of the phenomenon with which he is dealing.

Confronting the convinced Communist with the Party's inconsistencies on the Negro (or any other) question is a waste of time. He sees all issues as functionally related to the general Party line at any given time, and the line is inseparable from the advancement of the interests of the Soviet Union. The fight against the poll tax cannot be divorced from opposition to the "imperialist" Marshall Plan. Oppression of the Negro in the South is part and parcel of American intervention in Greece and China. The indictment and conviction of Communist Party leaders for conspiracy is an attack on every colored American. But the indictment of Trotskyites under the same law is a removal of "race baiters" and "white chauvinists." A Robeson speaking before a "civil rights" rally can deplore the abridgement of liberties when members of the Party are the victims; but his reply to "What about the Trotskyites?" is that they got what they deserved as fascists.

While tracing in considerable detail the fluctuations of the Communist Party analysis and program, we have made no startling new discoveries. Indeed, practically all the documents and other materials used have been available to the general public for a considerable time. But perhaps we have pointed up the mechanics whereby a monolithic political organization, whose orientation is supplied by an outside force, approaches a specific domestic question over a period of time. The remainder of this chapter is concerned with evaluating the motives and effectiveness of the Party's program for American Negroes. We shall try to summarize its influence on various aspects of Negro life—art, the press, the church, and so on. We shall also attempt to assess the Party's motives and its role in the movement for Negro rights. Basically, this procedure involves a recapitulation of the previous chapters.

The Communist Party is a bureaucratically controlled power center; because it is also a monolithic structure, it must necessarily politicize all aspects of life. Negro art, literature, theatre, or sports can claim no pluralistic values in themselves. They are judged in terms of their contribution to the realization of immediate— and vaguely ultimate—Party goals.* A Negro painter who does not depict Negro suffering may be considered a slave of "bastard modernism." A Negro novelist who does not take Negro struggles as a theme may be dismissed as an opportunist seeking acceptance by the white élite and concerning himself only with the large royalty checks that might come his way. The colored dramatist is not worth his salt if his plays do not portray revolt against existing racial patterns. (Of course, during the war period these dramas were expected to tone down the protest angle.) The race historian who fails to provide a radical past for the Negro is judged to be a conscious betrayer of the race—if the Party line at the time demands a radical past. The same for the Negro composer. And if there ever is a Negro circus, it too will be viewed with an eye to its "bourgeois contamination" or its "deviant sectarianism," and criticized accordingly.

But despite the monolithic character of the Party structure, it

---

* A Negro recreational director of my acquaintance was at one time a drama student at Northwestern University. During the 1930's he lived in the "Black Metropolis" of south Chicago, where a number of Communist Party units were functioning. He showed some promise as a playwright and several of his one-act dramas were presented locally. After the production of the first one, he noticed that a number of persons whom he had not met before congratulated him on his work. They invited him to parties where he was introduced to other Negro intellectuals and where white girls were present—"come-on bait," as he put it. They asked to see other plays he had written. When he asked for their comments, he was told that they showed "talent" but that the basic themes were wrong, the subject matter superficial. "You ought to write as a Negro dramatist," they told him, "and deal with the struggles of the Negro people." He replied that he just wanted to be a good dramatist, and select for himself the themes and ideas with which he dealt. A short time afterward he found himself being denounced as a "bourgeois" writer who was interested only in catering to middle-class tastes.

should be recognized that there are many individual Communists who are consistently concerned with winning full equality for Negroes and who are guilty of no discrimination in their personal attitudes and actions. Indeed, quite a few Party joiners, both Negro and white, were primarily motivated in the beginning by a desire to "do something" about segregation and discrimination per se; and they believed that they could accomplish this aim by identification with the Party, which patterned much of its program around the question of Negro rights. That many such Party joiners were so motivated is indicated by the numerous withdrawals when the line subsequently changed and these people became convinced that the Communists had either given up the struggle or subordinated it to other items on the agenda. In its thirty-year history the Communist Party of the United States has turned again and again to the attainment of Negro rights as a focal point for its program. This emphasis has stemmed in large part, of course, from the intermittent preoccupation of the Comintern with racial and colonial problems; but the American Party has also been influenced by the fact that many liberal and leftist Americans of both races feel strongly about discrimination and are willing to participate in organizations that develop action programs.

Another factor of importance in this connection is the need of the individual Communist for an emotional identification with oppressed groups. Negroes are the largest racial minority in this country. At times Communists have regarded the Negro as their burden, seeing themselves in the role of suffering missionaries lifting the black man to a higher plane. In shaking hands with a Negro, in sitting beside him at meetings, in participating with him in joint activities, and in calling him "comrade," the white Party member frequently feels that he is responding to as basic a principle as that of conformity to Party leadership. For he prefers to think that he is a Communist in the first place because of humanitarian impulses and moral conviction; and he is inclined to resist the idea that he pays lip service to, and goes through the motions of, racial equality because he is a Communist.

But the white Communist, like some other Caucasians, often misreads the psychology of Negroes when he attempts to approach them on this basis. Many Negroes resent—and under-standably so—those whites who pose as their friends and who attempt in their formal programs and in their personal relation-ships to break through the traditional race barriers. This is the case for several reasons. For one thing, there is the suspicion that such whites want to use Negroes for some ulterior purpose. Also, Negroes tend to accept the values of the dominant white major-ity: the idea of success, or getting ahead. And they are likely to view with skepticism and distaste those individuals who do not succeed in these terms. Negroes frequently want to know why any white man should be professionally interested in their plight when so many channels of economic and political advance are open to those having the requisite skin color.* And all too often Negroes accept the white man's valuation of their race. The phenomenon of self-hatred is not limited to Jews, Mexicans, or Indians. As a result, many black men cannot build up the requisite self-confidence for participating with Caucasians in protest and betterment movements.

The white Communist, of course, is frequently caught in cross-currents when dealing with Negroes. For example, a particular articulation of the Party line may require a soft-pedaling of the Negro question. But if the Party wants to hold its Negro mem-bership and gain more recruits, it must produce immediate and tangible results. During periods when broader Party strategy demands relegation of Negro rights to an order of secondary importance, it is difficult for the Communists to maintain their pose as "the responsible spokesmen of the Negro masses." In the united front period and during the war years (1941-45) this basic inconsistency plagued the Party. Added to these difficulties is the fact that the Party has sometimes been indiscreet in recruit-ing white members, with the result that anti-Negro elements have often been added to its ranks. The cross-pressure set up by prejudiced whites on the one hand and by Negroes on the other

* For a more detailed consideration of this phenomenon, see Henry Lee Moon, *op. cit.*, *passim*. The author points out that Negroes often hold poor whites in contempt and that there is a tendency to identify Communist spokesmen with this group. He emphasizes that Negroes resent the Party's regarding them as problems rather than as persons; a frequent consequence of the latter is hatred and suspicion on the part of the Negro.

has sometimes made it hard for the local Communist leader to maintain an effectively functioning internal organization. Discrimination within Communist ranks has always been a rather pressing problem for the Party élite; hence the periodic campaigns to "stamp out the virus of white chauvinism" within the Party itself. These crusades mirror the conflicting pressures operative in the internal structure. They have usually ended, however, in an effort to "stamp out the virus" without stamping out any white members.

Another source of dissension is found in the behavior of white Communists who advance occupationally, either within or outside the Party organization. Upgrading usually means a better income, which enables the Communist to live in a "bourgeois" community; and such residential areas are apt to exclude Negroes. The new position also may mean increased association with persons of middle-class status. Social success in these circles entails a denial of Party values, specifically in the sphere of racial discrimination. Residence in a bourgeois area usually means a loss of identity with the Negro at the lower-class level. The Party member so situated must develop some sort of rationalization, which is usually of doubtful persuasiveness even to himself, not to mention Negroes.

The Communist who advances as a Party functionary or as a trade union official is likely to be caught in these opposing currents. As his authority increases and his jurisdiction expands, he must necessarily secure acceptance in ever-widening groups. Often he can play his appointed role only by soft-pedaling his position on the Negro question and the specific issues it raises.

During several periods in the history of the American Communist Party the organization has been committed to a program of radical transformation of the underlying economic order, which it conceives to be the taproot of all social evil. For the Communist it logically follows that an attack on capitalism is an attack on its specific manifestations in the field of race relations. When the Party has opposed economic inequality, it has inherently opposed inequality in other areas of life. Hence the sometime popular quotation from Marx that "labor in the white skin cannot be free when that in the black is branded." With the exception of the 1941-45 period, the American Party has regarded race prejudice as both a product and a further instrument of capitalism. The solution to the problem of discrimination has been expressed in terms of the immediate (or at least the long-range) overthrow of the existing economic order. Under these circumstances the Party position on the Negro question becomes part and parcel of a basic economic determinism. The fact that national and race prejudice still exists in the anti-capitalist Soviet Union—and from some indications appears to be increasing—has made no noticeable imprint on Party theory in this realm.

The Party, of course, has not been blind to the fact that the Negro in the United States is a potential resource as well as a burden. It is not likely that the Communists in their thirty years of activity in this country would have given as much attention to the black minority had the Party not been convinced that Negroes could ultimately be used to serve Party ends. And in the Communist's mind, Party ends came in the course of time to be inseparable from the ends which Negroes should seek.

Lenin's theory of imperialism and national liberation played an important part in the Communists' approach to Negroes from the very outset; and this influence is perhaps stronger now than at any time since the late 1920's. Lenin was, if anything, an opportunist. And the American Party is cast in the image of the master Bolshevik. However, it would be an over-simplification to contend that the Party's interest in the Negro question has been a wholly opportunistic one. Communist recruitment could probably have advanced more rapidly among the southern white workers, for example, had the Party not placed so much emphasis on Negro rights. Its gains among white collar groups were somewhat hampered by its periodic preoccupation with the doctrine of racial equality, which conflicted with the social values of the middle class. Certainly opportunism will not account for the attitudes of many individual Communists who joined the Party because of a prior belief in racial equality and who have practiced racial brotherhood in their own social relationships. All this is not to suggest that principle, in the liberal sense, has played a determinant role in Party policy but rather to emphasize that the matter is considerably more complex than is generally supposed.

We must refer again to the structure of the Party and the psychology of the individual members if we want to comprehend the shifting program and attitudes on the Negro question. No convinced Communist would admit that the Party could be satisfied with anything less than full equality for American Negroes. But he insists that this goal is inseparable from the advancement of the interests of the Soviet Union; for the U.S.S.R. is the fatherland of racial and ethnic equality, and the realization of social equality can come only with the communization of the world. Though it may be temporarily necessary at times to tone down the struggle for Negro rights—to give up the fight for equality in the armed forces and in industry—the Communist sees these actions as in direct conformity with the ultimate goal of full equality. He need not necessarily place tongue in cheek or entertain Machiavellian thoughts when he no longer attempts to eliminate segregated blood banks. If segregated blood banks and industrial discrimination are a necessary compromise to gain unity for the American war production effort, and if the latter contributes to Russia's defense on the Eastern front, then racial equality in the United States has been done a good turn. What the Communist can't understand is why Negroes don't cotton to this obvious bit of logic.

Whatever his personal feeling on the Negro question may be, the individual Communist must not let it lead him into "deviations" from the current line or to a "reformist and cosmopolitan" approach. For the dedicated Communist recognizes that there is a higher purpose for his every act. Although the Party approach at the moment may go against his grain, he is consoled by the realization that it is ultimately contributing to the fundamental goal. And the longer his tenure with the Party, the more agile he becomes in such mental gymnastics. As a result of training, habit, and the ever-present need to be "politically correct" in all matters, he is able to dissolve his doubts and soothe his soul.

Thus the individual Communist could persuade himself that in attacking the March on Washington Movement he was actually advancing the fight for Negro job rights. The MOWM, he reasoned, was under Socialist influence; Socialists (to wit, "Social Fascists") were opposed to the U.S.S.R.; therefore, Socialists were inherently opposed to the best interests of the Negro; ergo, the MOWM was a betrayal of the Negro workers. Any good Communist knows that he rides the tide of history and that the ultimate interests of mankind lie with the communization of the world. He therefore has no patience with the liberal's weighing of goal and method. He understands that the end always justifies the means. It logically follows, then, that the Party line is always correct; and from adherence to it all blessings flow.

The Party cannot regard interracial betterment and Negro protest organizations as legitimate implements for the realization of Negro rights. While it may at times applaud their programs and leadership, and even point favorably to their accomplishments (indeed, even attempt to form alliances with them), it basically views them as instruments to be used for such purposes as will advance the program of the Party, whatever the latter may be at the time. When they fail to serve such purposes, they are characterized as exerting a traitorous influence on the Negro struggle; the Party then must aim either to destroy them or to convert them into Party vehicles. If the basic struggle for Negro rights is retarded or permanently injured as a result, this per se can evoke no concern on the part of the Communists.

Should the Party succeed in its present efforts to penetrate the NAACP, for example, it is highly probable that the latter would disintegrate in much the same manner as the National Negro Congress, the Southern Negro Youth Congress, and the United Negro and Allied Veterans of America of World War II. The Party would have no hesitation in destroying the NAACP if it could, even though the latter is the most effective Negro protest organization ever developed in the United States. One of its major faults, in the present view of the Party, is that it has failed to oppose the Marshall Plan or to denounce "American aggression" in Korea. This is sufficient cause to consign it to the grave.* The Party's opposition to the NAACP will continue until there is an abrupt change in line, such as might result from a slack in the cold war. Objective changes in the Negro question, if any, will have nothing whatsoever to do with it.

* Fortunately, Party strength in the NAACP is now at a minimum, and its chances of capturing the organization are remote.

In reviewing the history of the Communist Party of the United States for the past three decades it becomes apparent that it has largely failed in its prolonged effort to turn the Negro question to account for its own purposes. While it has claimed a monopoly on "fundamental analysis" of the problem, while it has devoted a startling amount of its energies to Negro work, while it has constantly identified itself with the specific issues affecting Negro rights, it has relatively little to show, from an organizational standpoint, for all its labors. As Henry Lee Moon has pointed out:

No other political Party, no branch of the Christian church, no labor organization, no other reform or revolutionary movement has devoted as great a share of its resources to gaining adherents and spreading its influence among Negroes as has the Communist Party.

Yet with all their untiring efforts—their dramatic fight for the freedom of the Scottsboro boys, their triumph in the Angelo Herndon case, their struggle for equal social, political and economic rights, as well as their day-to-day efforts along a far-flung front—with all this, the Communists have failed to gain and hold any considerable number of Negroes in the Party membership.[2]

Had the Party in fact been unrelenting and consistent in its pursuit of these objectives, it would now without doubt have more to show for its efforts. But by its very nature the American Communist Party is able to seek specific goals in the Negro struggle only insofar as these are consistent with the line at any given time. Negroes have become aware of this, which explains in part the failure of repeated attempts to build a larger Communist organization among them.

It is more or less axiomatic that any radical party in the United States will try to gain a following among oppressed racial and ethnic minorities—especially among Negroes, who are more important numerically and perhaps more inclined to protest than other groups. In this respect the Communist Party has been exceptional only in the degree of emphasis it has placed on the Negro group and in the detailed tactics for securing its support. What intrudes itself upon the observer, however, is the fact that the Party has worked so hard to glean so little. Negro membership in the Party has probably never exceeded 8,000 at any one time.

Its peak was reached during the united front period, at a time when the Communists were officially supporting "reformist" goals. True, many thousands of Negroes have joined the Party during the thirty years of its existence, but only a fraction of this number has seen fit to make any kind of permanent identification with the organization.

Every shift in the line, every change to conform with the "new situation," especially when the swing was toward a revolutionary orientation, has resulted in large-scale withdrawal of Negro members. Coupled with this has been the continuing inability of the Communists to integrate the Negro into the Party organization or to develop a Negro leadership that would attract any substantial following. The characteristic lament of Party spokesmen that "we are failing to build Negro cadres" and that "Negro comrades are not being brought forward as leaders" is a real one, reflecting a failure to attract Negroes of exceptional ability or provide them a mass membership with which to work.

This lack of success along organizational lines is further evidenced in the death a-borning or early collapse of those "front groups" which the Party has launched to implement its Negro work. The American Negro Labor Congress was an ineffectual grouping of the Party faithful. Despite the fact that Communists entertained great expectations for this outfit, it was never able to evoke any appreciable response from black workers. Its successor, the League of Struggle for Negro Rights, sought to build a mass movement around the self-determination doctrine, reaching not only the black proletariat but the Negro middle class and intelligentsia as well. But even the limited success which this group enjoyed was made possible only by concentrating on the immediate needs of Negroes. Its activities were known largely because of a few prominent Negro intellectuals who associated themselves with it.

While the National Negro Congress was the largest and most effective organization developed by the Communists around race issues, it had a significant life span of less than four years. Efforts to breathe new life into its limp carcass after the end of World War II were unavailing. The Southern Negro Youth Congress suffered a similar fate, although it was able to prolong its formal existence for more than a decade. Other specific organizations, such as the Negro People's Committee to Aid Spanish Democracy and the Negro Labor Victory Committee, were limited instruments that could not be converted to other Party purposes once their original aims were realized or lost. Still other Party-supported groups—which eventually came to be Party-controlled—sometimes recruited a substantial black membership and concerned themselves with various aspects of the Negro question, only to fail in the end. The most notable example in this category, of course, was the Southern Conference for Human Welfare.

When a shift in line occurs, the Party must convert its Negro organizations accordingly. If it is unable to do so, then these groups must be crushed and new ones established. As a consequence, Negroes have come to realize that when one joins or supports a Party agency, abrupt reversals of policy are a possibility. This hardly makes for confidence among a racial minority that wants equality and wants it all the time; such vacillations may prove to be a source of irritation to an oppressed group which wishes to pursue without detour the road to full equality.

But even so, the liberal often finds it difficult to avoid at least a modicum of amazement when confronted with the realization that out of half a dozen large-scale Negro organizations projected by the Communists during the past three decades, not one has survived to the present time. Numerous explanations can be advanced for these failures: political lethargy among Negroes, fear of identification with a revolutionary movement, preoccupation with the more immediate problems of survival, the peculiar hold of traditional religious beliefs, and the strong factionalism within Negro society itself. But one explanation demands primary attention; namely, the fact that Negroes are loath to support an organization whose orientation is supplied by the Politburo and which at any time might attempt to separate them from, or pose them against, the liberal forces in American life.

The repeated rejection of the Communist Party and its "fronts" by black America should suggest caution to those who are all too quick to bewail the Negro's being "duped" and misled by the "reds." Some have been taken in, to be sure. But the thing that impresses the thoughtful person is the fact that these victims have been so few. Even more noteworthy is the fact that even these few have been inclined to see the light rather quickly and gauge their own actions accordingly.

So long as we hold Negroes in a subordinate position while preaching the ideal of equality, they are going to protest. And they are apt to join, or at least cooperate with, those organizations which articulate this frustration. At times Communist "front" groups have performed this function. And red baiters notwithstanding, no Negro is going to be convinced that he must sit in the back of a bus merely because the Communists happen at the time to favor his sitting in the front seats. Nevertheless, the degree of loyalty which the Negro has given to the conservative society which discriminates against him is impressive; and though this loyalty is often undeserved, it has been peculiarly consistent, as attested by the fact that moderate organizations like the NAACP have steadily grown in prestige and strength while Communist instruments have bloomed and died quickly.

It has been for the most part only when the Communists have *joined in* rather than *initiated* demands for equal rights that the Party has given the appearance of speaking for a large Negro following. In this connection the recent statement by Jackie Robinson, the Negro baseball player, is highly revealing. Testifying before the House Un-American Activities Committee, he declared:

The white public should start toward real understanding by appreciating that every single Negro who is worth his salt is going to resent any kind of slurs and discrimination because of his race, and he is going to use every bit of intelligence such as he has to stop it. This has got absolutely nothing to do with what Communists may or may not be trying to do. And white people should realize that the more a Negro hates communism because it opposes democracy, the more he is going to hate any other influence that kills off democracy in this country—and that goes for racial discrimination in the Army, and segregation on trains and buses, and job discrimination because of religious beliefs or color or place of birth.

And one other thing the American public ought to understand, if we are to make progress in this matter; the fact it is a Communist who denounces injustice in the courts, police brutality, and lynching when it happens doesn't change the truth of his charges. Just because Communists kick up a big fuss over racial discrimination when it suits their purposes, a lot of people try to pretend that the whole issue is a creation of Communist imagination.

But they are not fooling anyone with this kind of pretense, and talk about "Communists stirring up Negroes to protest" only makes present misunderstanding worse than ever. Negroes were stirred up long before there was a Communist Party, and they will stay stirred up long after the party has disappeared—unless Jim Crow has disappeared by then as well.[3]

In the light of the record, it is sometimes hard for liberals to comprehend the Party's insistence on the correctness of its strategy and the depth of its influence. Correlatively, it may be difficult to understand why certain groups, notably the race baiters of the North and the white reactionaries of the South, can make a similar claim that the Communists have instigated and controlled Negro protest. We might venture the opinion, in the first situation, that Communists purposely create the illusion among Negroes and in the Party ranks that the Stalinists are the spearhead in the struggle for racial equality. In this connection the Communists have apparently been more successful in persuading themselves than in convincing the mass of Negroes. And this self-persuasion has often blinded the Party to the realities of the Negro struggle. As for the race baiters and reactionaries, the record does not matter. They are against change—any change—in the traditional pattern of race relations; and one way of combatting innovation is to label its proponents as "red." Tom Heflin knew this. So did Eugene Talmadge. So did Mr. Bilbo and the Dream House publishers. John Rankin and Gerald L. K. Smith know it now.

This tendency to overstate the influence of the Party is illustrated by the conservative literature on the trade unions. It has frequently been charged that because Communists controlled certain labor organizations, notably in the early CIO, the Party had large groups of Negro workers in its pocket, to do with as it saw fit. However, an examination of the record would show that Communists have been able to hold onto a Negro labor following only when they have devoted themselves to the cause of Negro rights in a limited trade union context. One of the foremost students of Negro labor in this country recently pointed out, for example, that the leftists in the UAW-CIO were never able to take Negro support for granted, Party prestige being dependent on what the Communists did about seniority, wages, and intra-union discrimination. In this connection, he said, Negroes could be just as opportunistic as the Stalinists, giving or withholding their support as it served their specific and immediate interests to do so.* This is a point that is often ignored by those who see only the Communist face of the coin. Opportunism, however, is a game that more than one can play. Negroes, because of their minority group status, have had to play it for decades. It would be presumptuous to suggest that they are any less skilled at it than the most practiced Party functionary.

The foregoing observations concerning the failure of the American Party in organizational terms are not meant to suggest that it has made no impact on Negro-white relations during the past thirty years. Henry Lee Moon has noted:

> It is a matter of record that the Communists have generally fought for full recognition of Negro rights. They have carried on this fight through their own organizations and through those organizations in which they exert influence. They have pushed the Negro to the forefront in Party work. They have consistently nominated him for office on the party ticket. They have dramatized his problem. They have risked social ostracism and physical violence in his behalf. They have challenged American hypocricy with the zeal, if not the high principle, of the abolitionists. In all this they have performed a vital function as an irritant on the American conscience.[4]

While one need not completely agree with Moon, it is easy to appreciate the suggestion that the Party has exerted a significant, though often indirect, influence on interracial patterns during the three decades it has been active.

Unfortunately this influence, because of its frequently indirect character, is difficult to measure. It remains for some competent

---

* A Negro student of the writer's acquaintance recently confided that he had attended a number of parties sponsored by the local branch of the Civil Rights Congress. In response to my inquiry as to whether he had been "converted," he exclaimed: "Hell, no! I know who they are and what they are up to and why they are pretending an interest in me. But the food they serve is good, and I like to dance; so I'll keep on going until they get wise to the fact that I am wise to them."

political sociologist to inquire into the matter in systematic fashion. Here we can only suggest some of the probable by-products of Communist action on the Negro question. The Party undoubtedly influenced a great many Negro intellectuals, particularly such writers as Claude MacKay, Langston Hughes, and Richard Wright. It affected them not only as men of letters but also as men of political action. The Party's mark upon such a figure as Paul Robeson is obvious. More recently the Communists have captured the loyalty of W. E. B. DuBois, the foremost intellectual in American Negro life two and three decades ago. Particularly during the 1930's, the Party made a substantial impact on the younger Negro students and intellectuals. This did not necessarily result in their joining the Party, but it did lead them to see that the solution of the complex problem of discrimination was intimately tied up with the success of the labor movement, thus impressing upon them the importance of organizing Negroes into militant trade unions.

The Communists also left their print on the Negro press. While few Negro journalists were Party members, they frequently found that much of the more dramatic material on Negro protest derived from the various struggles of the Party to secure Negro rights; such matters as court cases, relief demonstrations, and civil rights agitation were headline material and grist for the editorial mills. The Party influenced the Negro press in another way. Race papers in the United States are largely dependent for news items on the contributions of voluntary reporters. Local Party leaders made a point of supplying copy, writing it in an acceptable newspaper style, and forwarding it directly to Negro newspaper editors. The stories were slanted toward the Party view, of course, but editors were not always aware of this. Even the sophisticated editor, who saw the bias and was reluctant to use such items, had the problem of obtaining adequate news coverage. The precarious position of the Negro press, its shortage of competent reporting, and its need to emphasize Negro protest, all played into Party hands, especially prior to World War II.

Another important indirect influence of the Party was on the moderate protest and betterment organizations. While it has periodically alienated such organizations as the NAACP and the

NUL by denouncing or even seeking to destroy them, it has also forced them to initiate changes in their policies and programs. Moderate Negro leaders are inclined to fear a radical organization —be it the Garvey Movement or the Communist Party—which might appeal over their heads to the Negro masses. Moderate spokesmen display considerably less faith in the political acumen of the average Negro than one would suppose. Consequently, they have usually found it necessary to make what they may regard as unwise concessions in order to remain on top of and guide discontent. The growing identification of the NAACP with the labor movement, which dates back to the early 1930's, can be viewed as partly the result of Communist pressure. The greater concern of the National Urban League for educating Negro workers about trade union membership as well as for specific occupations also falls into this category. The growth of internal democracy within the NAACP has been in part a gratuitous by-product of the Communist threat to the existing administration. The Communists have sought to discredit the incumbent national leadership in order that the Party might capture local branches and, ultimately, the national organization. This threat has tended to increase the responsiveness of the NAACP officialdom to rank and file will.

The Party must also be credited with considerable impact on the racial policies of the trade unions which it controlled or in which it had a significant voice. While it is true that the CIO in order to be successful in the mass production industries would have had to organize Negro workers, it is not likely that union leaders would have given as much attention to the matter or developed the specific programs they did in the absence of prodding from Communist elements. The Party often made the question of Negro rights an intra-union political issue and consequently forced non-Communist groups to take practical cognizance of it. The existence of factions within the unions enhanced the bargaining position of the Negro membership. It is questionable, for example, whether the UAW-CIO would have developed its remarkably effective program for combating union and management discrimination had not the Communists served as a hair shirt.

In the major political parties, too, the Communists have made their pressure felt. The fact that the Progressive Party, ostensibly under the leadership of Henry Wallace but in reality an instrument of the Party, placed great emphasis on civil rights and made special appeals to the Negro minority was undoubtedly one reason for the Democratic Party's ultimate adoption of its civil rights platform in 1948. Other examples could be cited of indirect Communist influence on the shaping and modification of major-party positions. This impact, like all other indirect weights, is difficult to measure. All that is being suggested here is that it has been an influence of some importance and is worth further investigation.

No other organization in the United States, with the possible exception of the NAACP, has done more to publicize the Negro's plight than has the Communist Party. A glance at any Party publication will suggest that the editors do not consider an edition complete unless much of the available space is given over to a discussion of matters pertaining to the Negro question. No case of lynching, police brutality, court injustice, discrimination in employment, or other forms of discrimination does the Party permit to go unnoticed. And this has been generally true in the past, except for those periods when emphasis on such matters was considered inimical to more fundamental Party goals.

The Communists have not been content to publicize racial injustice to an exclusively American audience; they have carried the message to every corner of the globe through the world propaganda machine of the Kremlin. And the Party has not confined itself to the facts, though they are damaging enough in themselves as anti-American propaganda. Instead, the Communists have resorted to distortion, to exaggeration, to the technique of the big lie. This kind of propaganda serves to embarrass the U. S. State Department and compromise its prestige as it seeks to make friends for democracy among foreign racial and ethnic groups, particularly in Asia.

We have already discussed at length the influence of the Communists on the interpretation of American Negro history. While it is not easy to measure the Party's impact on non-Communist students of the Negro past, it is safe to say that new lines of inquiry, as well as specific problems for investigation, have been suggested by the Party historians.

While the Communist Party has been among the organizations stimulating an interest in the Negro past, it has frequently been as guilty of distorting this past as the conservative historians it opposes. The Party has been inclined to deduce from Negro history such findings as would support its particular bent at any given time. The net result has been to encumber rather than enhance understanding. The contribution which the Party might have made by a critical appraisal of the standard textbook treatment of the Negro past has been largely lost by its tendency to compound the errors of the conservatives. There is plenty for the American Negro to be proud of in his history. And he does not need to ground his pride in any overplaying of certain historical leaders and movements which the Communists have attempted to plug. One thing is certain; his protest and betterment efforts will ultimately be more effective if he harbors no illusions—or disillusions—as to what the historical record really shows.

It is exceedingly difficult to suggest just what dent the Communist Party has made on the Negro church. It is probable that the Party had some part in shaping the growing social and political awareness of Negro religious organizations. Church groups were at times drawn into active support of some of the front organizations which the Party created among Negroes. A number of individual Negro churchmen such as Max Yergan, were at one time involved in the articulation of the Party line. The Communists probably gained some loyalty from the younger Negro ministers and churchmen, particularly during the 1930's. But again this is a matter which does not lend itself to meaningful measurement, at least not here.

The exertion of these and other influences on the Negro question in the United States was not uncalculated. At times the Party attempted to slow down, even to stall the struggle for Negro rights when its general line required it. And even those actions which yielded positive results in terms of Negro welfare often carried a partial taint. Its blessings were always mixed. A good example of the negative by-product which always accompanied the positive contribution is to be found in the Party's relations with indigenous Negro protest groups. In periodically attacking these moderate organizations, the Party may have unwittingly fostered the liberalization of their internal political structures; and the Communist dynamos may have sharpened the concern of these groups for the Negro worker and the labor movement. On the other hand, the disruptive tactics of the Communists within the NAACP and similar agencies had a tendency to split the membership, to confuse issues, and to hamper the unity of action which a protest agency, and particularly that of a racial minority, requires. At the same time, these tactics forced the authentic leaders, of whom there is always a scarcity, to devote valuable time to countering the machinations of the Communists, not only at the national level but in local branch organizations as well. In killing off or permitting the demise of the Negro organizations which it created around the promise of a more militant struggle for Negro rights, the Party further frustrated Negro protest, sometimes setting its own Negro organizations against those of the larger community. The Negro Labor Victory Committee was established, for example, not for the primary purpose of improving the role of Negroes in the war effort but to offset the March on Washington Movement.

The Party indubitably had some following among the Negro intellectuals; but in the case of the individual savant the frequent result of such affinity was the compromise of his independence, the circumscription of his imagination, and the channeling of his idea-output into a rigid mould. One can only speculate on the number of Negro writers, for example, whose promising creativeness was choked off and whose subsequent efforts have produced nothing more than a mouthing of high-toned slogans. Doxey A. Wilkerson serves as a good example in the non-fiction field.

In the trade unions the Communists have at times fought effectively for the rights of Negroes, but here again the fight has not been waged consistently; and the results have not always been completely salutary from the Negro's point of view. Communists have frequently caused divisions of Negro workers within an individual trade union structure and within the larger labor movement. Such factionalism has made it possible for some trade union bureaucrats to play Negro against Negro and to vitiate the force which a unified racial minority might assert. In those unions which it controlled, the Party sometimes used Negroes for purposes largely divorced from trade union matters. In this connection it frequently diverted their attention from the primary goals and mischanneled their energies; to wit, toward opening a second front in 1942-1943, or opposing the Marshall Plan more recently. Finally, the Communists on occasion have made an effort to organize Negro "blocs" within the labor organizations, not for purposes of combatting discrimination but as a purely political power resource to be used in struggles for control. In this tactic, however, they have largely failed.

The Communists have attempted to groom certain of their own Negro members for positions of race leadership. But the black Communist holding a position of authority has always been a Party leader first and a Negro leader second. Since the Negro leader to be effective needs freedom to maneuver, to shift his appeals and strategy as circumstances require, and to compromise where compromise is called for, leadership candidates advanced by the Party have largely fizzled. For the Communists' black leader is bound by the Party line at any given time. Like any other Party agent, each decision is made for him. His "leadership" function involves leading others to an acceptance of this decision —whatever it may be. Any appeal or following he has built up always runs the risk of being immediately vitiated by the abrupt development of a "new situation," for example, the Stalin-Hitler pact. It is not for naught that Negroes familiar with radical movements in the United States often refer to James W. Ford as "Uncle Tom with a Party Card," ready to doff his hat before his white Communist masters.

In its intermittent struggle for Negro justice in the courts the Party has challenged numerous legal and political precepts; this challenge has been partly responsible for certain significant changes, as for example, in the method of selecting juries in the South and elsewhere. But the fight waged by the Party in this area, like those waged in others, has not been unrelenting. Its primary concern has not been for the fate of the victims in whose behalf it has intervened; rather these cases have been used to make propaganda hay, to "expose capitalist injustice"—when the line called for such exposés. Indeed, the Party's declared intention to use the courts as a political instrument has invoked counter moves on this level by conservatives. Because of the sensational publicity which often surrounds such a trial, the merits of the case are likely to get lost in the symbolism; the offensive techniques typically employed by the Communists may only reinforce the bias of a southern jury, thus augmenting the chances that justice will be flouted. The Negro is not impervious to the game that is being played. In his eyes the Party becomes just another organization attempting to use Negroes for ulterior motives, and therefore receives his loathing and distrust.

With respect to the Negro's general political interest and awareness, the Party has without doubt had a stimulating effect, though this influence has not always been constructive. Communists played a role in weaning Negroes away from the Republican Party in 1932 and in piling up the black vote for Roosevelt in 1936. It likewise had a hand in focusing attention on the political aspects of the Negro question during the 1930's. At other times, however, as in the 1940 elections, it has sought to effect a political divorcement of the Negro from the liberal movement, or, as in 1948, to place his energies behind "labor" and "progressive" parties neither labor nor progressive. And the basic issues around which efforts have been made to develop Negro political support frequently have had little to do with Negro rights; for example, opposition to the Economic Recovery Program. The Communists have visualized the Negro as an important cog in a third party apparatus such as the Progressive Party in 1948. However, Negroes are not now apt to support any Party which in effect poses them against the "liberal center."

While Negro advancement in this country is contingent on identification with white groups around a set of common problems, as exemplified by the initial Southern Conference for Human Welfare, the fact remains that Negroes must focus much of their activity on specific race questions. Above all, their political institutions cannot be constructed around an organization that does not want the same thing and want it all the time. The Communist Party has not filled this bill—at least insofar as racial issues are concerned. While Negro political movements must be flexible, while they must have the capacity to shift as opportunities develop and to deploy their forces as circumstances require, while they must be able to compromise and bargain and form alliances here and there as the immediate advancement of Negro rights indicates, they cannot be subject to the fitful gyrations that have characterized the Communist Party program. Though both the Communist Party and the Negro protest movement may be characterized by periodic shifts in tactics, the fluctuations of the latter belong to a different orbit, whose generating center is closer to Monticello than to the Kremlin.

Negroes would constitute a valuable resource for any authentic third party movement built around organized labor. To command the support of American workers—and of American Negroes—such a movement would have to be grounded in the native radical tradition. It would need more than a conglomeration of confused intellectuals, old-time pacifists, isolationists, and Communist hacks such as the Progressive Party represented. Negroes have played an important role in shaping the American radical tradition; they are by no means loath to participate in its extension. But their loyalty will not be won to a movement that uses the window dressings of such a tradition as a front for the expansion of world Communism.

The cold shoulder which black America has turned toward the Red enchantress cannot constitute a source of comfort for the reactionary defender of the status quo. As Jackie Robinson pointed out, "Negroes were stirred up long before there was a Communist Party, and they will stay stirred up long after the Party has disappeared—unless Jim Crow has disappeared by then as well." Nor can the lukewarm reception which Negroes have given the Communists be taken as an indication that Negro leadership is lacking in political awareness or acumen. On the contrary, in using the Communist Party when it could serve their immediate interests and in rejecting it when it tended to separate them from their friends, Negroes have displayed a rare political sharpness.

The failure of the Stalinists to capture the allegiance of colored America can be explained largely by the Party's umbilical attachment to the Kremlin, which inevitably relegates the question of Negro rights to a position of secondary importance. But behind this failure also lies the Communists' inability to see the black citizen for what he is. In his embracement of the ideal of equality, the Negro has shown that he is an American in the most fundamental sense, for the egalitarian aspiration stems from the deepest ideological streams of our culture. A striking paradox inheres in the fact that the most convincing demonstration of loyalty to the American system has come from a group which has reaped the least from it. Because of this orientation the Negro tends to define the "Negro question" in simple terms; namely, the attainment of full status, of all the rights and privileges and responsibilities of citizenship. When this goal is reached there will still be problems; but the Negro will attack these problems, not as a *Negro,* but as a worker or as a citizen.

The blank pages in the party's roll books are mute testimony of the Negro's failure to find in the Soviet Union or the Black Republic the thing he is seeking. This is the record and it stands as a challenge to those white reactionaries who attempt to convince an increasingly hysterical public that a merger of "red and black" threatens America. Paul Robeson's irresponsible remark that 15,000,000 Negro Americans would not fight against the Soviet Union is a windfall for such race-baiters. In the furor which such utterances can cause, two centuries of Negro loyalty to the principle of democracy can be momentarily obscured.

For the individual Negro living in his particular locality, this kind of white bigotry is apt to constitute a more real and immediate threat than Communism. Moon has put it rather well:

The black folk of America know the enemy, the *real* enemy. They have looked into his hard white face. It is the fiendish face of reaction. The face of death—death to the spirit as well as to the body. This is the deadly enemy they know first hand. They have met him face to face in the villages of South Carolina, in the swamps of Florida, on the banks of the Potomac, on the plains of Texas and Kansas and in the dark ghettoes of Detroit, Chicago and New York.[5]

Negro leaders are confident, on the basis of their experience, that they can balk any attempts by the Communists to convert native protest movements into Party instruments. They only wish that their self-proclaimed protectors from a foreign, leftist totalitarianism would be half as ardent in protecting them from the home-grown, rightist variety.

The disappearance tomorrow of the entire Communist Party apparatus in the United States—unless accompanied by a rightist dictatorship—would have little bearing on the volume or intensity of Negro protest. Negroes would be no less opposed to discrimination and the multitude of specific forms which it takes. Historically, Negro discontent cannot be attributed solely or even in large part to the stimulus provided by a radical ideology unless the Constitution and the Bill of Rights can be so interpreted. Karl Marx was only thirteen years old when Nat Turner led his fellow slaves in revolt against the planters of Southampton County, Virginia. W. E. B. DuBois was familiar with the works of Friedrich Engels, but this had nothing to do with his calling the Niagara Conference. A. Philip Randolph in his earlier days was a Socialist, but he did not become important as a leader of protest until he started acting like a Negro and a trade unionist. Walter White was organizing anti-lynching campaigns long before he read Stalin's *Marxism and the National and Colonial Question*. The NAACP was a going concern for a number of years before the establishment of the Communist dictatorship in the U.S.S.R. Negroes have never required the *Daily Worker* or a James W. Ford to tell them that discrimination was wrong and that something ought to be done about it.

Those who identify such organized discontent with an alien ideology are only obscuring the basic issues. They are also misreading the implications of the Constitution and the Bill of Rights, which suggest to Negroes as well as to Jews and Italians that equal ought to *mean* equal. In characterizing all protest and betterment efforts of Negroes as "Red-inspired," these persons play directly into the hands of those to whom they are presumably opposed. They enable the Communists to claim credit for ideas and movements which they did not develop or support; ideas and movements, in fact, which the Party frequently opposed. They also make it more difficult for home-grown, responsible Negro organizations to carry out their legitimate functions, thus impeding the channeling of Negro protest in terms of the pragmatic American tradition. The position in which they place the Negro leader was well described by Lester Granger when he declared recently:

Authentic Negro leadership in this country finds itself confronted by two enemies on opposite sides. One enemy is the Communist who seeks to destroy the democratic ideal and practice which constitute the Negro's sole hope of eventual victory in his fight for equal citizenship. The other enemy is that American racist who perverts and corrupts the democratic concept into a debased philosophy of life. In opposing the one enemy, Negro leadership must be careful not to give aid and comfort to the other.[6]

Negroes in the United States have had plenty of provocation to revolt. But they have chosen to protest within the constitutional framework. They have not succumbed, as a group, to any "siren song sung in bass." And because the aspirations of the American Negro are essentially egalitarian, a "bourgeois" document like the American Constitution has a liberating potential in the Black Belt of Alabama and in the ghetto of Harlem that the *Communist Manifesto* could never hope to have.

# NOTES

## NOTES TO CHAPTER I

1. E. Franklin Frazier, *The Negro in the United States* (New York: Macmillan Company, 1949), pp. 82-98.

2. Herbert Aptheker, *Negro Slave Revolts in the United States 1526-1860* (New York: International Publishers, 1939), pp. 17-18.

3. W. E. B. DuBois, *Black Reconstruction* (New York: Harcourt, Brace and Company, 1935), *passim.*

4. Louis M. Hacker, *The Triumph of American Capitalism* (New York: Columbia University Press, 1940), pp. 378-379. Frazier, *op. cit.*, Chap. VII.

5. Maurice R. Davie, *Negroes in American Society* (New York: McGraw Hill Book Company, 1949), Chap. II.

6. *Selected Speeches of Booker T. Washington* (New York: Doubleday and Company, 1932).

7. Allison Davis, Negro Churches and Associations in the Lower South, *passim.* Unpublished manuscript prepared as a part of the preliminary researches for Gunnar Myrdal's *An American Dilemma.* Available at the Schomburg Collection of the New York City Public Library.

8. Foster R. Dulles, *Labor In America* (New York: Thomas Y. Crowell Company, 1949), pp. 110-111.

9. *Ibid.*, p. 141; Charles H. Wesley, *Negro Labor in the United States* (New York: Vanguard Press, 1927), pp. 254-259; Sterling D. Spero and Abram L. Harris, *The Black Worker* (New York: Columbia University Press, 1931), p. 45.

10. Lois MacDonald, *Labor Problems and the American Scene* (New York: Harper and Brothers Publishers, 1938), pp. 255-264; Wesley, *op. cit.*, pp. 255-281; Spero and Harris, *op. cit.*, pp. 101-102.

11. W. E. B. DuBois, *Dusk of Dawn* (New York: Harcourt, Brace and Company, 1940), pp. 88-95; Gunnar Myrdal, *An American Dilemma* (New York: Harper and Brothers Publishers, 1944), pp. 742-744.

12. DuBois, *Dusk of Dawn*, p. 91; Mary White Ovington, *How the National Association for the Advancement of Colored People Began* (New York: NAACP, 1914).

13. Ralph J. Bunche, The Programs, Ideologies, Tactics and Achievement of Negro Betterment and Interracial Organizations, pp. 206-207. Unpublished manuscript pre-

pared as a part of the preliminary research for Gunnar Myrdal's *An American Dilemma*. Available at the Schomburg Collection of the New York City Public Library.

14. Spero and Harris, *op. cit.*, pp. 405-408.

15. Wesley, *op. cit.*, pp. 264-265.

16. Myrdal, *op. cit.*, pp. 191-201.

## NOTES TO CHAPTER II

1. Quoted from Charles H. Vail, *Socialism and the Negro Problem* in Spero and Harris, *The Black Worker*, p. 404.

2. Spero and Harris, p. 405.

3. *Ibid.*, p. 407.

4. *Ibid.*, p. 409.

5. St. Clair Drake and Horace R. Cayton, *Black Metropolis* (New York: Harcourt, Brace and Company, 1945), pp. 25-26; Spero and Harris, *op. cit.*, pp. 411-412.

6. Selig Perlman and Philip Taft, *History of the Labor Movement in the United States: Labor Movements, Vol. IV.* (New York: Macmillan Company, 1935), p. 423.

7. *Ibid.*, pp. 426-427.

8. Platform of the Communist Party, *American Labor Year Book* (1920), p. 419.

9. Jay Lovestone, "The Great Negro Migration," *Workers Monthly*, IV, No. 4 (February, 1926), 179-184.

10. Drake and Cayton, *op. cit.*, pp. 77-82; Myrdal, *An American Dilemma*, pp. 722-723; Spero and Harris, *op. cit.*, p. 386; Frazier, *The Negro in the United States*, pp. 527-531; Edward Byron Reuter, *The American Race Problem* (New York: Thomas Y. Crowell Company, 1927), pp. 406-409.

11. Harold F. Gosnell, *Negro Politicians* (Chicago: University of Chicago Press, 1935), *passim;* Spero and Harris, *op. cit.*, p. 412; Drake and Cayton, *op. cit.*, Chap. XIII; Davis, Negro Churches and Associations in the Lower South, pp. 504-505.

12. William F. Dunne, "The Negroes as an Oppressed People," *Workers Monthly*, IV, No. 9 (July, 1925), 295.

13. William F. Dunne, "Negroes in American Industries," *Workers Monthly*, IV, No. 6 (April, 1925), 260. *See also:* Earl Browder, "A Negro Labor Organizer," *Workers Monthly*, IV, No. 7 (May, 1925), 294; James W. Ford, "The Negro and the Struggle Against Imperialism," *Communist*, IX, No. 1 (January, 1930), 22.

14. Margaret I. Lamont, "The Negro's Stake in Socialism," *American Socialist Quarterly*, IV, No. 1 (March, 1935), 1.

15. Resolutions of the Central Executive Committee of the Communist Party of the United States. Quoted by John Pepper, "American Negro Problems," *Communist*, VII, No. 10 (October, 1928), 634.

16. J. Stachel, "Organization Report of the Sixth Convention of the Communist Party of the U.S.A.," *Communist*, VIII, No. 4 (April, 1929), 184.

17. Jay Lovestone, "Toward a World Bolshevik Party," *Workers Monthly*, V, No. 2 (December, 1925), 79.

18. Earl Browder, "New Steps in the United Front," Report on the Seventh World Congress of the Communist International (New York: Workers Library Publishers, 1935), pp. 20-25.

19. Dunne, "The Negroes as an Oppressed People," *loc. cit.*, pp. 295-298.

20. Dunne, "Negroes in American Industries," *loc. cit.*, p. 260.

21. Platform of the Workers (Communist) Party—1925. Quoted in Spero and Harris, *op. cit.*, p. 418.

22. Earl Browder, "A Negro Labor Organizer," *loc. cit.*, p. 294.

23. *Report of the Central Executive Committee of the Workers (Communist) Party, 1925* (Chicago: Daily Worker Publishing Company, 1925), p. 115.

24. William Z. Foster, "Company Unionism and Trade Unionism," *Workers Monthly*, V, No. 3 (January, 1926), 133.

25. *Labor Herald* (Organ of the Trade Union Educational League), III, No. 5 (July, 1924), 152.

26. *Report of the Central Executive Committee of the Workers (Communist) Party, 1925*, p. 115.

27. Robert Minor, "The First Negro Workers Congress," *Workers Monthly*, V, No. 2 (December, 1925), 71-72.

28. *Ibid.*, p. 73.

29. *Ibid.*, p. 68.

30. Spero and Harris, *op. cit.*, p. 411.

31. Minor, "The First Negro Workers Congress," *loc. cit.*, p. 73.

32. James W. Ford, *The Negro and the Democratic Front* (New York: International Publishers, 1938), pp. 81-83.

33. Bunche, The Programs, Ideologies, Tactics, . . . . , p. 695.

34. Ralph Chaplin, *Wobbly: The Rough and Tumble Story of an American Radical* (Chicago: University of Chicago Press, 1948), p. 333.

35. "Betrayal by the N.A.A.C.P.," *New Masses*, XIV, No. 2 (January 8, 1935), 6.

36. Dunne, "Negroes in American Industries," *loc. cit.*, *passim*.

37. Dunne, "The N.A.A.C.P. Takes A Step Backward," *Workers Monthly*, V, No. 10 (August, 1926), 460.

38. Drake and Cayton, *op. cit.*, p. 752.

39. Myrdal, *op. cit.*, p. 746; Ralph Bunche, Conceptions and Ideologies of the Negro Problems, p. 152. Unpublished manuscript prepared as a part of the preliminary researches for Gunnar Myrdal's *An American Dilemma*. Available at the Schomburg Collection of the New York City Public Library.

40. Robert Minor, "Death or a Program," *Workers Monthly*, V, No. 6 (April, 1926), 270.

41. Robert Minor, "After Garvey—What?" *Workers Monthly*, V, No. 8 (June, 1926), 365.

42. Programme of the Communist International 1928, *Handbook of Marxism*, Emile Burns, Editor (New York: International Publishers, 1935), p. 1032.

43. Bunche, The Programs, Ideologies, Tactics . . . . pp. 431-432.

44. Quoted in W. E. B. DuBois, "Opinion—The Negro and Radical Thought," *Crisis*, XXII, No. 3 (July, 1921), 103.

45. Spero and Harris, *op. cit.*, p. 423.

46. James Jackson, "The Negro in America," *Communist International* New Series, No. 8, p. 51.

47. Dunne, "Negroes in American Industries," *loc. cit.*, pp. 259-260.

48. Organization Report of the Sixth Convention of the Communist Party of the U.S.A.," *Communist*, VIII, No. 5 (May, 1929), 246.

49. Myrdal, *op. cit.*, pp. 60-61.

50. Drake and Cayton, *op. cit.*, Chap. VII.

51. George S. Schuyler, "Have the Communists Quit Fighting for Negro Rights?" *Negro Digest*, III, No. 2 (December, 1944), 61.

52. William L. Patterson, "Awake Negro Poets!" *New Masses*, IV, No. 5 (October, 1928), 10.

53. Myrdal, *op. cit.*, pp. 732-733.

## NOTES TO CHAPTER III

1. Perlman and Taft, *History of the Labor Movement in the United States*, p. 550.
2. "Editorial Comment on the 'Negro Question'," *Communist International*, No. 8, New Series, p. 54.
3. *Ibid.*
4. A. Shiek, "The Comintern Program and the Racial Problem," *Communist International*, V, No. 16 (August 15, 1928), 407; Wesley, *Negro Labor in the United States*, p. 278; Spero and Harris, *The Black Worker*, p. 417.
5. Shiek, "The Comintern Program and the Racial Problem," *loc. cit.*, p. 408.
6. *Ibid.*, p. 409
7. Communist International, *The Revolutionary Movement in the Colonies: Theses Adopted at the Sixth World Congress of the Communist International* (New York: International Publishers, 1929).
8. Communist International, "Resolutions on the Negro Question in the U. S. A.," *Daily Worker*, February 12, 1929, p. 3. Quoted in Spero and Harris, p. 417.
9. Jay Lovestone, "The Sixth World Congress of the Communist International," *Communist*, VII, No. 11 (November, 1928), 673-674.
10. John Pepper, "American Negro Problems," *Communist*, VII, No. 10 (October, 1928), 628.
11. *Ibid.*, p. 632.
12. *Ibid.*, p. 634.
13. James S. Allen, *The Negro Question in the United States* (New York: International Publishers, 1936); Harry Haywood, *Negro Liberation* (New York: International Publishers, 1948). (My emphasis, CWR)
14. Earl Browder, "Report of the Political Committee of The Twelfth Central Committee Plenum of the Communist Party of the United States," *Communist*, X, No. 1 (January, 1931), 7. (My emphasis, CWR)
15. *Ibid.*, p. 17.
16. William Winestone, "The Economic Crisis in the United States and Tasks of the Communist Party," *Communist International*, VI, No. 31 (February 15, 1930), 1230.
17. Henry Lee Moon, *Balance of Power: The Negro Vote* (Garden City, N. Y.: Doubleday and Company, Inc., 1948), pp. 129-130.
18. *Crisis*, XLII, No. 10 (October, 1935), 305.
19. David P. Berenberg, "The Bankruptcy of the Communist Party," *American Socialist Quarterly*, III, No. 4 (December, 1934), 46-47.
20. Harry Haywood, "The Theoretical Defenders of White Chauvinism in the Labor Movement," *Communist*, X, No. 6 (June, 1931), 504.
21. Browder, "For National Liberation of the Negroes," *Communist*, XI, No. 4 (April, 1932), 297; James S. Allen, *The American Negro* (New York: International Publishers, 1932); B. D. Amis, "For a Strict Leninist Analysis of the Negro Question," *Communist*, XI, No. 10 (October, 1932), 945.
22. Harry Haywood, "The Struggle for a Leninist Interpretation of the Negro Question in the U. S. A.," *Communist*, XII, No. 9 (September, 1933), 890-893; Joseph Prokopec, "Negroes as an Oppressed National Minority," *Communist*, IX, No. 3 (March, 1930), 239.
23. Communist Party of the United States, "Draft Program for the Negro Laborers in the Southern States," *Communist*, IX, No. 3 (March, 1930), 246-247.
24. *Ibid.*

25. *Ibid.;* Stuart Jamieson, *Labor Unionism in American Agriculture* (Washington, D. C.: United States Government Printing Office, 1945), p. 293.

26. Browder, *Report to the 8th Convention of the Communist Party* (New York: International Publishers, 1934), pp. 44-52.

27. Robert Minor, "The Negro and His Judases," *Communist,* X, No. 7 (July, 1931), 632.

28. Haywood, "The Crisis of Jim-Crow Nationalism of the Negro Bourgeoisie," *Communist,* X, No. 4 (April, 1931), 330.

29. *Ibid.,* p. 337.

30. Minor, "The Negro and His Judases," *loc. cit.,* p. 639.

31. Resolution, 8th Convention of the Communist Party of the United States, 1934. Quoted in Earl Browder, *The Way Out: A Program for American Labor* (New York: Workers Library Publishers, 1934). See also "The Roosevelt Program: An Attack Upon the Toiling Masses," *Communist,* XII, No. 5 (May, 1933), 419.

32. William Z. Foster, "The Workers (Communist) Party in the South," *Communist,* VII, No. 11 (November, 1928), 676-681.

33. Jamieson, *op. cit.,* 293-300.

34. John Howard Lawson, "In Dixieland We Take Our Stand," *New Masses,* XI, No. 9 (May 29, 1934), 8-10.

35. Bunche, The Programs, Ideologies, Tactics, . . . pp. 696-698.

36. Browder, *Build the United Peoples' Front* (New York: Workers Library Publishers, 1936), p. 60.

37. *American Labor Year Book,* XI, (1930), 96.

38. *Ibid.*

39. Otto Huiswood, "The Negro and the Trade Unions," *Communist,* VII, No. 12 (December, 1928), 775.

40. *The Negro Worker* (Organ of the International Trade Union Committee of Negro Workers, Hamburg, Germany), II, Nos. 1-2 (January-February, 1932). See inside of cover page.

41. *American Labor Year Book,* XI, (1930), 96-101.

42. Quoted in *American Labor Year Book,* XIII, (1932), 74.

43. Jamieson, *op. cit.,* Chap. III.

44. John Pepper, "American Negro Problems," *loc. cit.,* p. 637.

45. *Equality, Land and Freedom: A Program for Negro Liberation* (New York: League of Struggle for Negro Rights, 1933), pp. 12-13.

46. *Ibid.,* p. 7.

47. *Ibid.,* p. 11.

48. Ford, *The Negro and the Democratic Front,* p. 83.

49. *Equality, Land and Freedom: A Program for Negro Liberation,* pp. 16-17.

50. *The Negro Worker,* II, Nos. 1-2 (January-February, 1932). See inside cover page.

51. George Padmore, "An Open Letter to Earl Browder," *Crisis,* XLII, No. 10 (October, 1935), 320, 315.

52. Browder, "Earl Browder Replies," *Crisis,* XLII, No. 12 (December, 1935), 372.

53. Walter White, *A Man Called White* (New York: Viking Press, 1948), p. 128.

54. Moon, *op. cit.,* pp. 123-124.

55. *Ibid.,* p. 124.

56. *Crisis,* XLII, No. 12 (December, 1935), 369.

57. Harry Haywood, "The Scottsboro Decision," *Communist,* XI, No. 12 (December, 1932), 1075.

58. Minor, "The Negro and His Judases," *loc. cit., passim.*

59. Haywood, "The Crisis of Jim-Crow Nationalism of the Negro Bourgeosie," *loc. cit.*, p. 333.

60. Communist Party of the United States, *Draft Resolution Proposed for the 8th Convention of the Communist Party of the United States* (New York: Workers Library Publishers, 1934), pp. 21, 40, 41.

61. Drake and Cayton, *Black Metropolis*, pp. 735-736.

62. A. Nasanov, "Against Liberalism in the American Negro Question," *Communist*, IX, No. 4 (April, 1930), 296.

63. Bunche, The Programs, Ideologies, Tactics, . . . p. 428.

64. Oscar C. Brown, "What Chance Negro Freedom," *Crisis*, XLII, No. 4 (April, 1935), 134, 137, 149.

65. Bunche, The Programs, Ideologies, Tactics, . . . p. 429.

66. Minor, "The Negro and His Judases," *loc. cit.*, p. 639.

67. *Ibid.*, *passim*.

68. A. B. Magil, "The Socialist Party Convention," *New Masses*, XV, No. 11 (June 12, 1934), 12.

69. *Ibid.*; James S. Allen, "Thomas, Prince of Straddlers," *New Masses*, XVI, No. 11 (March 12, 1935), 9.

70. Sam Brown, "The Proposals of the Communist Party for a United Front With the S. P. in the U. S. A.," *Communist International*, XI, No. 21 (November 5, 1934), 740-741.

71. Ernest Doerfler, "Socialism and the Negro Problem," *American Socialist Quarterly*, III, No. 3 (Summer, 1933), 27-28.

72. *Declaration of Principles Adopted at the 1934 Convention of the Socialist Party*, *American Socialist Quarterly*, Special Supplement, III (July, 1934), 3.

73. Margaret I. Lamont, "The Negro's Stake in Socialism," *American Socialist Quarterly*, IV, No. 1 (March, 1935), 42.

74. *Ibid.*, p. 47.

75. Norman Thomas, "For the Socialists," in Symposium for 1932 Presidential Candidates, *Opportunity*, X, No. 11 (November, 1932), 340.

76. Doerfler, "Socialism and the Negro Problem," *loc. cit.*, p. 36.

77. Speech of Clarence Hathaway before the 1932 Convention of the Communist Party of the United States. Quoted in Joseph North, "The Communists Nominate," *New Masses*, VII, No. 1 (July, 1932), 4. (omissions in original)

78. Eugene Gordon, "Negro Novelists and the Negro Masses," *New Masses*, VIII, No. 11 (July, 1933), 16.

79. Richard Frank, "Negro Revolutionary Music," *New Masses*, XI, No. 7 (May 15, 1934), 29.

80. *Ibid.*, p. 30.

81. Stanley Burnshaw, "The Theatre: Toward a Genuine Negro Drama," *New Masses*, XVI, No. 2 (July 9, 1933), 29.

82. Gordon, "Negro Novelists and the Negro Masses," *loc. cit.*, p. 20.

83. E. Clay, "The Negro Writer and the Congress," *New Masses*, XIV, No. 12 (March 19, 1933), 22.

84. *Ibid.*

85. Quoted in North, "The Communists Nominate," *loc. cit.*, p. 6.

86. Joseph North, "The Communist Party Convention," *New Masses*, XI, No. 3 (April, 1934), 7.

87. *Ibid.*, *passim*.

## NOTES TO CHAPTER IV

1. "Manifesto Issued by the Executive Committee of the Communist International Proposing to Labor Organizations and Social-Democratic Parties to Join in a United Front Against Hunger and the Capitalist Offensive," (Adopted March 18, 1933), *Communist*, XII, No. 5 (May, 1933), 769-776.

2. Quoted in Adolph Sturmthal, *The Tragedy of European Labor* (New York: Columbia University Press, 1943), p. 73.

3. Brown, "The Proposals of the Communist Party for United Front with the S. P. in the U. S. A.," *Communist International*, XI, No. 21 (November 5, 1934), 740-741.

4. I. Amter, "The National Congress for Unemployment and Social Insurance—And After," *Communist*, XIV, No. 1 (January, 1935), 33-44.

5. Morris Childs, "Our Tasks in Light of Changed Conditions," *Communist*, XIV, No. 4 (April, 1935), 436.

6. Louise Scott, "Some Problems of Party Work in the Countryside," *Communist*, XIV, No. 2 (February, 1935), 436.

7. Earl Browder, "New Developments and Tasks in the U. S. A.," *Communist*, XIV, No. 10 (October, 1935), 1010-1011.

8. Nat Ross, "Next Steps in Alabama and the Lower South," *Communist*, XIV, No. 10 (October, 1935), 971.

9. James W. Ford, "The United Front in the Field of Negro Work," *Communist*, XIV, No. 2 (February, 1935), *passim*; North, "The Communists Nominate," *New Masses*, VII, No. 1 (July, 1932), 4.

10. George S. Schuyler, "The Separate State Hokum," *Crisis*, XLII, No. 4 (April, 1935), 135, 148; Moon, *Balance of Power: The Negro Vote*, pp. 123-124.

11. Browder, "For Working Class Unity! For a Workers' and Farmers' Labor Party!" (Speech before the Seventh World Congress of the Communist International, August, 1935), *Communist*, XIV, No. 9 (September, 1935), 787-789.

12. Seventh World Congress of the Communist International, "Resolution on the Offensive of Fascism and the Tasks of the Communist International in the Fight for the Unity of Working Class Against Fascism," *Communist International*, XII, No. 17-18 (September 20, 1935), 951.

13. George Dimitrov, "A Congress of the Mobilization of Forces on a Wide Scale Against Fascism and War," *Communist International*, XII, No. 17-18 (September 20, 1935), 951.

14. Marcel Cachin, "Fascism and the United Front in France," *Communist International*, XII, No. 15 (August 5, 1935), 733-737; Earl Browder, "New Steps in the United Front," *Communist*, XIV, No. 11 (November, 1935), 990-1014.

15. Dimitrov, "The Fascist Offensive and the Task of the Communist International in the Fight for the Unity of the Working Class Against Fascism," *Communist International*, XII, No. 17-18 (September 20, 1935), 838.

16. Earl Browder, "Recent Political Developments and Some Problems of the United Front," *Communist*, XIV, No. 7 (July, 1935), 619.

16-a. Earl Browder, *Build the United People's Front* (New York: Workers Library Publishers, 1936), pp. 59-60. (my emphasis, CWR)

17. Ford, *The Negro and the Democratic Front*, pp. 79-80.

18. Earl Browder, "New Steps in the United Front," *Communist*, XIV, No. 11 (November, 1935), 1005.

19. Ford, "Uniting the Negro People in the People's Front," *Communist*, XVI, No. 7 (August, 1937), 728.

20. Ford, *The Negro and the Democratic Front*, pp. 33-34.

21. *Daily Worker*, July 9, 1935, p. 6.

22. *Ibid.*, July 17, 1935, p. 6.

23. George Padmore, "Ethiopia and World Politics," *Crisis*, XLII, No. 5 (May, 1935), 138.

24. William L. Patterson, "World Politics and Ethiopia," *Communist*, XIV, No. 8 (August, 1935), 732.

25. *Ibid.*

26. *Daily Worker*, August 26, 1935, p. 2.

27. *New York Times*, September 8, 1935, p. 1.

28. *Daily Worker*, September 9, 1935, p. 2.

29. *Crisis*, XLII, No. 10 (October, 1935), 305.

30. Browder, "Earl Browder Replies," *Crisis*, XLII, No. 12 (December, 1935), 372.

31. Ford, *The Negro and the Democratic Front*, pp. 33-34.

32. Moon, *Balance of Power: The Negro Vote*, p. 126.

33. "The NAACP and the Communists," (Reprint) *Crisis*, LIV, No. 3 (March, 1949), *passim*.

34. Herbert R. Northrup, *Organized Labor and the Negro* (New York: Harper and Brothers Publishers, 1944), p. 15.

35. Browder, *The People's Front* (New York: International Publishers, 1938), p. 38.

36. *Ibid.*, p. 40. (my emphasis, CWR)

37. Ford, *The Negro and the Democratic Front*, p. 37.

38. Browder, *The People's Front*, *passim*.

39. Ford, *The Negro and the Democratic Front*, p. 89.

40. *Hearings Before the Committee on Un-American Activities*, United States House of Representatives, Eighty-First Congress, First Session (Washington, D. C.: United States Government Printing Office, 1949), p. 467.

41. Browder, *New Steps in the United Front* {New York: Workers Library Publishers, 1935), p. 20.

42. Browder, "Earl Browder Replies," *loc. cit.*, p. 372.

43. Ford, *The Negro and the Democratic Front*, pp. 135-136.

44. *Hearings Before the Committee on Un-American Activities*, pp. 467-468.

45. Myrdal, *An American Dilemma*, p. 817.

46. John P. Davis, *Let Us Build A National Negro Congress* (Washington, D. C.: Sponsoring Committee for a National Negro Congress, 1935).

47. Browder, "New Steps in the United Front," *loc. cit.*, p. 1005; Elanor Ryan, "Toward a National Negro Congress," *New Masses*, XV, No. 10 (June 4, 1935), 14-15.

48. Ford, *The Negro and the Democratic Front*, p. 25.

49. *Official Proceedings of the National Negro Congress, 1936* (Washington, D. C.: National Negro Congress, 1936), p. 41.

50. *Ibid.*, p. 42.

51. Horace R. Cayton and George S. Mitchell, *Black Workers and the New Unions* (Chapel Hill: University of North Carolina Press, 1939), p. 419.

52. *Ibid.*, p. 418.

53. *Official Proceedings of the National Negro Congress, 1936*, p. 19.

54. *Ibid.*, pp. 16-17.

55. Ford, *The Negro and the Democratic Front*, p. 76.

56. Browder, *The People's Front*, p. 47.

57. Richard Wright, "Two Million Black Voices," *New Masses*, XVIII, No. 9 (February 25, 1936), 15.

58. Cayton and Mitchell, *op. cit.*, pp. 420-421.

59. *Official Proceedings of the National Negro Congress, 1936*, pp. 39-41.

60. Cayton and Mitchell, *op. cit.*, p. 422.

61. Myrdal, *op. cit.*, p. 818.

62. *Official Proceedings of the National Negro Congress, 1936*, p. 37.

63. Ford, *The Negro and the Democratic Front*, p. 114.

64. Lee Coller, "Not Since Reconstruction," *New Masses*, XXXI, No. 10 (May 30, 1939).

65. Quoted in Myrdal, *op. cit.*, pp. 818-819.

66. *Report on the Economic Conditions of the South*, Prepared for the President by the National Emergency Council (Washington, D. C.: United States Government Printing Office, 1938).

67. Rob F. Hall, "The Southern Conference for Human Welfare," *Communist*, XVIII, No. 1 (January, 1939), 60.

68. Charles S. Johnson, "More Southerners Discover the South," *Crisis*, XLVI, No. 1 (January, 1939), 14-15.

69. Hall, "The Southern Conference for Human Welfare," *loc. cit.*, p. 60.

70. *Ibid.*, pp. 61-64.

71. Charles S. Johnson, "More Southerners Discover the South," *loc. cit.*, p. 14.

72. *Ibid.*, pp. 14-15.

73. James S. Allen, *The Negro Question in the United States*.

74. James W. Ford, "Our Oppressed Nation," *New Masses*, XIX, No. 12 (June 16, 1936), 25.

75. Herbert Aptheker, *Negro Slave Revolts in the United States* (New York: International Publishers, 1939); *The Negro in the American Revolution* (New York: International Publishers, 1940); *The Negro in the Abolitionist Movement* (New York: International Publishers, 1941); *The Negro in the Civil War* (New York: International Publishers, 1938).

76. Aptheker, *The Negro in the American Revolution*, p. 5.

77. *Ibid.*, p. 44.

78. Aptheker, *The Negro in the Abolitionist Movement*, pp. 40-41.

79. Aptheker, *The Negro in the Civil War*, pp. 44-45.

80. Ford, *The Negro and the Democratic Front*, p. 155.

81. Earl Browder, *Social and National Security* (New York: Workers Library Publishers, 1938), p. 28.

82. Browder, *The Democratic Front* (New York: Workers Library Publishers, 1938), p. 71.

83. Browder, *Social and National Security*, pp. 32-33.

## NOTES TO CHAPTER V

1. William Z. Foster, *Daily Worker*, April 2, 1941, p. 4.

2. *Daily Worker*, May 23, 1941, p. 7. (my emphasis, CWR)

3. *Daily Worker*, May 24, 1941.

4. *Daily Worker*, May 23, 1941, p. 7. (my emphasis, CWR)

5. Pat Toohey, "Greater Attention to the Problems of the Negro Masses," *Communist*, XIX, No. 3 (March, 1940), 279-280.

6. *Ibid.*, p. 280.

7. *Ibid.*, p. 280.

8. Resolution of the Third National Negro Congress, Washington, D. C., April, 1940. Quoted in: *Jim-Crow in National Defense* (Los Angeles: Los Angeles Council National Negro Congress, 1940), pp. 4-5.

9. A. Philip Randolph, "A. Philip Randolph Tells Why I Would Not Stand for Re-election as President of the National Negro Congress," *American Federationist*, XLVIII, No. 1 (July, 1940), 24.

10. Theodore R. Bassett, "The Third National Negro Congress," *Communist*, XIX, No. 6 (June, 1940), 548.

11. *Ibid.*, p. 542.

12. Ralph Bunche, The Programs, Ideologies, Tactics, . . . ., pp. 370-371.

13. Bassett, "The Third National Negro Congress," *loc. cit.*, p. 549.

14. Max Yergan, *Democracy and the Negro People Today* (New York: National Negro Congress, 1940), p. 9.

15. *Ibid.*, p. 13.

16. *Jim Crow in National Defense*, (Los Angeles: Los Angeles Council National Negro Congress, 1940); *Democracy Means: Jobs for Negroes* (Philadelphia, Communist Party of Philadelphia, 1941).

17. Rob Fowler Hall, "New Forces in the South," *Communist*, XIX, No. 8 (August, 1940), 702.

18. White, *A Man Called White*, pp. 186-194, 206-210, 235-261; Lester B. Granger, "Barriers to Negro Employment," *Annals*, 223 (September, 1942), 72-80.

19. Earl Browder, *The People Against the War Mongers* (New York: Workers Library Publishers, 1940), *passim*.

20. *Daily Worker*, May 23, 1941, p. 7.

21. T. R. Bassett, "The Negro People And the Fight for Jobs," *Communist*, XX, No. 9 (September, 1941), 806-807; James W. Ford, *The Negro People and the New World Situation* (New York: Workers Library Publishers, 1941), p. 12.

22. *Daily Worker*, April 2, 1941, pp. 3, 4; May 20, 1941, p. 3; May 23, 1941, p. 7.

23. *Daily Worker*, June 21, 1941, p. 3.

24. Max Weiss, *Youth's Road to Peace and Security* (New York: New Age Publishers, 1941), *passim*; Henry Winston, *Old Jim-Crow Has Got to Go* (New York: New Age Publishers, March, 1941), *passim*.

## NOTES TO CHAPTER VI

1. Earl Browder, *Victory Must Be Won* (New York: International Publishers, 1942), p. 4.

2. Earl Browder, "Partisanship—A Luxury America Cannot Afford," *Communist*, XXIII, No. 3 (March, 1944), 200.

3. *Daily Worker*, July 15, 1941, p. 6.

4. James W. Ford, *The Negro People and the New World Situation*, p. 11.

5. James W. Ford, "Some Problems of the Negro People in the National Front to Destroy Hitler and Hitlerism," *Communist*, XX, No. 10 (October, 1941), 888-896.

6. Ford, *The Negro People and the New World Situation*, p. 15

7. *Ibid.*, p. 13.

8. Max Weiss, *Youth Serves the Nation* (New York: Workers Library Publishers, 1942), pp. 22-23.

9. Benjamin J. Davis, Jr, *The Negro People and the Communist Party* (New York: International Publishers, 1943), pp. 9-10.

10. James W. Ford, "Teheran and the Negro People," *Communist*, XXIII, No. 8 (March, 1944), 260-266.

11. Benjamin J. Davis, Jr., "Reply to a Libel," *New Masses*, L, No. 7 (February 15, 1944), 9.

12. Doxey A. Wilkerson, *The Negro People and the Communists* (New York: Workers Library Publishers, April, 1944), p. 13.

13. *Ibid.*, p. 18.

14. Robert Minor, *The Heritage of the Communist Political Association* (New York: Workers Library Publishers, 1944), *passim*; For a more detailed outline of the CPA program see: David Goldway, *The Communist Political Association* (New York: New Century Publishers, 1945).

15. Minor, *The Heritage of the Communist Political Association*, p. 45.

16. Earl Browder, "On the Negroes and the Right of Self-Determination," *Communist*, XXIII, No. 1 (January, 1944), 84-85.

17. James W. Ford, "The Negro People Unite for Victory," *Communist*, XXII, No. 7 (July, 1943), 643.

18. Doxey A. Wilkerson, "The Negro in the War," *New Masses*, XLIX (December 14, 1943), 18.

19. Benjamin J. Davis, Jr., "Reply to a Libel," *loc. cit.*, p. 8.

20. Ford, *The Negro People and the New World Situation*, pp. 12-13.

21. Ford, "The Negro People Unite for Victory," *loc. cit.*, p. 643.

22. *Negro Digest*, III, No. 2 (December, 1944), 56.

23. George Schuyler in the symposium, "Have the Communists Quit Fighting for Negro Rights?" *Negro Digest*, III, No. 2 (December, 1944), 63-64.

24. Horace R. Cayton in *ibid.*, pp. 67-68.

25. A. Philip Randolph, "March on Washington Movement Presents Program for the Negro," *What the Negro Wants*, ed. Rayford W. Logan, (Chapel Hill: University of North Carolina Press, 1944), pp. 148-149.

26. Ernest Williams, "The Negro Struggle," *Militant*, VI, No. 8 (February 21, 1942), 3.

27. Doxey A. Wilkerson, "Speech on the Draft Resolution at the Plenary Meeting of the National Committee, CPA, June 18-20, 1945," *Communist*, XXIV, No. 7 (July, 1945), 621.

28. Wilkerson, "The Negro in the War," *loc. cit.*, p. 18.

## NOTES TO CHAPTER VII

1. *Daily Worker*, May 24, 1945, pp. 7, 9.

2. *Daily Worker*, June 3, 1945, p. 5.

3. James W. Ford, "Revisionist Policies Weakened Struggles for Negro Rights," *Daily Worker*, June 25, 1945, p. 7. (my emphasis, CWR)

4. Letter, Edna Lewis, East Harlem Club, Communist Political Association, *Daily Worker*, June 29, 1945, p. 7.

5. George Lohr, "Negro Struggle Weakened by Revisionism," *Daily Worker*, July 17, 1945, p. 7. (my emphasis, CWR)

6. H. V. Saunders, "Struggle for Negro Liberation," *Daily Worker*, July 23, 1945, p. 7.

7. Alice Burke, "The Dissolution of the C. P. in the South," *Daily Worker*, July 24, 1945, p. 3. (my emphasis, CWR)

8. See articles in the *Daily Worker* by individuals on dates as follows: Robert

Minor, June 16, 1945, p. 7; Robert Thompson, June 16, 1945, p. 7; Fred Blair, June 25, 1945, p. 7; Samuel Sillen, June 22, 1945, p. 7; William Norman, June 23, 1945, p. 7; Max Bedacht, July 5, 1945, p. 7; Israel Amter, July 6, 1945, p. 7; Elizabeth Gurley Flynn, July 23, 1945, p. 7.

9. *Daily Worker*, July 28, 1945, p. 2.

10. Resolution of the National Convention of the Communist Party of the United States of America, Adopted July 28, 1945, Communist Party Convention, New York City.

11. Thelma Dale, "Reconversion and the Negro People," *Communist*, XXIV, No. 10 (October, 1945), 896-897.

12. "The Present Situation and the Next Tasks," (Discussion by Doxey A. Wilkerson) *Communist*, XXIV, No. 7 (July, 1945), 619-623.

13. Earl Browder, "Speech to the National Committee of the CPA," June 18, 1945, *Daily Worker*, July 20, 1945, CPA Discussion Page Section, p. 1.

14. Frederick V. Field, "The Record of American Imperialism in China," *Political Affairs*, XX, No. 1 (January, 1946), 31-41; Tim Buck, "The Postwar Role of Canadian Imperialism," *Political Affairs*, XXV, No. 1 (January, 1946), 89-96; William Z. Foster, "Leninism and Some Practical Problems of the Postwar Period, *Political Affairs*, XXV, No. 2 (February, 1946), 99-109.

15. "The Imperialist Threat to World Peace," (Editorial) *Political Affairs*, XXV, No. 4 (April, 1946), 294-295.

16. Claudia Jones, "On the Right of Self Determination for the Negro People in the Black Belt," *Political Affairs*, XXV, No. 1 (January, 1946), 67.

17. Henry Winston, "Party Tasks Among the Negro People," (Report to the Plenary meeting of the National Committee CP, U.S.A., February 12-15, 1946), *Political Affairs*, XXV, No. 4 (April, 1946), 349.

18. *Ibid.*, p. 350.

19. *Ibid*, pp. 356-357.

20. Harry Haywood, "Toward a Program of Agrarian Reforms for the Black Belt," *Political Affairs*, XXV, No. 10 (October, 1946), 937-938.

21. *Ibid.*, p. 938.

22. *Ibid.*, pp. 938-939.

23. Robert Thompson, "Party Policy in the Veterans' Field," *Political Affairs*, XXV, No. 1 (January, 1946), 45.

24. *Ibid.*, pp. 45-46.

25. John Pittman, "The Negro People Spark the Fight for Peace," *Political Affairs*, XXV, No. 8 (August, 1946), 724-733.

26. Claudia Jones, "On the Right of Self Determination..." *loc. cit.*, p. 68.

27. "Resolution on the Question of Negro Rights and Self-Determination," Reprinted in *The Communist Position on the Negro Question* (New York: New Century Publishers, 1947), pp. 9-13.

28. Doxey A. Wilkerson, "The Negro and the American Nation," *Political Affairs*, XXV, No. 7 (July, 1946), 652-658.

29. James S. Allen, "The Negro Question," *Political Affairs*, XXV, No. 11 (November, 1946), 1046.

30. See the statements of William Z. Foster, Benjamin J. Davis, Jr., Eugene Dennis, James E. Jackson, James S. Allen, A. W. Berry, Homer Chase, Alexander Bittleman, Ray Hansborough, Max Weiss, Edward Strong, William L. Patterson, and Nat Ross in *The Communist Position on the Negro Question*. See also: Francis Franklin, "The Status of the Negro People in the Black Belt and How to Fight for the Right of Self-

Determination," and Max Weiss, "Toward Clarity on the Negro Question," *Political Affairs*, Vol. XXV, No. 5 (May, 1946).

31. Benjamin J. Davis, Jr., *The Path of Negro Liberation* (New York: New Century Publishers, 1947), pp. 21-22.

32. *Theory and Practice of the Communist Party*, Marxist Study Series I, First Course, Prepared by National Education Department of the Communist Party (New York: New Century Publishers, 1947), Fourth Printing, September, 1948, p. 31.

33. *Ibid.*, p. 32.

34. *Ibid.*, p. 33.

35. Pettis Perry, "Destroy the Virus of White Chauvinism," *Political Affairs*, XXVIII, No. 6 (June, 1946), 1-5; Robert Thompson, "Strengthen the Struggle Against White Chauvinism," *ibid.*, pp. 17-20.

36. Perry, "Destroy the Virus of White Chauvinism," *loc. cit.*, p. 5.

37. *Ibid.*, p. 6.

38. *Ibid.*, pp. 10-11; Thompson, "Strengthen the Struggle Against White Chauvinism," *loc. cit.*, pp. 22-24.

39. Perry, "Destroy the Virus of White Chauvinism," *loc. cit.*, p. 11; Thompson, "Strengthen the Struggle Against White Chauvinism," *loc. cit.*, p. 26.

40. Thompson, "Strengthen the Struggle Against White Chauvinism," *loc. cit.*, p. 16.

41. Perry, "Destroy the Virus of White Chauvinism," *loc. cit.*, p. 12.

42. Pittman, "The Negro People Spark the Fight for Peace," *loc. cit.*, p. 726.

43. *Ibid.*, p. 727.

44. *Ibid.*, pp. 727-728.

45. *Ibid.*, p. 732.

46. Interview, Atlanta, Georgia, May 10, 1946.

47. Letters, Birmingham, Alabama, July 26, 27, 1949.

48. *Veterans' Handbook* (New York: National Association for the Advancement of Colored People).

49. Richard Gladstein, *Argument to the Jury in the New York Communist Trial* (San Francisco: Civil Rights Congress, 1949); Elwood Dean, *The Story of the Trenton Six* (New York: New Century Publishers, 1949); *Freedom for the Ingram Family* (New York: National Committee to Free the Ingram Family, 1949).

50. Dean, *op. cit.*, p. 15.

51. *Freedom for the Ingram Family*, p. 3.

52. *Ibid.*

53. *Ibid.*

54. *Ibid.*

55. Quoted in the *New Leader*, XXXII, No. 52 (December 24, 1949), 1.

56. Edward Strong, "On the 40th Anniversary of the N.A.A.C.P.," *Political Affairs*, XXIX, No. 2 (February, 1950), 28; cf. Howard Johnson, "Aspects of Negro History and the Struggle Against White Chauvinism," *Political Affairs*, XXIX, No. 2 (February, 1950), 13-22.

57. Benjamin J. Davis, Jr., "The Negro People's Liberation Movement," *Political Affairs*, Special Convention Issue, September, 1948, pp. 885, 887.

58. White, *A Man Called White*, pp. 344-349; For the line of the Party on the NAACP see: Pittman, "The Negro People Spark the Fight for Peace," *loc. cit.*, p. 728; Winston, "Party Tasks Among the Negro People," *loc. cit.*, pp. 351-352; William Z. Foster, "On Self-Determination for the Negro People," *Political Affairs*, XXV, No. 6 (June, 1946), 552; Benjamin J. Davis, Jr., "The Negro People's Liberation Movement," *loc. cit.*, pp. 885-887; James W. Ford, "The Communist Party: Champion Fighter for Negro Rights," *Political Affairs*, XXVIII, No. 6 (June, 1949), 48-49; Norman

Ross, "The Struggle for the Negro-Labor Alliance," *Political Affairs*, XXVIII, No. 6 (June, 1949), 86.

59. "NAACP: A Perspective," *Communist Campanile*, VI, No. 4 (May, 1949), 1. (Published by the Berkeley Campus Section Communist Party.)

60. *Crisis*, LVI, No. 6 (June, 1949), 185-186.

61. "The NAACP and the Communists," (editorial) *Crisis*, LVI, No. 3 (March, 1949).

62. *Ibid.*

63. Strong, "On the 40th Anniversary of the N.A.A.C.P.," *loc. cit.*, p. 27.

64. *Hearings Before the Un-American Activities Committee*, pp. 459-471.

65. Interview, San Francisco, California, July 7, 1949.

66. Harry Haywood, *Negro Liberation* (New York: International Publishers, 1948), pp. 137-167; Herbert Aptheker, "Consciousness of Negro Nationality: An Historical Survey," *Political Affairs*, XXVIII, No. 6 (June, 1949), 88-95; *The Communist Position on the Negro Question* (Excerpts from the major speeches in discussion of the Negro question at the plenary meeting of the National Committee of the Communist Party, December 3-5, 1946.) (New York: Century Publishers, 1947), *passim.*

67. Doxey A. Wilkerson, "Negro Culture: Heritage and Weapon," *Masses and Mainstream*, II, No. 8 (August, 1949), 5.

68. *Ibid.*, pp. 13-14.

69. *Ibid.*, pp. 20-21.

70. Hal Simon, "The Struggle for Jobs and for Negro Rights in the Trade Unions," *Political Affairs*, XXIX, No. 2 (February, 1950), p. 33-48.

71. *Report of the Director, CIO Committee to Abolish Discrimination* (Washington, D. C., Congress of Industrial Organizations, 1949); Philip Murray, *Report to the Congress of Industrial Organizations, Eleventh Constitutional Convention* (Washington, D. C., Congress of Industrial Organizations, 1949), pp. 56-59; National CIO Committee To Abolish Discrimination, *Working and Fighting Together, CIO Wants FEPC, What Is the Law, Facing the Job of Negro Housing, Turn-over Talk on Fair Practices*, Series of pamphlets published by the Committee; dates not indicated.

72. Walter P. Reuther, *Justice on the Job Front* (Detroit: International Union, United Automobile, Aircraft and Agricultural Implement Workers of America—CIO, 1947); UAW Fair Practices and Anti-Discrimination Department: (Detroit); *Handbook For Local Union Fair Practices Committees* (1946); *A Girl's Best Friend is Her Union* (1947); *Discrimination Costs You Money* (1948); *Democracy's Cross Roads* (1949).

73. John Williamson, "The Trade Unions and the Negro Workers," *Political Affairs*, XXVI, No. 11 (November, 1947), 1007-1008; Perry, "Destroy the Virus of White Chauvinism," *loc. cit*, p. 5.

74. John Williamson, "Only Militant United Action Can Defeat the Drive Against the Unions!" *Political Affairs*, Special Convention Issue, September, 1948, pp. 857-859; Benjamin J. Davis, Jr., "The Negro People's Liberation Movement," *loc. cit.*, p. 888.

75. George Murphy, "Henry Wallace" (In a series of statements by representatives of the various political parties), *Crisis*, LV, No. 10 (October, 1948), 299.

76. *Ibid.*, p. 315.

77. *Ibid.*, p. 315.

78. *Ibid.*, p. 316

79. *Ibid.*, p. 315.

80. 1948 Election Platform of the Communist Party, *Political Affairs*, Special Convention Issue, September, 1948, pp. 941-942.

81. Benjamin J. Davis, Jr., "The Negro People's Liberation Movement," *loc. cit.*, p. 898.

82. 1948 Election Platform of the Communist Party, *loc. cit.*, p. 943; For a detailed elaboration of the Communist Party's position on the Progressive Party's Negro rights platform see the following articles, all of which appeared in *Political Affairs*, the official Communist Party publication, volume, number and dates as indicated: Jack Stachel, "The Third Party Movement in the 1948 Elections," XXVI, No. 9 (September, 1947); S. W. Gerson, "Electoral Coalition Problems in New York," XXVI, No. 10 (October, 1947); Benjamin J. Davis, Jr., "Build the United Negro People's Movement," XXVI, No. 11 (November, 1947); Theodore R. Bassett, "The New People's Party and the Negro People," XXVII, No. 7 (July, 1948); Max Gordon, "The 'Grand' Old Party," XXVII, No. 8 (August, 1948).

83. George Murphy, "Henry Wallace," *loc. cit.*, p. 299.

84. *Crisis*, LV, No. 10 (October, 1948), 297.

85. Doris Fleeson, "His Albatross," *Oakland Tribune*, November 10, 1948.

86. *Crisis*, LV, No. 12 (December, 1948), 361.

## NOTES TO CHAPTER VIII

1. Harold Rosenberg, "The Communist: His Mentality and His Morals," *Commentary*, VIII, No. 1 (July, 1949), 5.

2. Moon, *Balance of Power: The Negro Vote*, p. 120.

3. *Hearings Before the Committee on Un-American Activities*, p. 481.

4. Moon, *op. cit.*, p. 127.

5. *Ibid.*, p. 121.

6. *Hearings Before the Committee on Un-American Activities*, p. 464.

# INDEX

Wilson Record is Professor of Sociology
at Portland State University in Portland, Oregon.